COMPETITION AND CURRENCY

A CATO INSTITUTE BOOK

COMPETITION AND CURRENCY

Essays on Free Banking and Money

Lawrence H. White

NEW YORK UNIVERSITY PRESS
New York and London

Library of Congress Cataloging-in-Publication Data
White, Lawrence H. (Lawrence Henry)
    Competition and currency: essays on free banking and money/
Lawrence H. White.
    p.   cm.
    ''A Cato Institute book.''
    Includes bibliography and index.
    ISBN 0–8147–9224–3
    1. Free banking. 2. Money. 3. Free enterprise. I. Title.
HG1588.W46 1989
332.1--dc19   89–3211
                                                           CIP

New York University Press books are printed on acid-free paper, and
their binding materials are chosen for strength and durability.

To my parents

Contents

Acknowledgments

The initial inspiration for this volume was simply the conjunction of the thoughts that (1) the number of articles I had written on competitive banking and money had grown large enough to constitute a not-too-slim collection, (2) it would be useful to have them widely available together, and (3) there was no harm in seeing whether someone might not be persuaded to publish such a collection. I am very pleased that New York University Press has proven receptive. I am indebted to David Boaz of Cato Institute for being instrumental in the process of matching author to publisher. I thank Colin Jones of NYU Press for his patience in awaiting the completion of the Introduction. The press agreed to publish this book just as I was preparing to leave the university's economics department for my present position at the University of Georgia.

Most of all I wish to thank my former colleague Israel Kirzner, who, through the Austrian Economics program at NYU, provided research support which gave me the time to pursue these ideas. His intellectual support, encouragement, and scholarly criticism, together with those of our colleagues Mario Rizzo and Ludwig Lachmann, were the best things about being at NYU. I am deeply grateful to all three.

Acknowledgments

Introduction

The competitive provision of currency by private banks is part of
what Adam Smith (1976 2:687) called "the obvious and simple
system of natural liberty." Free banking is therefore an obvious and
simple idea. Or so it seems to me, having spent the last decade or so
thinking about it. It may well seem an outlandish idea to readers for
whom it is still new. I ask them to suspend disbelief at least until the
end of the book. If by then the idea that motivates my discussion of
free banking—that open competition among private firms could provide a monetary system better than one provided by a state monopoly central bank—at least seems *worth arguing* about, my efforts here
will have succeeded as far as I can reasonably hope.

The essays in Part 1 represent consecutive attempts to deal with
the most important issues raised by the idea of free banking. Some
of these issues are policy-oriented (or "normative"), some analytical
(or "positive"), and the arguments concerning them are likewise of
two types. Because normative concerns about monetary systems are
generally based on analytical beliefs about how the systems work, I
have mixed both types of arguments in these essays—possibly to a
greater extent than I ought to have. The current of advocacy that
runs through these essays will not, I hope, put off economists interested primarily in the analytical matters. Conversely, I hope that
policy-oriented readers will not find the attention to analytical details
too great an obstacle.

I am painfully aware that I have not been able to anticipate every
argument that has been or could be made against the idea of free
banking. Nor have I thought of every argument that can be made in
its favor. (Novel arguments are made by George Selgin and by Kevin
Dowd in important recent monographs.) In particular, while the

1

essays below focus on rebutting the natural-monopoly and public-good arguments for a government role in the payments system, sophisticated critics have lately argued that unregulated banking results in suboptimal outcomes because of informational asymmetries (e.g., Cothren 1987, Mullineaux 1987). I remain unpersuaded at present (1) that these problems are an important feature of the real world, and not just of particular hypothetical models; (2) that if they were, banking contracts could not be structured to remedy them to an efficient extent; and (3) that even contractually irremediable informational imperfections can rationalize any government involvement other than the provision of information. Private commercial bank clearinghouses, given their historical role in mixed banking systems (Timberlake 1984, Gorton and Mullineaux 1987), may well have an important "quasi-regulatory" role to play in enhancing the performance of a free banking system by internalizing informational externalities. The scope of this role is open to question (Selgin and White 1988), but in any case it does not seem to require the political grant of authority which is the kernel of central banking.

Whatever conclusions are eventually drawn, it is encouraging to see that increasing amounts of theoretical and historical research are being done on the feasibility of free-market institutions for the provision of monetary services. This research, and the greater interest of policy analysts in alternative monetary institutions, constitutes in large measure a predictable response (after a long and variable lag) to the sorry record of the monetary regime under which we now live. The experience of the United States with unbridled fiat money has included the double-digit inflation of the 1970s, the painful disinflation of the early 1980s, and the rampant uncertainty of the present. No one can say precisely when the next bout of high inflation will begin, but no one can say that it will not happen.

The number of reform plans now on the table is perhaps even greater than the number of interested authors: some authors have offered multiple proposals. The proposed alternative regimes range from binding guidelines for the path of central bank liabilities, to competitive currency systems which eliminate the central bank, to cashless competitive payments systems which eliminate money as we know it. (My own sympathies lie primarily within the second group.) Despite their diversity, all these proposals call for restriction of the power of the central bank authorities to alter the path of monetary policy purely at their own discretion. A sizable number of old-school economists have yet to recognize the desirability of *any* constitutional limits on government's monetary role, but that is no reason for putting off discussion of whether the role should be zero.

THE CASE FOR FREE BANKING

The essay here reprinted as Chapter 1, "Free Banking as an Alternative Monetary System," was written for a Pacific Research Institute conference held in November 1981. It first appeared in Siegel (1984). It sandwiches the core of my doctoral dissertation's first chapter between slices of its fifth chapter. Although the essay was originally meant to provide a preview of the work I was doing in my dissertation, it appeared in print almost simultaneously with the 1984 book based on my dissertation (which book contained a different fifth chapter).

The essay argues that the proper regulator of the supply of money is neither "rules" nor "discretion" for a central bank, but competition. Convertibility of inside money into a commodity outside money, which I view as a natural institutional product of competition among issuing banks, restrains the supply of currency and deposits without relying on the wisdom and beneficence of monetary authorities or on artificial devices for restraining them. Convertibility is a matter of private contract, unlike a politically imposed monetary policy rule, and thus it is far easier to enforce. A private bank that fails to honor its obligations can be taken to court by any customer who holds them. A central bank that evades its restraints can only be disciplined through cumbersome political channels. If it is in cahoots with the legislature, what recourse does an ordinary citizen then have?

Chapter 2, "Competitive Money, Inside and Out," argues directly for repeal of legislative barriers to competitive supply of inside and outside monies. Originally written for the Cato Institute's annual monetary conference of January 1983, and published in the *Cato Journal* in that year, the version here incorporates revisions made for its re-publication in Dorn and Schwartz (1987). The case for deregulation of the inside money industry (i.e., banking) is a straightforward microeconomic case for eliminating the distortions created by subsidies, taxes, and blunt restrictions on what banks do, where they do it, and how they price it. Regulations on banking activity are not necessary for monetary stability. The contrary view is based, I believe, on a misreading of history.

The essay cites an early work by Milton Friedman (1960) as the most explicit and respectable critique of laissez-faire banking. The revised version contains new footnotes and some new wording in the text to acknowledge that Friedman (1984) has recently expressed greater openness toward laissez-faire banking. I find it encouraging that Friedman, in a piece coauthored with Anna J. Schwartz (Friedman and Schwartz 1986), has explicitly reconsidered his 1960 views. I am much happier to have a scholar of Friedman's stature as an intellectual ally, albeit a skeptical one, than as an opponent.

The next two essays were first drafted in 1985 and have recently been published in a Pacific Institute volume edited by Thomas Willett (1988). The first essay considers the problems with government supply of money; the second various solutions. The problems with government provision of money are formalized in the theories of (1) seigniorage maximization, (2) central banks as bureaucracies, and (3) political business cycles. I intend to treat these theories at greater length in a subsequent book on the theory of monetary institutions.

The policy reforms falling under the rubric of "depoliticization" of the money supply range from greater autonomy for the central bank to its elimination. I argue that only the more fundamental reforms are likely to accomplish any noticeable improvement. So as not to fall prey to the danger that "the best may become the enemy of the good," I should reiterate here that I would regard a genuine constitutional limitation on the central bank's money-creation powers as an improvement even if it did not mean the abolition of central banking. But I have never considered it a would-be reformer's duty to offer plans more politically palatable than the one he sincerely believes best. I am mindful of William Lloyd Garrison's admonition that gradualism in theory is perpetuity in practice.

The standard sort of argument economists make for government provision of a good or service is that it constitutes a "public good" which will inherently be underprovided by the market. It would be a poor reflection on the creativity of economists if none had applied this argument to money. (It would also suggest that the many economists affiliated with central banks and international monetary agencies had been unable to justify their own employment.) My reasons for disagreeing with the argument are spread across the first three chapters, together with arguments against the proposition that money is somehow a natural monopoly.

The final chapter in Part 1, originally an essay commissioned by the Sequoia Institute for presentation at the International Conference on Privatization sponsored by the United States Agency for International Development (USAID) in February 1986, appeared in Hanke (1987). The essay applies the argument for competitive currency to the case of the less-developed countries. I find that the argument fits there just as well, perhaps better: private issue of currency is an efficient way to promote monetization, which is yet lacking (for good reason, given inflation rates) in the rural areas of many LDCs. One may think of this argument as extending one step further Ronald McKinnon's (1973) well-known brief for financial liberalization.

THE QUESTION OF THE MONETARY STANDARD

The first piece in Part 2 was written for the Cato Institute's newsletter, *Policy Report,* where it appeared in 1981. It is the earliest piece in this volume, written while I was still thinking through the issues for the first time. It takes a more skeptical attitude toward gold than do the next two chapters.

The next piece, "Fix or Float?", is pitched at a more popular level than most of the others in the volume. It originally appeared in *Inquiry* magazine, and has been reprinted several times in economics anthologies for undergraduates. The essay explores the choice between fixed and floating exchange rates from the perspective of free banking and concludes that the choice is a false one. The question "fix or float?" presupposes the monopoly provision of money by national governments. With an international commodity money, neither fixing nor floating is necessary.

The essay "Free Banking and the Gold Standard" was written for a 1983 conference on the gold standard organized by the Ludwig von Mises Institute, and appeared in the resulting volume edited by Llewellyn Rockwell (1985). It explores the range of affinity between the gold standard, which is one possible and (history shows) practicable commodity money standard, and the competitive private issue of currency.

Perhaps this is as good a place as any to comment on the role played by "Austrian economics" in my work. I do not believe that any particular monetary policy outlook is an integral part of Austrian economics, which, strictly speaking, is an analytical and not a normative body of work. The analytical tradition, from Carl Menger to Ludwig von Mises to F. A. Hayek, is one I find extremely useful for thinking about monetary institutions. Needless to say, there are many important insights to be gained from non-Austrian monetary economists as well, but the work of these three is essential.

In their work one finds the insights that (1) the institution of money is the result, not of state action, but of market convergence with regard to goods widely accepted in trade; (2) the characteristic which distinguishes money from all other assets, is its *general* or routine acceptance in exchange; and (3) central banks can and do generate business cycles through changes in money supply, so that boom and bust represent the transitory real effects of nonneutral monetary injections. The influence of the evolutionary perspective is most evident in Chapters 9 and 12, where I discuss the evolution of an unregulated banking system. The view that money is uniquely marketable figures prominently in my attempt to define and identify money in Chapter 11 and in Chapter 13, which criticizes the idea that bonds could serve as a medium of payment. The monetary theory of the business cycle figures in the critique of political money supply regimes advanced in Chapter 3.

Mises and Hayek, of course, have gone beyond purely analytical work to consider policy questions. My normative outlook also owes something to theirs. Mises (1978) persuasively drew from his analysis conclusions favorable to free banking. Hayek (1978) introduced into contemporary debate the idea of denationalization of money, thereby drawing attention to the fundamental question of monetary policy: Why have a central bank? Why allow government to become involved with the supplying of money?

THE THEORY OF COMPETITIVE MONETARY ARRANGEMENTS

Having arrived at a view of what laissez-faire in monetary arrangements would mean, I discovered that other contemporary economists had developed alternative visions. The first two chapters in Part

3 are an attempt to grapple with the "pure accounting system of exchange" or "new monetary economics" or "BFH system" discussed by Fischer Black, Eugene Fama, Robert Hall, Robert Greenfield, and Leland Yeager. I am particularly indebted to Greenfield and Yeager for many patient discussions and letters on these topics. The three of us spent the summer of 1981 at the Institute for Humane Studies, which was then in Menlo Park, California. They were then just developing the ideas that appeared in print in 1983. I was skeptical of the BFH view of what a laissez-faire system would look like, but then so were they. My critique of the literature began as an attempt, in fact, to coauthor a piece with Rob Greenfield. I have been gratified by the scholarly openness to criticism of their ideas that Greenfield and Yeager have shown.

My differences with Greenfield and Yeager are small, I think, in comparison with our agreements. I may have been guilty of overemphasizing the differences, so let me here stress the common ground. We agree that the current monetary system is radically defective, even absurd. It places the dangerous power to create monetary disequilibrium in the hands of political authorities. We agree that desirable reform lies in the direction of laissez-faire: barriers against private competitive payments systems should be dismantled. Our only real differences are over the shape a laissez-faire system could and should take, and correspondingly over how to get from here to there.

Chapter 11 provides a bit of a change of pace, having little directly to do with alternative monetary regimes. Written for the Ludwig Lachmann festschrift edited by Israel Kirzner (1986), it is my attempt to hash out the long-debated issue of how best to distinguish money from nonmoney. It was directly inspired by at least partial dissatisfaction with the attempts by Dale Osborne and Murray Rothbard that it cites. I argue for what I think is a common-sense approach to identifying what is money and what is not. I differ from Osborne by not identifying money exclusively with outside money, even though for many analytical purposes that is indeed the type of money on which it is appropriate to focus. I differ from Rothbard by consistently adhering to a single criterion of moneyness, namely general acceptance as a medium of exchange, and thereby excluding assets, such as passbook accounts, which are not directly spendable even though redeemable on demand for exchange media.

The essay titled "The Evolution of a Free Banking System," coauthored with George A. Selgin, began as a chapter of Selgin's doctoral dissertation, which I supervised at NYU. To a large extent it further develops, and provides historical support for, the evolutionary analysis in Chapter 9. Selgin undertook the bulk of historical research and wrote the first draft. I wrote subsequent drafts. The piece first appeared in the July 1987 issue of *Economic Inquiry*. An alternate version, shaped to fit into a book-length monograph rather than into a referred journal, appears in Selgin (1988), a revised version of his dissertation.

Our primary interest in this essay is not to bolster the critique of alternative visions of free-market payments systems, but to logically reconstruct the process through which competitive payments systems have (or would have) evolved.

The final chapter was first published in the November 1987 issue of *Journal of Money, Credit, and Banking*. Like Chapters 9 and 10, it is an attempt to come to grips with a vision contrary to my own concerning the institutional features of a laissez-faire payments system: in this case, the "legal restrictions theory" of money developed by Neil Wallace of the University of Minnesota and Federal Reserve Bank of Minneapolis and his coauthors. The "legal restrictions theory" predicts that in the absence of government regulation of private banking activity there would be no asset like money as we now know it, that is, non-interest-bearing non-commodity money would cease to exist. This prediction seems so obviously contrary to what we know from historical experience with virtually free banking systems—non-interest-bearing bank notes existed in all of them—that it cries out for an explanation. My explanation is that the legal restrictions theorists have overlooked some very simple features of transactions technologies in the real world that account for the survival of non-interest-bearing currency. My critique is deliberately quite narrowly focused, for I by no means wish to dismiss the legal restrictions theory as uninteresting or unworthy of serious attention. To show that it has implications which run contrary to the facts is not to show that rival equilibrium models of the rationale for money are any less flawed.

References

Cothren, Richard. 1987. "Asymmetric Information and Optimal Bank Reserves." *Journal of Money, Credit, and Banking* 19: 68–77.

Dorn, James A., and Anna J. Schwartz, eds. 1987. *The Search for Stable Money*. Chicago: University of Chicago Press.

Dowd, Kevin, Forthcoming. *The State and the Monetary System*. Oxford: Philip Allan.

Friedman, Milton. 1960. *A Program for Monetary Stability*. New York: Fordham University Press.

———. 1984. "Monetary Policy for the 1980s." In *To Promote Prosperity*, edited by John H. Moore. Stanford: Hoover Institution Press.

Friedman, Milton, and Anna J. Schwartz. 1986. "Has Government any Role in Money?" *Journal of Monetary Economics* 17: 37–62.

Gorton, Gary, and Donald J. Mullineaux. 1987. "The Joint Production of Confidence: Endogenous Regulation and Nineteenth Century Commercial-Bank Clearinghouses." *Journal of Money, Credit, and Banking* 19: 457–68.

Hanke, Steve H., ed. 1987. *Privatization and Development*. San Francisco: Institute for Contemporary Studies Press.

Hayek, F. A. 1978. *The Denationalisation of Money*, 2d ed. London: Institute of Economic Affairs.

Kirzner, Israel M., ed. 1986. *Subjectivism, Intelligibility, and Economic Understanding*. New York: New York University Press.

McKinnon, Ronald I. 1973. *Money and Capital in Economic Development*. Washington, D.C.: Brookings Institution.

Mises, Ludwig von. 1978. "Monetary Stabilization and Cyclical Policy." [1928]. In *On the Manipulation of Money and Credit*, translated by Bettina Bien Greaves, edited by Percy L. Greaves, Jr. Dobbs Ferry, N.Y.: Free Market Books.

Mullineaux, Donald J. 1987. "Competing Monies and the Suffolk Bank System: A Contractual Perspective." *Southern Economic Journal* 53: 884–97.

Rockwell, Llewellyn H., Jr., ed. 1985. *The Gold Standard: An Austrian Perspective*. Lexington, Mass.: Lexington Books.

Selgin, George A. 1988. *The Theory of Free Banking: Money Supply Under Competitive Note Issue*. Totowa, N.J.: Rowman and Littlefield.

Selgin, George A., and Lawrence H. White. 1988. "Competitive Monies and the Suffolk Bank System: Comment." *Southern Economic Journal* 54: 215–19.

Siegel, Barry N., ed. 1984. *Money in Crisis: The Federal Reserve, the Economy, and Monetary Reform*. Cambridge, Mass.: Ballinger.

Smith, Adam. 1976. *An Inquiry into the Nature and Causes of the Wealth of Nations* [1776], edited by R. H. Cambell, A. S. Skinner, and W. B. Todd. 2 vols. Oxford: Oxford University Press.

Timberlake, Richard H., Jr. 1984. "The Central Banking Role of Clearing-house Assocations." *Journal of Money, Credit, and Banking* 16: 1–15.
Willett, Thomas, ed. 1988. *Political Business Cycles: The Political Economy of Money, Inflation, and Unemployment.* Durham, N.C.: Duke University Press.

I

The Case for Free Banking

1

Free Banking as an Alternative Monetary System

Our current stagflationary malaise has reactivated the interest of American and European economists and policy analysts in the topic of alternative monetary institutions. Many economists and other observers perceive—and perceive rightly—that the institutions of their national monetary authorities are responsible for monetary disorder. The stress on *institutions* reflects the recognition—again correct—that monetary trends can neither be explained by reference to the personalities in positions of monetary authority nor be corrected by mere substitution of one set of faces for another. Nor can improvement be made by offering the existing authorities yet more good advice. In order to understand present conditions and to reform them, one must instead look to the incentive structure and the effective constraints surrounding the suppliers of money and credit.

This essay aims to contribute to the debate over alternative monetary institutions by discussing the features of a particular alternative system—free banking—that has not yet received professional or public attention commensurate with its attractiveness and importance. By "free banking" I refer generally to the unrestricted competitive issue of currency and deposit money by private banks on a convertible basis, not to the so-called free-banking systems adopted by a number of American state governments between the late 1830s and the Civil War. For the sake of easy conceptualization, I will focus on specie (full-bodied gold or silver coin) as the base money for which bank money is redeemable. What I say below is nonetheless

Reprinted, with changes, from *Money in Crisis: The Federal Reserve, the Economy, and Monetary Reform*, ed. Barry N. Siegel (Cambridge, Mass.: Ballinger, 1984), by permission of the publisher.

applicable, with suitable modification, to any system with a commodity or other base money whose quantity is not subject to manipulation by a government monetary authority (for example, a paper-based system in which the stock of irredeemable paper currency is permanently frozen).

THE RELEVANCE OF FREE BANKING

It may be helpful as a preface to our discussion to locate free banking within the framework of the debates over monetary institutions. In decades past, the issue of alternative monetary frameworks was treated primarily as a question of the desirability of "rules" or "discretion" for a monetary authority, the rationale for whose existence was not questioned.

Today it is widely recognized that allowing a monetary authority to pursue discretionary monetary policy carries two dangers that are not mutually exclusive. The first danger, one which has long been stressed by Milton Friedman and other monetarists,[1] is that the activist pursuit of policy objectives by use of monetary "tools" is almost certain to do more harm than good. Fine-tuning is impossible because of the inherently insufficient predictability of the impact of policy actions. The Federal Reserve Board's discretionary actions have proven historically to be a major cause of instability in the American economy. Stop-go monetary policy, because it makes business conditions unpredictable, inhibits long-term investment. The Fed has also proven susceptible to political pressure for cheaper credit.

This line of thought has been given new emphasis by writers adopting the rational-expectations perspective.[2] Only unanticipated policy has a systematic impact on real variables, and its impact is typically to *dis*coordinate an otherwise self-righting economy by misleading agents who are trying to read price signals. An activist policy only adds noise to the signals.

The second danger of discretionary policy, one which has recently been stressed by public-choice theorists, is that a government unconstrained in its power over the creation of base money can be expected systematically to abuse that power.[3] Inflationary creation of base money serves to enlarge the government's command over real resources in a way hidden from the populace. The wealth-redistributive character of monetary injections makes them suitable for use as a vote-buying tool.

These groups of economists who recognize the dangers of discretionary monetary policy typically propose as an alternative that the monetary authority be bound to obey a fixed rule of conduct, sometimes called a "monetary constitution." The particular rule commonly suggested by monetarists in the United States is that the Fed be duty-bound to manipuulate the monetary base so that some particular monetary aggregate conforms to a fixed growth rate of k percent, where k is a predetermined magnitude chosen for its consistency with price stability or some other goal. The dangers of this sort of rule, and of fixed monetary rules in general, have not been much emphasized in recent years. It therefore seems appropriate to review them at some length. One may wholeheartedly agree with the monetarist, rational-expectations, and public-choice arguments against discretionary policy, and even agree that almost any constraint that made the behavior of the monetary authority steadier and less inflationary would be an improvement, and yet be alive to the hazards of fixed rules and to the existence of other alternatives.

The primary hazard of putting the monetary authority on automatic pilot is that the economic system lacks an unchanging magnetic north pole. An inflexible rule of conduct will have consequences unintended by its designer should the orientation points of the monetary environment move in ways unanticipated at the time of design. Allowing that the rule may be modified when conditions dictate is equivalent to having no fixed rule at all.

For the sake of specificity, let us focus on the monetarist suggestion that the growth path of some monetary aggregate be dictated in advance. In practice, a particular monetary aggregate—the monetary base, M_1, M_2, M_3, or something larger—must be singled out. The limits of permissible deviation must be specified, either for the aggregate's growth rate over any period of a particular length or for its magnitude at particular dates stretching indefinitely into the future.[4] It is considered desirable to peg the growth of a monetary aggregate not because this is an end in itself, of course, but because the growth rates of prices and nominal income are believed to be geared to the growth rate of the monetary aggregate in a fairly constant ratio. The ratio is, however, unlikely to stay constant for any particular monetary aggregate. It is subject both to short-term volatility and to long-term structural change. Monetarists used to speak of pegging the growth rate of M_1. The recent meiosis of M_1 into M_{1A} and M_{1B}—and its even more recent reversal—should at least alert them to the fact that any particular monetary aggregate is a statistical artifact, liable to lapse eventually into irrelevance with further steps in the ongoing evolution of the payments mechanism and financial markets. The likelihood of such developments is enhanced by steps toward the deregulation of the banking and financial industries. It hardly need be added that the ultimate effect of electronic funds transfer systems on the income velocity of M_1, for example, can hardly be predicted with the confidence necessary for the drafting of a lasting monetary constitution.

To choose one of today's broader monetary aggregates as the permanent pivot upon which the entire monetary system is to swing hereafter must surely be an act of alarming boldness in the light of recent evidence of the mutability of commercial monetary institutions. The more perceptive monetarists have begun to acknowledge the danger. Leland B. Yeager has noted "the institutional developments that seem to be blurring distinctions between banks and other financial institutions and between the medium of exchange and near-moneys and even blurring the very concepts of money and its quantity." He recognizes that "if control over the quantity of money *does* become impractical and even conceptually elusive, some substitute must be found." We might add that those who wish to elevate the *k* percent rule to the status of a constitutional amendment must be willing to turn a blind eye to such possibilities. Yeager goes on correctly to point out that some nominal magnitude must be set exogenously to the banking system in order to render the purchasing power of money determinate. He concludes with this confession:

The method whose possible obsolescence has been worrying us is control of the number of units of medium of exchange in existence. Another is specification of the money price of some commodity or composite of commodities, with that price being kept meaningful by unrestricted two-way convertibility. Belatedly I must admit that the arguments for the gold standard or a composite-commodity standard are more intellectually respectable than I used to think and teach.[5]

Convertibility into gold or silver coin pins down nominal prices without reliance on an obsolescent quantity rule. Indeed, it carries no presumption that a monetary authority even exists.

Quite apart from the unpredictability that technical change imposes on the relationship between any particular monetary aggregate and other nominal variables, we should note another source of unpredictability. The introduction of this element is, ironically, quite in the spirit of rational expectations.[6] It is this: The estimated coefficients of the relationships between monetary aggregates and other nominal variables are, strictly regarded, relevant only to the past monetary regime under which they were observed. They are liable to change under the impact of such a policy innovation as the adoption of a k percent M_i growth rule. The choice of particular values of k and i can hardly be based with confidence upon such estimates. This objection was raised to the monetarist proposal by Jacob Viner more than twenty years ago:

Even if we accept an empirical constancy of relations discovered in the past as demonstrating a logical relation in that period, the introduction into the economic universe of a specific rule of behavior for the money supply would constitute an alteration of potential significance in the nature of that universe, and . . . we must not take for granted that the relation of the price level to the supply of money will be even approximately the same after such a rule is adopted and effectively enforced as it was before. The transformation of a hitherto unpredictable economic variable to one which everyone can predict with certainty is almost certain to have some effect, though one unpredictable in advance, on the pattern of its relations to other economic variables.[7]

In addition to these questions of unforeseeable change in the long-term trend of the velocity of any particular monetary aggregate, there is the distinct question of the short-run variability of the money multiplier, the relationship between a monetary target variable and the monetary base that the authority can directly manipulate. The M−1 money multiplier as measured by the Federal Reserve Bank of St. Louis has looked fairly stable even since the introduction of money-market deposit accounts in December 1982 and "super NOW" accounts in January 1983. But this appearance is misleading: it is primarily due to the fact that shifts in bank reserve ratios, properly counted as shifts in the money multiplier, are incorporated into the

St. Louis Fed's measure of the "adjusted" monetary base through a component called the "reserve adjustment magnitude." Hence recent shifts in funds from high-reserve to low-reserve accounts have shown up as changes in the adjusted monetary base rather than as shifts in the money multiplier.[8]

It is generally said that although variations in money multipliers prevent the Federal Reserve from accurately hitting monetary targets on a short-term (month-to-month or quarter-to-quarter) basis, it can on a sufficiently long-term basis hit its targets with reasonable accuracy. The very vagueness of this formulation should alert us to the question of whether the permissible band around the Fed's target can be drawn tightly enough to neutralize the disruptive swings in monetary growth rates that have characterized Fed policy in the past. If a past quarter's deviation of M_1 from target were treated entirely as a bygone, in practice there would be no rule constraining the path of M_1. The rule must dictate correction of errors to get M_1 back within the permissible band or cone. It must also dictate the speed of correction. The framers of a monetary growth rule must recognize an unfortunate trade-off between short-term money-market instability caused by veering back to path more sharply and medium-term general instability caused by correcting course more slowly. F. A. Hayek has pointed out the extreme danger of erring in the first direction:

As regards Professor Friedman's proposal of a legal limit on the rate at which a monopolistic issuer of money was to be allowed to increase the quantity in circulation, I can only say that I would not like to see what would happen if under such a provision it ever became known that the amount of cash in circulation was approaching the upper limit and that therefore a need for increased liquidity could not be met.[9]

Public knowledge of the approach to the limit would create an alarm that would temporarily raise desired cash balances and so exacerbate the liquidity crunch.

There is a simple way to enhance the predictability of velocity and the money multiplier, of course: tighten the rein of banking regulation in order to block out financial innovations and all other sources of variation. The reserve requirements of Federal Reserve System member banks were sometimes defended on this basis. The onerousness of these requirements prompted an exodus of banks from the system. The Fed's predictably bureaucratic response was to demand an end to the banks' freedom to leave the system on the grounds that a loss of member banks was weakening its control over the money supply. Those provisions of the Monetary Control Act of 1980 that extended reserve requirements to all banks were then a step in the direction of tighter regulation for the sake of firmer control.[10] So were recent extensions of reserve requirements to new forms of bank-issued interest-bearing certificates. Whether these controls achieve their ostensible end or not—it is likely that frequent regulatory changes *decrease* the predictability of the monetary system —they hamper domestic banks in their competition with other financial institutions and with foreign banks, and they harm the interests of the consumers of banking services.

Unfortunately, achievement of a workable, rigid, specific monetary rule may be inconsistent with deregulation of the banking industry.[11] The likelihood that this is indeed the case should give pause to those who, like Milton Friedman, support the fixed monetary rule as a device for enhancing economic liberty.[12] It would certainly be a perversion of policy, from the viewpoint of one sympathetic to the free working of markets, to restrict the banking industry's ability to serve consumers so that those administering monetary policy might have an easier time of it.

Free banking offers an escape from this policy box. The rules-discretion conundrum presupposes the existence of a monetary authority whose behavior must be either dangerously inflexible or dangerously flexible. An evident means of resolving this dilemma is to cultivate a monetary system not under the rule of a central authority. The most readily conceived system of this sort is that of free banking. A leading virtue of a free banking system is that it steers clear of both the hazards of discretionary monetary policy and the hazards of rigid monetary policy by freeing the monetary system entirely from bureaucratic control. Free banking is at the same time consistent with both determinateness of the purchasing power of the monetary unit and deregulation of the banking industry.

Some might object to this way of framing the alternatives because they view the convertibility of currency—into gold or silver coin, for example—as the imposition of a "rule." Several recent advocates of various forms of the gold standard have fostered this view by referring to convertibility as a "price rule" in contrast to the monetarist quantity rule. This way of speaking ceases to be helpful once we move beyond designing devices for channeling the behavior of a monetary authority. It obliterates an important distinction between designed order and spontaneous order.[13] Within a free-banking system, where there are many issuing banks but no government-sponsored central bank, convertibility prevails naturally without any legislature imposing it. Convertibility arises simply from the contractual agreement made by each issuer on the face of each note to redeem that note on demand for a specific quantity of specie.

We may briefly note the relevance of free banking to more recent discussions of alternative monetary frameworks. Two alternatives, in particular, have attracted attention in the United States: the gold standard and the system of competing private currencies proposed by Hayek. Roy W. Jastram has pertinently remarked on the new-found respectability of the gold standard among professional economists.[14] Readers of the *Wall Street Journal* in recent years have confronted a spate of columns and opinion pieces on the gold standard, pro and con. The question of gold gained widespread attention with the creation of the United States Gold Commission by the federal government.[15]

The boomlet of interest in the possibilities of private provision of currency has taken place mostly within academia. Professor Hayek deserves our recognition for opening this field to policy discussion, though earlier work of a less polemical sort had been done by others.[16] Free banking should be of interest to students both of the gold standard and of free currency competition. The system of competitive currencies under a specie standard has received scant notice in the recent literature, though it lies in an area of intersection between the gold standard and free currency competition.

We need not dwell here on the historical record of free banking, impressive though it is. I have elsewhere examined the most clear-cut case of the free banking on record, that of Scotland from 1716 to 1844.[17] During its free banking era, Scotland experienced remarkable economic growth with relatively little macroeconomic instability. The banking system enjoyed complete immunity from panics and runs. The American free banking era is not a clear-cut case, because of the tangle of regulations and entry requirements variously placed on banks of issue from state to state and because of the prohibition on interstate branch banking (which survives in large part even today). Vera Smith has aptly characterized the American system during this era as "decentralization without freedom."[18]

THE THEORY OF A FREE BANKING SYSTEM

Several authors have claimed that freedom to issue bank notes, even when issuers are bound to redeem notes for specie, implies either (1) an unlimited supply of bank notes and a correspondingly unlimited depreciation of the currency or (2) a perpetual and undampened oscillation in the quantity and value of the currency.[19] The most thorough way to evaluate these claims is to examine generally the operation of a free banking system, seeking to discover whether the self-interested actions of individual agents in that system give rise to equilibrating or disequilibrating processes.

In what follows, we first consider the equilibrium of an individual bank of issue within a free banking system. The bank issuing gold-convertible bank notes may be thought of as a profit-maximizing firm. For simplicity, we may assume that the firm holds only specie (gold and silver coin) and interest-earning commercial bills as assets and that it issues only bank notes and deposits as liabilities. The bank maximizes its profits subject to the accounting constraint that assets equal liabilities plus equity.

The upshot of this exercise is that the desired note circulation of the bank, considered as a choice variable for the bank, is limited by cost considerations. The rising marginal costs of maintaining notes in circulation set a limit to the bank's ability to expand permanently its holdings of bills and specie through issue of its notes. It may be nearly costless to print up additional notes and to *initiate* their circulation through bill purchases, but it is quite another matter to *maintain* their circulation in a competitive environment under convertibility. We discuss the various investments that a bank must undertake to make its notes relatively attractive for the public to hold.

We next consider the equilibrium of a free banking system as a whole. We assume that it operates within a small, open economy on an international specie standard. In this case, the domestic purchasing power of money is determined by the world purchasing power of specie. The demand for real currency balances by the domestic public then determines the desired nominal currency stock. The total stock of specie in the economy is determined by the conjunction of (1) this desired currency stock with (2) the public's desired ratio of coin to notes, (3) the desired specie-to-note reserve ratios of the various issuing banks, and (4) the shares of the circulation supplied by those banks. Changes in these four variables will change the domestic stock of specie in predictable directions, with the adjustment taking place through international specie flows.

We then examine the market mechanisms that move the banks within a free banking system toward equilibrium and so restrain them from overissuing. Having seen that the public's desired quantity of a particular bank's notes is a determinate magnitude, given that bank's optimizing expenditures, we consider the process by which the actual quantity is adjusted to the desired quantity. We show that the overissuing bank will find excess notes returning to it for redemption as note holders shed their excess notes. Reflux occurs either (1) through direct customer redemption or, more commonly, (2) through redemption demands from other banks that have accepted the excess notes as deposits. The second route involves the note-exchange system, an interbank clearing mechanism that we discuss.

However the excess notes return, the overexpansive bank will find its specie reserve dwindling. It must end its expansion and contract to protect itself from running out of reserves. The process by which the notes return may involve temporary changes in domestic prices and self-reversing international specie flows. These will be of greater magnitude the greater the relative size of the expansive bank (or group of banks acting in concert), suggesting the preferability of free banking to central banking under a specie standard.

Finally, we explain why independent issuing banks left to their own devices in a free banking system will be led, as if by an invisible hand, to participate in a note-exchange system.

The Individual Bank of Issue

Considered as an economic agent, a business firm is conventionally depicted in economic theory as pursuing self-interest in the specific

Table 1
Balance Sheet of the Issuing Bank

Assets		Liabilities plus Equity	
(Specie)	S	N	(Notes)
(Bills)	B	D	(Deposits)
		K	(Equity capital)

sense of profit maximization. Recent literature has sought to model the banking firm in this manner, drawing on the familiar optimization techniques of the neoclassical theory of the firm. The object of the literature has been to derive the formal conditions for the bank's optimal size and balance sheet composition.[20] We shall here adapt this approach to the situation of a note-issuing bank, treating the volume of its notes in circulation and the volume of its deposits as choice variables. With the aid of our model, we shall demonstrate that a profit-maximizing bank under the constraints of a free banking system does not attempt to push its notes into circulation ad infinitum. Rather, the issuing bank seeks to maintain a definitely limited circulation. In this section, we pursue the argument verbally. The mathematics of the optimization problem may be found in the chapter Appendix.

Consider a simplified version of the balance sheet of the issuing bank (Table 1), listing just two assets: specie and bills. The specie (precious metal in coined form) of the bank is its vault cash. Bills are its interest-earning assets. Purchase of commercial bills, or equivalently the granting of loans, is the usual means by which our bank issues its notes. The balance sheet lists three liabilities: notes, deposits, and equity capital. The outstanding notes of the bank constitute non-interest-bearing sight claims against its specie. Its deposits (which may be thought of either as demand deposits or as time deposits) are interest-bearing claims against its specie. Its capital is the fund originally contributed to the bank by its shareholders plus its accumulated earings.

Double-entry bookkeeping imposes the balance sheet constraint that assets equal the sum of liabilities plus equity: $S + B = N + D + K$. Taking equity as given, this implies that the bank cannot make additional loans (acquire more bills) without also either attracting additional depositors and note holders or losing specie. Although a greater volume of interest-earning assets taken by itself means a greater gross income for the bank, the bank must weigh this against the negative income factors (typically called "costs")[21] that necessarily accompany it. Conceptually, we may distinguish three sorts of costs that the bank faces: simple operating costs, liquidity costs, and interest payments to liability holders. All three costs naturally increase with the volume of the bank's assets and liabilities. Beyond some point, their sum increases faster than revenue, and so expansion beyond that point is unprofitable.

We may offer a more concrete interpretation to the various operating costs that the bank faces. The operating costs associated with discounting and holding commercial bills of exchange are costs of information, transaction, and self-insurance. They are expenses incurred in ascertaining the creditworthiness of bill issuers, in enforceing the repayment obligation upon maturation of the bills, and in absorbing some percentage of bad debts. These costs presumably rise at the margin, since as the bank expands its discounting, it must resort to borrowers whose creditworthiness it knows less well. The bank must either incur greater unit costs to screen these borrowers or suffer a great percentage of defaulters among them. The operating costs of holding specie are costs of storage and security.

It is important to understand the costs associated with maintaining notes in circulation, if only because in the past century the opponents of free banking so often built their case on the implicit assumption that a bank of issue could extend its circulation gratuitously. It is one thing to print up notes and to *initiate* their circulation; it is quite another to *maintain* their circulation in a competitive environment. Where the plurality of competing issuers gives the public a choice among brands of bank notes, each issuer must expend resources in giving its brand the qualities most attractive to at least some members of the public. Notes beyond the quantity wanted by the public will not remain in circulation but will return to the issuer upon whom they are claims. We should expect the rivalry among note issuers to be in many ways similar to the present-day rivalry among issuers of checking accounts.

Perhaps the most elementary quality dimension on which the

public may be expected to distinguish among bank note brands, as it does now among checking account brands, is ease of redemption. To attract a greater clientele requires, therefore, such expenses as longer operating hours, a greater number of tellers, additional local branch offices, and more extensive advertising of the availability of these conveniences. A second area of quality competition, one that Benjamin Klein has stressed with regard to inconvertible currencies, is public confidence in the reliability of an issuer's notes.[22] Individuals will be less disposed to hold the notes of a less trustworthy issuer, and so issuers must compete to convince the public of their superior reliability. Under a system of private bank notes convertible at par into specie, the primary aspect of reliability is the assurance that convertibility will not be delayed or denied on account of the bankruptcy, illiquidity, or fraud of the issuing bank. Confidence-bolstering expenditures would include the construction and maintenance of an impressive bank edifice, publicity of the bank's sound financial health, "image" advertising, and whatever else might reassure note holders that theirs are not the notes of a fly-by-night outfit. A secondary aspect of reliability is the ease with which the authenticity of individual notes may be ascertained. Enhancing public confidence in their genuine character might call for greater expenditures on designing, engraving, watermarking, and signing of notes, or for a more generous (costly) policy toward counterfeit notes tendered by innocent parties.

A potential third area of circulation-promoting expense is the payment of an explicit interest yield to note holders.[23] For competition to compel an issuer to make such payments in practice, the payment must more than compensate the note holder for the trouble of collecting the payment, and the operating cost of making the payment should not render interest-bearing notes unprofitable for the issuer. A characteristic feature of hand-to-hand currency, however—a feature that helps sustain the demand to hold it even where interest-bearing checking accounts are available—is the comparative ease associated with using it in small transactions. To collect interest for the holding of a bank note would require going through a bothersome procedure such as having the date of original issue stamped upon it and having the accumulated interest calculated with each paying over of the note. Since the bother involved is the same for any denomination of note, whereas the interest yield rises with the magnitude of the denomination and the length of time between transfers, we would be more likely to observe interest payments on notes of large denominations and notes that circulate more slowly (these are likely to coincide) than on notes of smaller denominations and notes that circulate more rapidly. The use of large bank notes in a modern economy, however, is itself likely to be less convenient than the use of checking deposits. Competitive free banking is therefore not inconsistent with an absence of interest-bearing currency. Notice that traveler's checks today, even though they are paid over only once and are issued competitively, do not bear interest.

The operating costs associated with deposits are similar to those associated with notes. Depositors, like note holders, must be assured of the trustworthinesss of the bank whose liabilities they hold. Deposit and withdrawal flows, like demands to change notes for specie and vice versa, must be serviced.

We call "liquidity costs" the expenses that the bank must bear in the event of an impending exhaustion of specie. These costs may be thought of concretely as the transactions and shipping costs of arranging to purchase (or to borrow) specie and have it delivered on short notice. Should a temporary deficiency not result in an immediate declaration of bankruptcy, these costs may also include whatever expense is necessary to compensate inconvenienced customers. Expected liquidity costs increase with an increase in the volume of notes or deposits (for a given volume of specie reserves) and decrease with an increase in specie reserves (for a given volume of notes and deposits).

Profit-maximizing equilibrium requires that the bank meet a number of equimarginal conditions. Its marginal net revenue from holding bills (yield minus the marginal operating costs of bill holding) must be equated to its marginal net benefit from holding specie (reduction in expected liquidity cost minus the marginal operating costs of specie holding). The bank must be indifferent between holding extra bills and holding extra specie of the same market value, for it can trade one for the other in the market. The marginal net revenue from holding bills must also be equated to the sum of the marginal operating cost and the marginal expected liquidity cost of maintaining notes in circulation. The rising marginal costs associated with a growing volume of bank notes outstanding set a limit to the extent of the bank's discounting operations (i.e., its purchases of bills with its notes). The marginal net revenue from holding bills must also be equated to the sum of the interest payments, operating costs, and expected liquidity costs associated with a marginal addition to the stock of deposits. The rising marginal costs of attracting and servicing deposits set a limit to the extent of the bank's purchases of bills with funds from that source.

Profit maximization similarly requires that the marginal net benefit from holding specie is equated to the total marginal cost of maintaining notes in circulation. The rising marginal costs of maintaining a note circulation set a limit to the bank's ability profitably to effect permanent purchases of specie with its notes, just as they set a limit to its purchases of bills. The marginal net benefit from holding specie must also be equated to the total marginal cost of acquiring it by attracting and maintaining an increased stock of deposits. The rising marginal costs of expanding the bank's deposit business set a limit to the bank's ability profitably to acquire specie from depositors. Finally, the marginal cost of enlarging the bank's assets by an expansion of its note circulation is equated to the marginal cost of enlargement by expansion of deposits. At the margin, the two sources of funds are equally costly.

Beyond the point defined by these conditions, the bank's marginal costs of expansion will rise, although its marginal revenue from bill holding will not. The profit-maximizing bank in a freely competitive banking system will therefore seek to issue definitely limited quantities of notes and deposits. It cannot expand the volume of its notes or deposits gratuitously.

The System as a Whole

Having considered the equilibrium position of an individual bank of issue, we now consider the equilibrium position of the system as a whole. We may illuminate certain properties of a free banking system by analyzing the relationship between the quantity of money (the nonbank public's holdings of specie plus bank notes plus checking deposits) and the total stock of specie held by banks and the public. The specie stock is in some respects the analogue of what in the present system is called the monetary base or the stock of high-powered money. A free banking system differs from the present American banking system in having its reserve ratios determined entirely by bankers' prudence rather than by a monetary authority's requirements or by a combination of required reserve ratios plus some prudential margin. This difference makes the system no less determinate.

The free-banking model differs more fundamentally in being a small open economy with fixed exchange rates and hence having nominal money stock determined "outside" the banking system by the conjunction of the public's desired real money balances and the purchasing power of specie, both regarded as data for the system. This difference means that the banking system would not determine the domestic quantity of money given the monetary base, as it does today, but would determine instead the quantity of specie. The nominal quantity of bank reserves plus basic currency would not be determined by a monetary authority, as in a fiat money central banking system. Hence, no central authority would have the power to create monetary disturbances by altering the quantity of high-powered money.

Under present-day conditions of flexible exchange rates, the size of the monetary base is determined by the monetary authority. Changes in the domestic monetary base, given the fractional reserve ratios of the banks, lead to even larger changes in the nominal stock of currency and bank deposits held by the public. Prices rise until the expanded stock of money is willingly held. It is more natural for a free banking system, however, to operate within a small, open economy with fixed exchange rates, as Scotland did during its free-banking period. We accordingly assume that the basic money of our free banking system, gold and silver coin, is money throughout the world economy. Precious metals may be freely imported and exported, with a negligible impact on the worldwide purchasing power of the metals. Interregional specie flows bring the actual specie stock of the region into adjustment with its equilibrium stock in accordance with David Hume's specie flow mechanism.[24] In this case, with the purchasing power of money given to our economy by the world market, the public's desired stock of real money balances determines the desired nominal money stock.[25] Exogenous changes in desired real money balances lead, ceteris paribus, to changes in the desired stock of specie, both directly and by their effect on desired bank specie reserves. The new desires will be met by interregional specie flows.

The relationship of the money stock to the quantity of specie depends, for a given desired stock of money, upon the relative quantities of specie, notes, and checking deposits desired by members of the public and upon the various quantities of specie reserves relative to notes in circulation and checking deposits desired by the issuing banks, weighted by their respective shares of total note circulation and total checking deposits. The *actual* quantity of specie relative to notes and checking deposits tends toward the public's specific *desired* quantity. Should the actual quantity be below the desired quantity, the public will convert notes and deposits with the issuing banks. We may similarly assume that each bank adjusts its actual quantity of vault specie relative to outstanding note circulation and checking deposits in accordance with the specific relationships it desires to maintain and that members of the public adjust their note holdings so that the various issuing banks' shares of the total circulation tend toward the specific shares desired in the aggregate by the public. We examine below the mechanisms of adjustment in this last case.

When the public desires to hold a greater share of its money in the form of specie rather than in notes or deposits, and when particular banks desire to hold a greater quantity of specie reserves relative to notes and deposits in circulation, a short-run equilibrating tendency will arise for specie to flow in from outside the region. As a particular bank's percentage share of the total note circulation increases, a tendency for specie to flow in will arise if and only if the consequent addition to the bank's desired specie reserves is greater than the consequent reduction in desired reserves of the banks whose market shares decline. The converse propositions also hold.

Mechanisms Regulating the Currency Stock

We are now in a position to examine generally the working of a note-exchange mechanism and other processes regulating the issue of bank notes. We saw above that the solution of the issuing bank's optimization problem determined, under reasonable assumptions concerning cost functions, a unique profit-maximizing magnitude for the stock of its notes in circulation. For issuer i, we denote this value N^{i*}. Because we have treated the "selling" costs of promoting the demand to hold its notes as simple production costs, which indeed they are from the banking firm's point of view, N^{i*} represents the public's desired quantity of bank i notes given that bank's optimizing expenditures. (We need not bother to distinguish in this section between nominal and real quantities of notes, given the context of convertibility of notes into a medium whose purchasing power is determined on a global basis.)

A general consideration of the possibilities for quality competition among bank note issuers, then, is sufficient to demonstrate that the desired stock of any particular bank's notes is a determinate magnitude under free banking. We do not have to resort to a special assumption that each issuer enjoys a geographic monopoly or that for some other reason each member of the public holds the notes only of a single bank. We do not have to suppose that within a region of many issuers some individuals refuse to accept the notes of some banks in payments,[26] so long as individuals do refuse to *hold* various brands of notes indefinitely in any but particular desired quantities.

Let us now consider the process by which the actual stock of notes issued by an individual bank—call it bank A—is adjusted to the public's desired stock. We consider the case in which the actual stock exceeds the desired stock, $N^A > N^{A*}$. This situation of an excess stock of notes may arise either because bank A has expanded its issue of notes without warrant or because the demand to hold them has fallen. Perhaps the most readily conceived scenario is one in which bank A, beginning from an initial optimum, expands its loans and discounts of bills, placing additional notes into the hands of its loan customers and the persons to whom they in turn spend away their loan proceeds, but does nothing to increase N^{A*}. We assume that bank A is one of many issuing banks within a region, all accepting one another's notes and participating in a regular note exchange. The region is defined as the geographic area of circulation of the participating banks' notes. We begin from an equilibrium situation in which neither specie nor any other banks' notes are in excess supply. We make the ceteris paribus assumption that underlying money-holding preferences do not shift.

There are three ways in which individual agents may in the immediate run respond to an excess holding of bank *A* notes: (1) They may redeem the notes for specie at the counter of the issuing bank; (2) they may place the notes into a deposit account, possibly interest-bearing, at their preferred banks; (3) they may hold the notes as buffer stock with the intention of spending the notes away to other agents within the region. This last action spreads the impact of the overissue over time. In general, agents will choose a combination of these courses of action in the light of their preferences and perceived situations.

Under the first course of action, direct redemption for specie, the reflux of the excess notes is immediate. The issuing bank immediately experiences a loss of specie reserves as they are paid across the counter. In actual experience, we may expect this path of reflux to be of minor importance. In the typical case, individual agents would probably find it more convenient to deal with their regular banks (assuming that their banks accept the notes of bank *A*), depositing the notes and withdrawing coin from their deposit accounts if desired.

The second course of action, deposit of the notes, brings the note exchange into play, supposing that the bank receiving the deposit is not the bank of issue in question. The note exchange is simply the periodic settlement among participating banks of the claims represented by their notes. These claims are collected by the banks when they accept deposits and loan repayments in one another's notes. (We examine below why issuing banks may be expected to agree to mutual acceptance and to join in a note exchange.) The deposit of an unusually large volume of bank *A* notes in other banks will result in an adverse clearings balance against bank *A* at the note exchange. The balance must be settled by the transfer of an agreed-upon medium—we may assume it to be specie—from bank *A* to the other banks. Thus the reflux of excess notes placed on deposit at other banks is delayed only until the date of the next note clearing. At that time, the expansive bank *A* suffers a loss of reserves, whereas the more conservative banks enjoy a corresponding gain of reserves.

Note that neither of these courses necessarily brings the individual agents to final portfolio equilibrium: They may hold an excess stock of specie or deposits. But we have traced the process far enough to show that bank *A* has begun to feel a loss of reserves.

Excess notes redeposited with bank *A* do not immediately subject it to a loss of reserves. Thus, the immediate check on overissue is attenuated according to the share of excess notes held by those who do their deposit banking with bank *A*. But redeposited notes do subject bank *A* to greater expenses in interest payments without bringing the added reserves that deposits of specie or another banks' notes bring.

Notes held or spent within the region by agents following the third course of action do not immediately return to the issuer. Instead, they remain in circulation for the time being, exerting upward pressure on prices. In due course, these excess notes will be returned to the issuing bank through the first and second routes, redemption and deposit, as note holders reassert their preferences. But we must trace the intervening sequence.

To some extent, the excess stock of notes will bring about increased spending on goods imported from outside the region we have been considering. This spending will result directly as agents draw down excess currency balances and may also result indirectly as they respond to the rise in local prices brought about by increased spending on local goods. Increased spending on imports will in turn give rise to a balance of payments deficit for the region. Because local notes are not acceptable outside the region, the balance must be settled in specie. Local banks will temporarily lose specie to the rest of the world during the adjustment process. The loss will not be permanent under the ceteris paribus assumption that there are no underlying shifts in money-holding preferences. The regional efflux of specie (or "external drain") will instead be self-reversing.[27]

The expansive bank *A* will bear the brunt of the specie lost through direct spending, since by hypothesis the excess currency balances consist exclusively of its notes. Since these notes do not circulate outside the region, they must first be redeemed for specie, either directly (course 1) or indirectly via deposits in other banks (course 2). Since holders of all brands of notes within the region face higher prices, the shift in spending in response to higher local prices will impinge upon the reserves of other banks in the region. Recall, however, that these banks simultaneously enjoy positive clearings from the reflux of notes through the deposit route.

We thus conclude that the overexpansive bank in a free banking system will sooner or later be disciplined by a loss of its reserves. The process will run its course sooner, to the extent that excess notes are immediately vented in the first two ways, or later, to the extent that they are initially vented in the third way (which must eventually result in their being returned to the issuer in the first two ways). Having started from an initial profit-maximizing equilibrium position, bank *A*, with smaller reserves, is now placed in a suboptimal position. Its reduced specie holding subjects it to an unacceptably high risk of exhausting its liquid reserve and consequently defaulting on its note obligations. In terms of our model, the net benefit from holding additional specie now exceeds the marginal net revenue from holding bills. An increase in specie reserves and a decrease in bill holdings is called for.

To reestablish its initial equilibrium position following a period of overissue, the expansive bank must reverse course. It may replenish its reserves by pursuing a relatively restrictive policy for a period, thereby enjoying positive clearings against the other banks. Or it may simply sell off bills for specie. At the same time, the region as a whole will experience an influx of specie to restore the holdings of its inhabitants and banks to their equilibrium levels.

We have thus far confined ourselves to the case of an overissuing bank acting alone. In the case of overissue by a group of banks or all banks within a region acting in concert, the process leading back to equilibrium through disciplinary reserve losses is the same. There is, however, a potentially important difference of degree: the larger the share of total circulation and deposits supplied by the overissuing banks, the greater the role of disruptive external drain in bringing the expansion to an end.

That reflux through the note exchange will not check a joint expansion should be clear. Supposing a group of banks within a region to expand by a common factor, no adverse clearings will arise because each member of the group will meet the increased volume of notes returned to it by way of deposit in other member banks with an equally increased volume of notes of those other banks deposited with it. There will of course be a loss of reserves from members of the group to any nonexpansive banks. Should all the banks in a region overissue, the system as a whole will lose reserves to the world beyond the region and to the public (who will desire additional specie holdings as prices rise in the short run). If the region comprises the world, only the public's demand for real specie acts as a drain on bank reserves.

The Genesis of the Note Exchange

Our discussion in the previous section presupposed the existence of an effectively functioning note-exchange system embracing a number of independent banks of issue. Here we attempt to explain why the independent issuing banks in a free banking system will be led, as if by an invisible hand, to promote the institution of a general note-exchange system. Our method of explanation follows that of Carl Menger, who offered an invisible-hand explanation for the emergence of the institution of money.[28] This method of explaining the origins of social institutions, and of course the term "invisible hand," may be traced to Adam Smith and earlier writers of the Scottish enlightenment. An invisible-hand explanation shows how the decentralized actions of purely self-interested agents may, without their intending it, give rise to a cohesive order.[29]

Consider an initial situation in which several banks in a region issue convertible bank notes, yet none accepts any other's notes for deposit or loan repayment. Holders of bank i notes who wish to pay the notes into a different bank must go through a costly intermediate step: either returning the notes to bank i for redemption in specie or engaging the services of an agent who does so for a fee (a local money changer). The salability of bank i notes is limited in comparison with specie: specie can, but the notes cannot, buy deposits in other banks. This limitation has both a minor direct and a major indirect effect on N^{i*}, because N^{i*} is presumably a function of the salability of bank i notes. The indirect effect is that sellers who regularly deposit their currency receipts in bank j will likely refuse to exchange their merchandise for bank i notes at par. The salability of bank i notes is thus further impeded and N^{i*} further reduced.

If other banks accepted bank i notes, those notes would enjoy increased salability and consequently a greater demand to hold them in preference to specie. In this situation, a pair of issuers—call them banks F and G—would find that each improves its position by agreeing to accept the other's notes at par. Mutual acceptance increases both N^{F*} and N^{G*}. Both banks would find it profitable to enter into a regular note-exchange arrangement. Neither bank would wish to accumulate the other's notes ad infinitum or to reissue them in place of its own. If the banks demanded redemption from one another without arranging a note exchange—for example, if bank F presented its bank G notes for redemption without allowing bank G to offset its liability by relinquishing its accumulated bank F notes—both banks would incur greater expected liquidity costs from the increased variance of net specie outflow, not to mention greater transportation costs of bringing the specie back home, than they would if they arranged a note exchange. Bank F's claims on bank G's specie are then offset by bank G's reciprocal claims. Each bank would want to set the regularity or frequency of the exchange in order to equate the marginal reduction in expected liquidity costs from more frequent exchange to the marginal increase in operating costs from more frequent exchange.[30]

The prospect of increasing the salability of their notes will make other banks join the note-exchange arrangement. They may join singly, or they may enter into separate arrangements that later merge with the first note exchange. Eventually a single note exchange will include all profit-seeking banks within a region.[31] Banks do not aim to establish a systemwide note exchange—bank C would benefit as much and possibly more if banks D, E, and F did not exchange among themselves—yet their profit-seeking actions have that unintentional.

The arrangements among the banks need not be symmetrical. Bilateral dealings of this sort exhibit an indeterminacy in distributing the gains from trade.[32] All banks voluntarily joining a note exchange presumably gain from its existence, however. The mutual acceptance arrangement improves the negotiability of every participant's notes. There is room for every bank to enjoy an increase in the demand to hold its notes, since the public substitutes holdings of notes for holdings of specie at the margin.[33]

In a bilateral note exchange, the clearing balance is computed simply between the two participants. Where third and further banks enter the arrangement, it is likely to be cheaper to conduct the exchange multilaterally than as a series of bilateral exchanges. A single clearing balance is computed to each bank against all other banks, and settlements are paid into and out of a central pool. We assumed above that adverse clearing balances at the note exchange were settled in specie. Certainly, a bank with a positive balance could insist upon specie, given the legal commitments of other issuers to convertibility of their notes into specie. But the costs of settlement can likely be economized by agreeing to substitute for specie shipments the transfer of some other agreed-upon medium. All banks might, for example, hold specie reserves on deposit with a single institution, which clears note-exchange balances by transferring the deposits on its books. Or they might transfer holdings of an especially liquid interest-earning asset issued outside the banking system.[34] In either case the disciplinary power of the note exchange against overissues by an individual bank would not be attenuated. A bank could still not permit an outflow of reserves to persist. Unanticipated reserve losses would still place the bank in a suboptimal position and signal it to contract its issues.

The Rationale of Free Banking

Having developed an account of the self-regulating manner in which a free banking system operates, we may in this final section attempt briefly to answer likely criticisms and misinterpretations of the case for free banking. In doing so, we will suggest what we consider the compelling advantages of free banking as a monetary system.

We do not claim on behalf of free banking that it uniquely or most effectively serves any particular macroeconomic policy goal such as price-level stability, price-level predictability, interest-rate stability, or reduced opportunity costs of holding currency (though it is consistent with each of these goals). On the contrary, its special virtue is that it frees money from use as a tool by those of constructivist bent who would impose tidy designs upon the economy. A free banking system is subservient only to the forces of competition among the producers of monetary services attempting to meet consumers' demands profitably. For that reason, it will not be popular with the economist who believes that a monetary system ought to be designed (that is, ought by rational construction) to promote the ends this economist finds desirable. It is no doubt possible to design a monetary system that would—so long as the real world conforms to the ceteris paribus conditions of the designer's model and so long as the monetary authorities behave virtuously—out-perform a free banking system in respect to achieving a specific target.[35] One designer's target, however, may be inconsistent with another's target, and both may be inconsistent with the preferences of the consumers of monetary services.

Proponents of managed fiat money of often argue that it is "inefficient" to allow a commodity stock to serve as the monetary base. Efficiency or inefficiency, however, is a property of alternative means considered in relation to the same end. A designed government-run monetary system may be more efficient than free banking in serving the narrow goals of the designer, of the monetary authority created, or of the government that adopts the design. But this judgment has no bearing on the question of whether the system is efficient in the usual economic sense, where the satisfaction of given consumer preferences is taken as the relevant goal. An example should illustrate this point. David Ricardo, one of the earliest monetary constructivists, denounced as wastefully inefficient the use of gold coins of large denominations as currency when paper currency could be made to serve in their stead. He admitted, however, that consumers offered a choice preferred to hold the coins.[36] Under those circumstances, a forced substitution of paper currency for coins would not have been efficient in serving the ends of monetary consumers.

Benjamin Klein has emphasized the important point that, where consumers have a choice, their willingness to hold a particular brand of currency depends on the confidence they have that its issuer will not cheat them. An issuer of inconvertible currency must be trusted not to inflate its supply unexpectedly.[37] An issuer of convertible currency must correspondingly be trusted not to refuse redemption. An issuer of specie must be trusted not to debase its metallic content. The metal itself must be trusted not to fall in relative value. Put another way, trustworthiness is an important quality of the economic good we call money.

Klein applies the criterion of consumer confidence to the question of the efficiency of substituting bank notes for specie. Bank note producers did not gain a foothold in the currency industry until they could produce trustworthy currency cheaply enough in competition with specie. Klein comments: "A forced movement from commodity to pure fiduciary money, for example, in the nineteenth century, would have implied a negative social saving."[38]

We may take this argument a step further. The forced substitution of fiat currency for convertible currency, like the Ricardian forced substitution of convertible currency for coin, is by no means efficient when it contravenes consumer preference for what is considered a more trustworthy currency. Lowering production costs does not constitute efficiency when the resulting product if one of lower quality in consumers' eyes. The actual forced movement in the twentieth century from a gold-convertible dollar to an inconvertible dollar must have represented a "negative social saving," to use Klein's phrase, if currency users would have preferred to continue using gold and gold-convertible currency. The federal government's resort to confiscation of gold and prohibition of gold-clause contracts in 1933 indicated its awareness of such a preference.

A comparison of the dollar's purchasing power before and after the termination of its gold-convertibility suggests that the public's trust in gold-convertible currency rather than in fiat currency was not misplaced.[39] George Bernard Shaw gave a succinct statement of the rationale for trusting gold over paper:

> To sum up, the most important thing about money is to maintain its stability. . . . With paper money this stability has to be maintained by the Government. With a gold currency it tends to maintain itself. . . . You have to choose (as a voter) between trusting to the natural stability of gold and the natural stability of the honesty and intelligence of the members of the Government. And, with due respect for these gentlemen, I advise you, as long as the Capitalist system lasts, to vote for gold.[40]

It might be argued that today the shoe is on the other foot—that specie-convertible currency must bear the burden of proving itself to be the currency most efficient at meeting consumer wants in a free market. This argument has some force. It applies especially to novel alternative monetary systems such as F. A. Hayek's private inconvertible currencies and Robert E. Hall's composite commodity standard, to name two recent proposals.[41] Only the market can adjudicate among competing claimants to the status of most desirable currency. It cannot be said, however, that the continued dominance of the Federal Reserve note represents a free market verdict.

In the United States today, competition among currencies remains closed despite the re-legalization of gold ownership and gold-clause contracts. Unrestricted competition among currencies would require at least the following reforms: (1) an end to any forced tender laws that compel acceptance of government currency in discharge of debt and thereby prevent private contracts in other media of exchange from being legally enforced; (2) an end to any legal restrictions on entry into banking and finance that prevent private entrepreneurs from offering, for example, specie-convertible notes and deposits; and (3) changes in any tax laws that restrict accounting or transactions using alternative currency units. As concrete evidence of legal barriers to entry, we note that an experiment with privately issued indexed currency and deposits in Exeter, New Hampshire, from June 1972 to January 1974 was ended under legal pressure from the Securities and Exchange Commission.[42]

One could not justify legal barriers to entry even if the production of money were a natural monopoly, because a natural monopoly needs no such barriers to support it. But more importantly, the idea that money production is in fact a natural monopoly rests on a confusion. Consideration of free banking on a commodity-convertible basis allows us to recognize that the question of a natural monopoly in the production of money is distinct from the question of an inherent market tendency toward convergence on a single monetary standard. The latter does exist, for the reasons Carl Menger spelled out: every transactor promotes his self-interest by using the single most salable commodity in the economy as a medium of exchange.[43] Roland Vaubel finds characteristics of a natural monopoly in the production of currency because he fails to make this distinction.[44] He confines his attention to competing inconvertible currencies, each currency constituting its own standard. Benjamin Klein, although he takes note of free banking as a case of "multiple monies convertible into a single dominant money," unfortunately persists in asserting that "the money industry is essentially a natural monopoly," as though this were the same as asserting the existence of a tendency toward a single dominant money.[45]

Where the single dominant money is a commodity like gold or silver coin, there is no reason to suppose that a natural monopoly—in the standard sense of continually falling average costs—exists at any level: mining of the metal, coinage, issue of convertible bank notes, or issue of deposit monies. There is no reason to suppose that a single producer could capture the entire market for ore, coins, bank notes, or deposits. That all coins are manufactured of like metals in like weights, and that all notes and deposits are redeemable for standard coin, no more indicates a natural monopoly in money production that the standardization of brick composition and size indicates a natural monopoly in brick production.

Nor should it be argued that the recent volatility of gold and silver prices indicates that precious metals are no longer suitable for use as a monetary base.[46] That price volatility has resulted largely from speculation concerning the profitability of holding metals relative to that of holding dollar-denominated assets. If the dollar were redefined as so many grams of silver, say, or if silver supplanted the Federal Reserve note as the dominant money, this motive for speculation in silver would cease. There would no longer be any scope for buying or selling silver in hopes that its dollar price might rise or fall. The silver market would become one with the market in U.S. currency. There might still be speculation in silver against other currencies, but only for the motives that spur dollar speculation in currency markets today. There is no reason to believe that the market for a specie-convertible money would be more subject to price volatility than the market for a fiat money. In fact, there is good reason to believe the reverse. As is well known, the relative price elasticity of both the supply and the nonmonetary (industrial and consumer) demand for the precious metal would add elements tending to stabilize the metal's purchasing power in the face of shifts in the demand to hold specie and specie-convertible money.

Our theoretical discussion assumed that the monetary base consisted of coins minted of a metal used worldwide as currency. For the first area to move from a fiat money system to a free banking system, this worldwide use of its basic money would not yet obtain. Our model of a small, open economy would have to be modified to recognize that the purchasing power of the monetary unit would be determined jointly with the equilibrium nominal domestic monetary base. The determinateness of the system would by no means be impaired. The free banking area would continue to have floating exhange rates against other currency areas and so would continue to be insulated against monetary shocks emitted by foreign suppliers of fiat currency. Undeniably, it would experience a new susceptibility to shifts in the supply curve for the monetary metal, but, as argued above, this is less worrisome than the present susceptibility of the system to shifts in the behavior of the monetary authority. Were other areas to adopt the specie standard of the original free banking area, money holders in the original area would profit from an appreciation in the value of their money on world markets.

The rationale for implementing the reforms necessary for free currency competition, apart from their other obvious microeconomic benefits, is simply this: If government-produced fiat money really does suit consumers best, there is no rationale for impediments to its potential competitors. It may be that the inherent tendency of the market to converge upon a single standard money or monetary base would allow the government-produced fiat currency unit to retain its monetary role even if all such impediments were removed.[47] The central section of this chapter supports the position that doubts about the stability of a free banking system on a specie standard are unwarranted, and therefore provide no basis for resisting its emergence. Further argument would be necessary to establish the case that the dollar ought to be made redeemable for gold or silver coin or bullion in order to facilitate the emergence of free banking on a specie standard. That argument would have to appeal to redemption of outstanding currency as the best way to make the transition to a monetary system built upon a base money freely chosen by the market. If one believes that the particular brand of inconvertible currency issued by government ought to be allowed to compete with other base monies, there is no reason that any gold the government holds—in the United States it is held primarily at Fort Knox—should not be distributed to the public, as Richard H. Timberlake has suggested.[48]

Unlike other proposals for denationalizing money, free banking has a history. It developed naturally, where permitted, out of a pure specie monetary system, which had developed naturally out of barter. There is no question that free banking on a specie standard is a viable system. Were it not for the legislative creation of central banks, primarily to meet the demands of central governments for inflationary finance, free banking would be with us today.

Appendix: Mathematics of the Optimization Problem

Double-entry bookkeeping imposes the balance sheet constraint

$$S + B = N + D + \overline{K}$$

The bank's expected profit function is:

$$\pi = r_b B - r_d D - C - L$$

where

$\pi \equiv$ expected profit
$r_b \equiv$ the yield rate earned on bills held
$r_d \equiv$ the yield rate paid on deposits
$C \equiv$ total operating costs
$L \equiv$ expected liquidity costs.

The yield rate r_b and r_d are treated as exogenously given to the bank, that is, as invariant with respect to the quantity of bills in purchases and deposits it attracts. This price-taking assumption could easily be modified to allow for price-searching behavior. Operating costs are assumed to be a twice-differentiable function of the balance sheet entries:

$$C = f(S, B, N, D)$$

We may assume the expected liquidity cost function $L = g(S, N, D)$ to take a somewhat specific form:

$$L = \int_S^\infty p(X - S)\, \phi\,(X/N, D)\, dX$$

where

$p \equiv$ percentage adjustment cost for impending specie deficiency, for simplicity assumed constant, so that realized cost $p(X - S)$ is linear in the size of the deficiency, $X - S$
$X \equiv$ net specie outflow during the period

$\emptyset(X/N,D)\equiv$ the probability density function over X, conditional on N and D.

The practical import of this equation is that expected liquidity costs decrease with an increase in S (N and D held constant). It is natural to assume in addition that $\emptyset$ $(X/N,D)$ behaves in such a way that expected liquidity costs increase with an increase in N or D (S held constant). Letting a subscript denote partial differentiation with respect to the subscripted variable, we may therefore write:

$$L_S<0, L_N>0, L_D>0.$$

The implications of profit maximization for the bank may be derived most clearly by setting out its choice problem as a Lagrangean constrained maximization problem:

$$\pi(S,B,N,D,\overline{K}) = r_bB - r_dD - C - L + \lambda(\overline{K} - S - B + N + D)$$
$$\pi_s = -C_s - L_s - \lambda = 0$$
$$\pi_B = r_b - C_B - \lambda = 0$$
$$\pi_N = -C_N - L_N + \lambda = 0$$
$$\pi_D = -r_d - C_D - L_D + \lambda = 0$$
$$\pi_\lambda = \overline{K} - S - B + N + D = 0$$
$$\therefore r_b - C_B = -C_S - L_S = C_N + L_N = r_d + C_D + L_D.$$

Notes

Axel Leijonhufvud and Robert E. Hall made constructive criticisms of an earlier draft of this essay. Jack High and Jennifer Roback offered useful comments on its theoretical section.

1. Milton Friedman, "The Case for a Monetary Rule," in *An Economist's Garden* (Glen Ridge, N.J.: Thomas Horton, 1972), 65–67.
2. Robert E. Lucas, "An Equilibrium Model of the Business Cycle," *Journal of Political Economy* 83 (1975): 1139; Bennett T. McCallum, "Price-Level Stickiness and the Feasibility of Monetary Stabilization Policy with Rational Expectations," *Journal of Political Economy* 85 (1977): 631–32.
3. H. Geoffrey Brennan and James M. Buchanan, *Monopoly in Money and Inflation* (London: Institute of Economic Affairs, 1981); Richard E. Wagner, "Boom and Bust: The Political Economy of Economic Disorder," *Journal of Libertarian Studies* 4 (1980): 1–37. For a guide through the policy-relevant aspects of the rational-expectations and political business cycle literatures, see Gerald P. O'Driscoll, Jr., "Rational Expecta-

tions, Politics, and Stagflation," in *Time, Uncertainty, and Disequilibrium,* ed. Mario J. Rizzo (Lexington, Mass.: D. C. Heath, 1979), 153–76.

4. The former method of specification projects an ever-widening cone of permissible magnitudes into the future, the latter only a band, around the desired trend.

5. Leland B. Yeager, "What are Banks?" *Atlantic Economic Journal* 4 (December 1978): 13.

6. Robert E. Lucas, "Econometric Policy Evaluation: A Critique," in *The Phillips Curve and Labor Markets,* ed. K. Brunner and A. H. Meltzer (New York: North-Holland, 1976), 19–46.

7. Jacob Viner, "The Necessary and the Desirable Range of Discretion to be Allowed to a Monetary Authority," in *In Search of a Monetary Constitution,* ed. Leland B. Yeager (Cambridge: Harvard University Press, 1962), 255.

8. Federal Reserve Bank of St. Louis, *U.S. Financial Data* (29 April 1983), pp. 1, 5. It should be noted, however, that the ratio of currency to total checkable deposits, another component of the multiplier, seems genuinely to have been little affected by the new accounts. See Federal Reserve Bank of St. Louis, *U.S. Financial Data* (6 May 1983), p. 1.

9. F. A. Hayek, *The Denationalisation of Money,* 2d ed. (London: Institute of Economic Affairs, 1978), 77.

10. For a thorough account of the act, see Jeffrey Rogers Hummel, "The Deregulation and Monetary Control Act of 1980," *Policy Report* 2 (December 1980): 1–11.

11. On deregulation and technical change in the banking industry, see Joe Cobb, "Deregulation of Banking: How Far, How Fast?" *Journal of Retail Banking* (September 1981).

12. See Milton Friedman, "Should There Be an Independent Authority?" in *In Search of a Monetary Constitution,* ed. Yeager, 243.

13. For an extended discussion of this distinction, see F. A. Hayek, *Rules and Order,* vol. 1 of *Law, Legislation, and Liberty* (Chicago: Chicago University Press, 1973), chap. 2.

14. Jastram's remarks are quoted by Lindley H. Clark, Jr., "Creating an Adequate Scarcity of Dollars," *Wall Street Journal,* 28 July 1981, 27.

15. The Commission's findings, primarily authored by the economist Anna J. Schwartz, appear in *The Report to the Congress of The Commission on the Role of Gold in International Monetary Systems,* 2 vols. (Washington, D.C.: Government Printing Office, 1982). The "minority report" submitted by the Commission's two pro-gold members has been published under separate cover: Ron Paul and Lewis E. Lehrman, *The Case for Gold* (Washington, D.C.: Cato Institute, 1982).

16. See particularly Benjamin Klein, "The Competitive Supply of Money," *Journal of Money, Credit, and Banking* 6 (1974): 423–53. For surveys of the literature on competing currencies, see Pamela J. Brown, "Constitution or Competition? Alternative Views on Monetary Reform," *Literature of Liberty* 5 (1982): 7–52, and James Rolph Edwards, "Monopoly

and Competition in Money," *Journal of Libertarian Studies* 4 (1980): 107–17.

17. See Lawrence H. White, *Free Banking in Britain* (Cambridge: Cambridge University Press, 1984), chap. 2. For another summary of the Scottish experience, see Rondo Cameron, *Banking in the Early Stages of Industrialization* (New York: Oxford University Press, 1967), chap. 3.

18. Vera C. Smith, *The Rationale of Central Banking* (London: P. S. King & Son, 1936), chap. 4. See also Hugh Rockoff, "The Free Banking Era: A Reexamination," *Journal of Money, Credit, and Banking* 6 (1974): 141–67.

19. For a recent example of the second claim, see Brennan and Buchanan, *Monopoly in Money*, 17–18.

20. For a survey of economic literature on the profit-maximizing model of bank behavior, see Ernst Baltensperger, "Alternative Approaches to the Theory of the Banking Firm," *Journal of Monetary Economics* 6 (1980): 1–37.

21. Strictly speaking, these are not always costs in the sense of opportunity costs.

22. Klein, "Competitive Supply of Money"; idem, "Money, Wealth, and Seignorage," in *Redistribution Through the Financial System*, ed. K. E. Boulding and T. F. Wilson (New York: Praeger, 1978), chap. 1; idem, "Competing Monies, European Monetary Union, and the Dollar," in *One Money for Europe*, ed. M. Fratianni and T. Peeters (London: Macmillan, 1978), chap. 4.

23. Klein raises this possibility in "Competitive Supply of Money," 441.

24. David Hume, "Of the Balance of Trade," in *Writings on Economics*, ed. E. Rotwein (Madison: University of Wisconsin Press, 1955). Or, if one prefers, in accordance with that version of the monetary approach to the balance of payments wherein purchasing power parity holds even in the immediate run. For that approach, see Donald N. McCloskey and J. Richard Zecher, "How the Gold Standard Worked, 1880–1913," in *The Monetary Approach to the Balance of Payments*, ed. J. A. Frenkel and H. G. Johnson (London: Allen & Unwin, 1976).

25. Adam Smith had this in mind in postulating his so-called law of reflux, that is, the long-run invariance of the total nominal currency stock to changes in the volume of bank notes; see his *Inquiry into the Nature and Causes of the Wealth of Nations*, ed. R. H. Campbell, A. S. Skinner, and W. B. Todd, (Indianapolis: Liberty Classics, 1981), 1: 300–302.

26. Ludwig von Mises operates on this assumption; see *Human Action*, 3d rev. ed. (Chicago: Henry Regnery, 1966), 437. Our account parallels his in other respects. Mises notes (p. 438) that the assumption can be relaxed for the case where excess notes return via innerbank settlements, but he does not develop this case.

27. This statement is made in the spirit of the monetary approach to the balance of payments. See Ludwig von Mises, *The Theory of Money and Credit*, trans. H. E. Batson, new enl. ed. (Irvington-on-Hudson, N.Y.:

Foundation for Economic Education, 1971), 184–85, for the argument that interregional gold flows must be self-reversing when arising from shocks not accompanied by shifts in relative demands to hold money.

28. Carl Menger, *Principles of Economics*, trans. James Dingwall and Bert F. Hozelitz (New York: New York University Press, 1981), chap. 8.

29. Smith, *Wealth of Nations*, 1: 456. For a brief philosophical discussion of the attractiveness of invisible-hand explanations, together with a list of examples, see Robert Nozick, *Anarchy, State, and Utopia* (New York: Basic Books, 1974), 18–22. See also the essays by Hayek cited there.

30. As this trade-off may not be the same for both banks, no particular frequency may satisfy the equimarginal condition for both banks. There may, therefore, be room for implicit or explicit side payments to reach a joint optimum.

31. The region will extend to the perimeter beyond which banks find that the augmentation of note demand from participation is too slight to offset the operating costs of participation. These operating costs include losses from accepting forged notes of other banks, losses that likely will increase at the geographic margin as the region expands.

32. We may cite historical examples: Although the Scottish note-exchange system seems to have been completely symmetrical, the Suffolk Bank note-exchange system in Boston was asymmetrical and may be viewed as involving a transfer to the Suffolk Bank of some portion of the other banks' gains from the arrangement. On the Suffolk system, see George Trivoli, *The Suffolk Bank* (Leesburg, Va.: Adam Smith Institute, 1979).

33. We therefore strongly question the suggestion that the Suffolk system imposed a net loss on the rural banks and that the city banks constituted a cartel formed for the purpose of extracting a transfer from the rural banks. See, for example, Gerald Gunderson, *A New Economic History of America* (New York: McGraw-Hill, 1976), 195.

34. The Suffolk system operated in the former way, the Scottish system in the latter.

35. If that target involves the magnitude of an index number, such as the consumer price index used as a proxy for the purchasing power of money, the government's index compilers must also behave virtuously. For a critique of Irving Fisher's plan to stabilize the price index, see Mises, *Money and Credit*, 401–6.

36. David Ricardo, *Pamphlets and Papers, 1815–1823*, vol. 4 of *The Works and Correspondence of David Ricardo*, ed. Pierro Sraffa (Cambridge: Cambridge University Press, 1951), 65–66.

37. That is, inflate its supply to a degree not compensated by the nominal interest yield of the currency. An anticipated 5 percent drop in purchasing power per unit is of no concern provided that the money yields an offsetting 5 percent in explicit interest. On confidence, see Klein, "Competitive Supply of Money," 432–38.

38. Klein, "Money, Wealth, and Seignorage," 10. Virtually an identical statement appears in Klein, "Competing Monies," 77. I have interpreted

Klein's use of the terms "fiduciary money" and "credit money" as references to convertible bank notes. I interpret the term "pure fiduciary money" in the quoted passage as a reference to inconvertible or fiat money. It is important not to blur the distinction between the sort of confidence involved in convertible currency and that involved in fiat currency.

39. Michael David Bordo, "The Classical Gold Standard: Some Lessons for Today," *Federal Reserve Bank of St. Louis Review* 63 (May 1981): 2–17. See also Table 7-2 in Richard H. Timberlake, "Federal Reserve Policy Since 1945: The Results of Authority in the Absence of Rules," in *Money in Crisis: The Federal Reserve, the Economy, and Monetary Reform*, ed. Barry N. Siegel (Cambridge, Mass.: Ballinger, 1984).

40. George Bernard Shaw, *The Intelligent Woman's Guide to Socialism and Capitalism* (New York: Brentano's, 1928), 263.

41. See Hayek, *Denationalisation of Money;* and Robert E. Hall, "Explorations in the Gold Standard and Related Policies for Stabilizing the Dollar," in *Inflation: Causes and Effects*, ed. Robert E. Hall (Chicago: University of Chicago Press for the National Bureau of Economic Research, 1982).

42. "Paying with Constants Instead of Dollars," *Business Week*, 4 May 1974, 29.

43. Menger, *Principles of Economics*, chap. 8. For a modern version of Menger's theory, see Robert A. Jones, "The Origin and Development of Media of Exchange," *Journal of Political Economy* 4 (1976): 757–75.

44. See Roland Vaubel, "Free Currency Competition," *Weltwirtschaftliches Archiv* 113 (1977): 437.

45. Klein, "Competitive Supply of Money," 439–42; idem, "Competing Monies," 78–79.

46. Hall, "Explorations in the Gold Standard," 7–8. Although Hall concedes that "a U.S. gold standard might have stabilized the gold market" in recent times, he claims groundlessly that "large changes in the price level would certainly have occurred" anyway had the U.S. currency been gold-based.

47. For the author's suspicion that this might be the case, see Lawrence H. White, "Gold, Dollars, and Private Currencies," *Policy Report* 3 (June 1981): 9. In this case, a free banking system might build upon a permanently frozen stock of paper currency previously issued by government.

48. Richard H. Timberlake, Jr., "Government Gold," *Banker's Magazine* 163 (March–April 1980): 22–23.

2

Competitive Money, Inside and Out

The aim of this essay, unlike that of so many works on monetary policy, is not to argue that government monetary authorities ought to behave in a proper manner rather than the improper manner they have so often behaved in. Instead, it argues that the public ought not be forcibly subject to the vagaries of government monetary control. The way in which Federal Reserve officials choose to act is by no means a matter of indifference. It is, on the contrary, a matter of grave concern for anyone concerned about the values of his assets and the health of the economy. Monetary policy matters very much. But precisely because the public is so vulnerable to the errors of monetary policy, it is vital that some means of real protection be available. Attempts to elicit better behavior from the Fed do not go far enough in the way of vindicating the public's interest. Members of a free society should not have to suffer government control over their money at all.

The most fundamental question of monetary policy is whether government has any legitimate role to play in producing, or regulating the private production of, monetary assets. The question is especially crucial for those who, in the tradition of classical or real liberalism, are wary of the encroachment of coercive state power in areas competently handled by voluntary market interaction. As Milton Friedman has put it, "one question that a liberal must answer is whether monetary and banking arrangements cannot be left to the market, subject only to the general rules applying to all other economic activity."[1] Enthusiasm for monetary policy x or monetary policy y presupposes the belief that government involvement is better than free markets in money and banking. Yet the reasoning behind

Reprinted, with permission, from *Cato Journal*, vol. 3, no. 1 (Spring 1983).

this belief has been little explained by monetary policy enthusiasts, too few of whom have been troubled by the question.

DEREGULATION OF INSIDE MONEY

Note the conjunctive phrase used by Friedman, "monetary and banking arrangements." There are two types of money used in the U.S. economy, as in other advanced monetary economies the world has known. They are (1) basic cash, today produced only by the Treasury (coins) and the Federal Reserve System (dollar bills), and (2) bank liabilities such as deposits transferable by check, usually privately produced, whose value derives from their being redeemable for basic cash. The distinction between these two types of money is usefully expressed by calling them outside money and inside money. The question of market or government provision of money therefore resolves into two questions, each dealing with one of the two types of money. It is possible to support deregulation of inside money without necessarily questioning the government position as sole producer of outside money. It is also possible to favor a system of privately produced outside money, for example a specie standard, without questioning bank regulation.

Deregulation of banking is properly a microeconomic issue, not an issue of monetary policy. The economic argument for abolishing any of the numerous ill-considered restrictions on banking is that free and open competition would better serve consumer wants. Full deregulation would eliminate the obvious waste created by erecting barriers around which competitors must maneuver. Numerous examples come to mind. Elimination of the interest ceiling on all deposits—now underway—will clearly benefit depositors. Clearing away the barriers that prevent non-bank financial firms and even non-financial firms from engaging in "banking" practices would widen the array of financial services and suppliers available to individuals and businesses. Legalization of interstate branch banking would permit the convenience of getting cash or paying by check away from home. The agenda for decontrol is a long one even after interest ceilings are lifted.

To summarize it briefly, the agenda for banking deregulation includes as its major items (1) repeal of lingering restrictions on loan and deposit interest rates and other pricing variables such as minimum balances, (2) elimination of restrictions on the asset portfolios of banks and especially thrift institutions (the difference between banks and thrifts in this regard is entirely artificial and should be eliminated by freeing the asset-holding choices of both), (3) lifting of archaic geographic restrictions, (4) removal of regulatory barriers to entry into all aspects of the banking and financial industries, (5) an end to the peculiar taxes on deposits known as "reserve requirements," (6) privatization of deposit insurance, and (7) phasing out of the Federal Reserve System's roles as holder of bank reserves, including the closing of the discount window at which the Fed loans reserves to commercial banks and the privatization of check-clearing services.[2]

One would expect some resistance to decontrol of banking to come from bankers themselves. Like the members of any industry, they enjoy restrictions that dampen the need to compete. Given the instability of private cartels, regulatory controls combined with closed entry are the only way to secure extra-competitive profits. And, in fact, there has been some pressure from banking industry groups to moderate the extent and slow the pace of deregulation. In 1982, the Depository Institutions Deregulation Committee narrowly approved the checking accounts paying competitive interest rates that began in January 1983. For no apparent reason other than to retain in cartel-enforcing fashion some producer surplus for the banking industry, the committee imposed a $2500 minimum balance on the accounts and barred corporations from holding the accounts.

Resistance to decontrol has recently arisen, however, from a more ominous source—the Federal Reserve System—on the grounds that deregulation of inside money poses a threat to the effectiveness of monetary policy. In 1982, for example, the Deregulation Committee issued regulations governing "money market" deposit accounts. The committee laudably introduced no reserve requirements. Nonetheless, it arbitrarily imposed a minimum balance of $2500 per account and a maximum of six transfers per month from an account to third parties, only three of them by check. Press reports noted that Paul Volcker, Chairman of the Federal Reserve, had favored the limit on transfers and had argued for an even higher minimum balance of $5000, the highest Congress would allow. Volcker's argument: Greater freedom from restrictions would allow the accounts to become more attractive to consumers than ordinary savings and checking ac-counts. This, he believed, would render more difficult the Fed's policy of controlling statistical measures of the money supply.[3]

Thus we see illiberal and inefficient regulations on banking activity defended as a means toward accomplishing the goal of targeted monetary growth. This is sadly ironic. The monetarist program of targeting monetary aggregates has long been advocated by Friedman not as an end in itself, but as "the only feasible device currently available for converting monetary policy into a pillar of a free society rather than a threat to its foundations."[4] If it is true that targeting broader monetary aggregates such as M_1 and M_2 requires restrictions on the freedom of banks and financial institutions to serve consum-ers efficiently, the game is not worth the candle, given the stated values of the game's best-known advocate. It would be more consis-tent for a free-market monetarist to favor targeting of the stock of government currency liabilities alone. I refer here to the stock of currency held by banks and the public rather than the aggregate presently called the monetary base (the sum of currency plus bank reserves held as currency-redeemable deposits at the Fed) only be-cause full deregulation of inside money would fully privatize check-clearing and the holding of reserves.

Friedman, in fact, long ago acknowledged that "merit" exists in the proposal, which he attributed to Gary Becker, "to keep currency issue as a government monopoly, but to permit 'free' deposit bank-ing, without any requirement about reserves, or supervision over assets or liabilities, and with a strict *caveat emptor* policy."[5] And he still acknowledges it. Friedman would replace the Federal Reserve System either with a fixed money supply growth rule *or* a frozen stock of currency, with no regulatory restrictions on private bank deposit creation.[6] Why then have Friedman, other free-market mon-etarists, and a fortiori other monetary economists been reluctant to endorse free deposit banking? What are the arguments, explicit or implicit, against free competition in the production of inside money?

In large part the skepticism or hostility of even free-market-ori-ented economists toward free markets in banking appears to be the result of their accepting at face value the myths that prevail with regard to the historical record of unregulated banking in the last century. The following statement by Friedman is perhaps representative of a widely shared reading of history:

The very performance of its central function requires money to be generally acceptable and to pass from hand to hand. As a result, individuals may be led to enter into contracts with persons [i.e., to accept the notes of bankers] far removed in space and acquaintance, and a long period may elapse between the issue of a promise and the demand for its fulfillment. In fraud as in other activities, opportunities for profit are not likely to go unexploited. A fiduciary currency ostensibly convertible into the monetary commodity is therefore likely to be overissued from time to time and convertibility is likely to become impossible. Historically, this is what happened under so-called "free banking" in the United States and under similar circumstances in other countries.[7]

In fact, according to the recent work of the economic historians who have seriously investigated the question, losses to noteholders under most state "free banking" systems in the United States were a much more minor problem than once supposed. The evidence "presents a serious challenge to the prevailing view that free banking led to financial chaos."[8] Nor did other nations' free banking systems show an inherent tendency toward overissue.

The convertibility problems that did exist in a few states were not due to some inherent instability in unregulated banking. On the contrary, those problems may be traced to the state regulations that framed the systems. While the so-called free banking systems did provide for entry into banking without the need to obtain a special charter from the legislature, their leading feature was the requirement that issuers deposit approved bonds with state officials as collateral against their notes. Because this requirement forced banks to devote a major share of their assets to state bonds, it made banks failure-prone during periods when prices of state bonds declined. This requirement was the principal source of the banks' notoriously frequent inability to redeem their notes at par.[9] Unregulated banks would naturally diversify their asset portfolios. In addition, perhaps because the banks provided a market for state debt, state legislatures sometimes intervened by passing suspension acts to block the enforcement of redemption obligations against overextended banks. This encouraged overissue by reducing the legal penalty for it. There also remained in place restrictions against interregional branch banking, a development that would have promoted stability and the wide circulation of trustworthy notes. For these reasons, "free-banking" as applied to these systems is a misnomer; "bond-deposit systems" would be more accurate.

For evidence of the stability or instability of a virtually unregulated banking system it is instructive to turn to Scotland, which had a genuinely free and remarkably stable banking system for more than a century prior to amalgamation with the English system in 1844.[10] There, due to vigorous competition among widely branched banks, the notes of bankers "far removed in space and acquaintance" could not gain currency. A very short period elapsed between the issue of any note and its return to the issuer for redemption. Competition had led all issuers to accept one another's notes at par and to join in a single note-exchange (clearinghouse) system. Notes issued by Bank A in a loan would, after being spent by the borrower, soon come into the possession of individuals who deposited them with Banks B through Z; these banks would return the notes to Bank A through the note-exchange system and demand redemption of them. No individual bank could overissue without rapidly being disciplined by adverse clearing balances. The case of the Ayr Bank, discussed at length by Adam Smith,[11] bears witness to the efficacy of the note-exchange mechanism.

In the United States, as Friedman's quote suggests, the situation of distant bankers overissuing notes with poor homing power was experienced in a few states. These issuers were the "wild-cat" banks, so called because the bank offices were supposedly located out in the untamed forests among the wildcats. It is clear that today's advanced communications networks eliminate a necessary condition for wild-cat banking.[12] Even in the last century, however, wildcat banking was by no means inevitable. It did not occur in Scotland. It was made possible in the United States only by the reluctance of state governments to prosecute fraud where it did occur. It was abetted by the prohibition of interstate branch banking. Bank notes could find their way beyond the areas where they could be redeemed only because redemption areas were circumscribed. In cities outside the area of redeemability bank notes traded at a discount. Individuals were willing to bear the loss in value from carrying notes from the area of redeemability, where the notes traded at par, to an outside city, where the notes traded at a discount, only because the superior alternative—a bank note redeemable in both locations and therefore valued at par in both locations—was ruled out by the ban on interstate banking.

The pyramiding of reserves, which has been thought to make banking inherently unstable and in particular to have produced the panics of late nineteenth-century America, was the product of the artificial unit banking system.[13] That a large group of banks came to trust their reserves to a single bank or to a smaller group of banks was, as it was in England, the result of artificially excluding banks from regional and national financial centers. In Scotland each bank held its own reserves; there was no pyramiding. No less an authority than Walter Bagehot pointed out that each bank holding its own reserves was the natural system that would emerge in the absence of intervention. Bagehot was unequivocal in saying that one central bank holding reserves for the entire system was a poor idea. It had grown up in England as the perverse consequence of unwise banking legislation.[14]

If the objections to full deregulation of inside money creation are largely based on a misreading of history, as I believe they are, the case in favor of it, based on its enhancement of liberty and efficiency, is a strong one. I see no inherent reason why monetarists, gold-standard advocates, and denationalization-of-money advocates cannot all join in supporting deregulation of banking.

For monetarists, as already indicated, this would mean shifting to a monetary rule based on the growth of the monetary base, or stock of currency, from one that is based on the growth of a broader monetary aggregate.[15] If some monetarists in the past have favored targeting a broader aggregate, it is because historically they have found its measured velocity to have been slightly more stable than the velocity of the monetary base. In an era of major innovations in the payments system and the variety of near-money instruments— the past few years have already seen two redefinitions of the broader aggregates—the monetary base is a safer bet.

Gold-standard advocates should also find deregulation of inside money congenial with their free-market outlook. Some have, it is true, defended 100 percent reserve requirements on bank notes and demand deposits on the grounds that fractional-reserve banking is somehow inherently fraudulent.[16] But it is difficult to see why fraud is inherent in the issue of—as opposed to the failure to redeem—ready claims to gold against which less than 100 percent reserve is held at any moment, provided that the claim holders are not misled about the arrangement. If it is inherently fraudulent for a bank, is it also inherently fradulent for an insurance company to issue more claims than it could redeem were all to come due at a single moment? It seems more just to say that a claim holder suffers an actionable breach of contract only when the claim issuer actually fails to honor the claim, not when the issuer's ability to honor all its claims (in the event of their arriving simultaneously and unexpectedly) falls below 100 percent. It is at least not clear why such a non-bailment contract between bank and customer is inadmissible. The legal prohibition of fractional-reserve banking would mean an abridgment of freedom of contract and a blockage of opportunities for mutually beneficial exchange. Under a gold coin standard with dregulation of inside money, those individuals who insist on 100 percent bank liquidity could have their wants satisfied by 100 percent-reserve institutions. Individuals who prefer the higher interest that a fractional-reserve bank can pay (because it holds some interest-earning assets) would likewise be free to hold contractual claims to gold issued by those institutions. Historical experience with free banking in Scotland indicates that fractional-reserve banks under conditions of free contract can operate with sufficient security to outcompete 100 percent-reserve banks totally, though this fact of course does not answer the normative jurisprudential question of whether such freedom of contract should be allowed.

DENATIONALIZATION OF OUTSIDE MONEY

Even more fundamental—and hence more controversial—than deregulation of inside money is the question of denationalization of outside money. F. A. Hayek raised this question to prominence by publication of his booklet *Denationalisation of Money* in 1976, with a second edition in 1978.[17] The advocate of competitive market provision of outside money is somewhat at a disadvantage in stating his case. In contrast with the advocate of a specific government monetary policy, he cannot with certainty spell out in exhaustive detail the institutional change his program would bring. That is because an essential part of free-market provision is the freedom of institutions to develop and adapt themselves to consumer wants in unforeseeable ways. Market competition is a discovery procedure, as Hayek has remarked.[18] Its results are different from what anyone could predict or deliberately bring about, and therein lies its virtue. Its unpredictability is due to its aptitude for discovering that goods and ways of providing goods not previously known, or at least not previously known to be profitable, are in fact profitable. This is true of competition in the provision of outside money as in the provision of any good. Only through the competitive process can we discover what sorts of outside money, and what ways of supplying it, are best suited to consumer preferences.

Any scenario of a future free-market monetary system, then, should be considered conjectural in its details. The suppositions the scenarist makes concerning the dominant forms of outside money are necessarily no more than suppositions, whose purpose is simply to illustrate the idea of privately produced money. (Some forms of outside money are more plausible than others, of course.) This is worth keeping in mind because the advocacy of monetary freedom should not be identified with the advocacy of particular forms of money. There is a danger, for example, that Hayek's conjectures concerning the type of outside money that might come to dominate under open competition (namely, privately issued inconvertible currencies whose purchasing powers are kept stable in terms of market baskets of wholesale commodities by means of quantity control) will give his work an air of what we may call social-science fiction. Hayek's attempt to forecast "the future unit of value" can only be regarded as an entrepreneurial speculation, not as a prediction derivable from economic theory.[19]

Such speculation should not be allowed to distract attention from Hayek's most valuable message:

[T]here is no reason whatever why people should not be free to make contracts, including ordinary purchases and sales, in any kind of money they choose, or why they should be obliged to sell against any particular kind of money. There could be no more effective check against the abuse of money by government than if people were free to refuse any money they distrusted and to prefer money in which they had confidence.[20]

Economists have recently explored the properties of three systems under which government would not produce outside money. Hayek and Benjamin Klein have conceived of a multiplicity of privately produced non-commodity outside monies.[21] Fischer Black, Eugene F. Fama, Robert L. Greenfield, and Leland B. Yeager have conceived of a payments system, based on checkable mutual funds, that is devoid of outside money.[22] Elsewhere I have discussed a free-banking system based on convertibility into a commodity money, such as coined precious metal, which could be privately produced.[23]

History has seen privately produced commodity money, in particular privately minted gold and silver coins,[24] but so far as I know has not seen competition among privately produced non-commodity outside monies, nor sophisticated payments systems devoid of outside money. For this reason free banking on a specie standard is the most plausible monetary system free of government involvement. (Again, this is not to suggest that markets should not be open to other forms of private money or barter.) It clearly is the system that would have emerged in the absence of the state interventions of past centuries. We today have a system of government-issued fiat currencies only because governments successively monopolized the coinage, monopolized the issue of bank note currency through the creation of central banks, and permanently suspended convertibility for central bank liabilities. No private firm under open competition could have taken the first two of these steps in the absence of "natural-monopoly" conditions. Suspension is a breach of contract that only a government or government-sheltered agency can commit with impunity. Economists who defend the government's monopoly provision of outside money presumably defend each of these steps, or think it not advisable to reverse them once they have been taken.

The standard approach used by economists to justify government production of a good, or regulation of its private production, is to argue that the good in question is a "public good," or a good that generates Pareto-relevant positive externalities. Because the potential producer of a public good cannot sell the external benefits he would generate, the good may be underproduced or not produced at all if left to the profit-driven free market. It is possible to challenge this approach on the scientific ground that its theoretical concepts are lacking, or on the ethical ground that the production of an external benefit does not create a right to seize compensation from those benefited.[25] In the case at hand neither challenge is necessary because it is obvious that money—being simply an asset generally accepted in payment—is not a public good. The market did not fail to produce money. Money satisfies neither the non-rivalry-in-consumption criterion nor the non-excludability criterion associated with public goods. The money one individual owns is excluded from ownership by anyone else, and the liquidity services provided by that money cannot simultaneously be enjoyed by anyone else.[26] It is true that government monetary policy can affect the serviceability of money when government controls the production of money, but that does not justify government production of money or show money to be a public good. The public-goods argument for government production of money boils down to the claim that government can produce a money with desired characteristics that private firms cannot produce. There is no evidence that this is the case, although there is plenty of evidence that a government monopoly can stay in business producing a money worse than any private producer could.

It may be argued that uniformity of money is a public good because it reduces informational burdens on transactors, and that government may provide that good by suppressing the variety of monies that prevails under open competition.[27] The argument proves too much, however: It holds equally against proliferation of a variety of products or brands in any industry. It amounts to arguing that too much choice makes life difficult for consumers and ought to be suppressed by letting government choose for them. This sort of intervention in fact eliminates the only process available—market competition—for discovering which products and how many brands best serve consumer preferences. Even if the market process will eventually converge on a single type of money—e.g., converge out of a state of barter on a single precious metal as the outside money commodity—the time spent converging is not a wasteful aspect of competition that may efficiently be supplanted by government edict. Government would not be in a position to know what the market process would have selected as most suitable. If the market will support a number of brands, as it has under competitive conditions in the production of coins and inside money, entry barriers serve no welfare-enchancing purpose.

The question of the optimal number of money producers may be approached in another way. Proponents of government production of money have argued that "the production of a fiduciary currency is, as it were, a technical monopoly," or a "natural monopoly," so that competition is not feasible.[28] If the phrase "fiduciary currency" is intended to cover fractionally backed inside currencies such as specie-redeemable bank notes or dollar-redeemable traveler's checks, then the natural-monopoly argument is empirically false. No tendency toward the dominance of a single producer due to unlimited economies of scale was seen in the Scottish free-banking system; nor is such a tendency evident among producers of traveler's checks today.

There is more room for believing that the production of fiat outside money, if this is all that "fiduciary currency" means, is akin to a natural monopoly. This is because there is an inherent tendency for traders in an economy to converge on a single good (or a very small number of goods) as outside money. Carl Menger long ago explained why: Each individual in pursuit of the easiest way of completing his desired trades finds it advantageous to accept and hold an inventory of the good or goods that other individuals will most readily accept.[29] Where traders converge on a commodity money, as they naturally will out of a barter setting, no natural-monopoly problems arise. Neither the mining nor minting of precious metals gives indication of being a natural monopoly.

Where government has suppressed commodity money in favor of fiat money the question of natural monopoly does arise. Whether the production of fiat money is in fact a natural monopoly, i.e., whether traders in the region would in fact use a single fiat money were they free to use any potentially available, is not a priori obvious. Even if the answer were positive, there would be no rationale for legal barriers to entry. Nor would it follow inevitably that production of fiat money should be nationalized; a private monopoly disciplined by potential competition and competition at the borders might be better. Most importantly, to argue from potential natural monopoly in fiat money production that government should provide fiat money is to beg the question: Why fiat money at all rather than commodity outside money? I do not know of a single historical case of fiat money supplanting commodity money through competition rather than compulsion. Where then is the evidence that consumers prefer fiat outside money to commodity outside money?

It might be argued that inconvertibility of money confers social benefits because it reduces the costs of producing money, and that these cost savings cannot be realized through market processes because fiat money cannot emerge in piecemeal fashion. An established monetary standard spontaneously persists as a social convention because no trader by himself finds it advantageous to abandon it. All money users must be compelled to switch over simultaneously if inconvertible paper is to gain currency. A deliberate public choice between standards supposes something like a binding constitutional plebiscite. It cannot be claimed that one standard is Pareto-superior to another unless the other has no partisans in this choice setting. A compulsory switchover robs us of any assurance that the change is for the better as consumers view it. The argument that compulsion is justified because it is necessary to reach a new social convention might be made not only with regard to money, but also language (e.g., a compulsory switchover to Esperanto) or weights and measures (e.g., compulsory metrification). Yet a social engineer's confidence that his blueprint will prove superior to a system evolved spontaneously out of the interaction of many minds must rest in large measure on constructivist hubris. Seldom if ever does a complex social institution operate according to a blueprint.

Many economists believe that the replacement of commodity money by paper money constitutes a social savings because paper is cheaper than precious metal. Yet they may be overlooking the possibility that consumers prefer commodity money to fiat money strongly enough to consider the resource costs worth bearing. Monetary theorists may assume that what consumers care about is simply the quantity of real money balances, or that plus the first and second moments of a probability-density function over rates of change in the purchasing power of money. For many analytical purposes these assumptions are useful. But to use such assumptions in comparing alternative outside monies is illegitimate. Economists are not in a position to divine consumers' true preferences in a hypothetical constitution-like choice and thereby to design optimal social institutions for them. In particular, it cannot be taken for granted that money users are unwilling to forgo some alternative uses of a precious metal (or the resources necessary to supply the metal) in order to use some of it as outside money.[30]

Consumers would conceivably consent to the replacement of a commodity currency by a fiat currency only if they themselves enjoyed the resource savings. A government earnestly desiring to make a Pareto improvement might then offer fiat currency in proportion to a citizen's holdings of specie, but allow him to retain the specie. Historically, the introduction of fiat money has not come about in this way. Instead, it has come about by permanent suspension of redeemability of the central bank's liabilities, enriching only the government. The hypothesis that fiat money is potentially Pareto-superior, even if true (which is doubtful), would therefore not explain historical transitions to fiat money. Those who agree with Milton Friedman that government expenditures will rise to dissipate any level of income that government can extract should doubt that government passes on the savings from fiat money to the citizenry through lower overt taxation. Transition to fiat money gives government opportunities through inflationary finance to further enrich itself at the clear expense of the populace. It enables government to commandeer resources from the private sector simply by printing the greenbacks to pay for them. Fear of this possibility would rationally create a preference for hard outside money were a constitutional choice between standards actually offered to the public.[31] America's Founding Fathers placed a prohibition on fiat currency into the U.S. Constitution, for whatever that fact is worth. It cannot be said that the fear of reckless monetary expansion under irredeemable currency is historically groundless.[32]

A final argument made for nationalization of outside money is that it is necessary to the existence of a lender of last resort, that is, a central bank standing ready to lend reserves to solvent but illiquid commercial banks. But one cannot argue that illiquid banks would have no recourse in the absence of a central bank: there would exist a system of interbank lending of existing reserves, such as the Federal funds market that operates today. If a temporarily illiquid bank is solvent and worth saving, a profit can be made lending to it, and lenders will be forthcoming. If the bank is insolvent and not worth saving, its dissolution will free up real resources for more productive uses elsewhere. Certainly, there are wealth losses associated with the failure of a bank, as with the failure of any business firm, but these are not Pareto-relevant externalities. The failure of one bank should not lower public confidence in other banks where banks are free to invest in establishing distinct identities in the public's mind. No runs on the banking system occurred in Scotland under free banking.

It is not even true that a lender of last resort (i.e., an institution able to increase the system's total existing reserves) for a regional banking system can exist only if some central body can create outside money at will. Under an international specie standard, for instance, it is possible for banks of one nation to borrow reserves from banks or other specie holders of another nation. Only when a banking system is coextensive with the currency area of its outside money can the volume of total outside money reserves be augmented for the banking system as a whole solely through the agency of a lender of last resort able to create outside money at will. The power to create outside money at will is consistent only with fiat money. It is doubtful that an unconstrained power to print cash can be created without being subject to abuse. The lender-of-last-resort function is clearly inconsistent with a strict quantity rule governing the creation of outside money. Monetarists who advocate both a lender-of-last-resort role for the Federal Reserve System and a rule-bound path for bank reserves or outside money (a.k.a. the monetary base) must have in mind a less-than-strict quantity rule.

Milton Friedman, to his credit, has called for a permanent closing of the Fed's discount window.[33] This change would eliminate the Fed's capacity to function as a lender of last resort in one sense. Under Friedman's proposal of an M_1 or M_2 quantity rule, the Fed could deliberately vary the stock of outside money in an attempt to offset temporary changes in the real demand to hold outside money. But this policy seems no different in principle from that of deliberately varying the stock of M_1 or M_2 (via the monetary base) in an attempt to offset temporary changes in the real demand to hold one of those aggregates, a policy Friedman would properly criticize.

The injection of new outside money by a central bank acting as lender of last resort, like the injection of outside money in any way other than through a perfectly anticipated proportional addition to every person's holdings of outside money, redistributes wealth involuntarily. Rather than having to induce holders of existing outside money to lend money voluntarily by offering an attractive interest rate, the illiquid bank receives new cash loaned at a below-market rate that tacitly dilutes the purchasing power of existing holdings. That an increased public demand to hold cash may make cash scarcer for banks is a pecuniary externality, not a Pareto-relevant externality that could be invoked to justify subsidization of banks. At bottom, the lender-of-last-resort function is a device for shifting from bank shareholders to the money-holding public the burden of a risk associated with banking.

Because the lender of last resort relieves bank shareholders of some of the risk of illiquidity from bad loans, profit-maximizing banks can be expected to take on loans riskier than those they otherwise would have. Western banks would not have made such large loans to governments of less-developed countries—loans that have been much in the news since their riskiness became manifest— had they not believed that an international lender of last resort, namely the International Monetary Fund, would absorb the risk.[34] The question now is whether that belief will be vindicated, or whether the American taxpayer or dollar holder will be forced to pick up the tab for loan losses that should properly fall on bank shareholders.

THE AGENDA FOR DENATIONALIZATION OF OUTSIDE MONEY

There is no justification in benefits to the public for government production of outside money. In fact, political control over the quantity of outside money is responsible for the monetary ills of inflation and recession we suffer. What then is to be done? The very least to be done is to open the production of outside money to potential competition from commodity monies, private inconvertible currencies as envisioned by Hayek, and foreign currencies. The legal and regulatory barriers to private production of alternative outside monies are greater than is typically recognized by economists considering the possibility. The following list of barriers present in the United States is probably not exhaustive: (1) private minting of coins has been illegal since 1864; (2) purchases of commodity monies are subject to sales taxes; (3) holdings of non-dollar currencies are subject to capital gains taxation; (4) though gold clauses are legal for indexing dollar obligations, it is doubtful that courts would compel specific performance of an obligation to pay something other than dollars; and perhaps most importantly (5) the unwarranted power of state and federal regulatory bodies to restrict entry into banking can (and has been) used to suppress the establishment of alternative monetary systems.[35]

Should these restrictions be eliminated, transactors would at least be free to use outside monies other than the one produced by the domestic government. None of the arguments above that seek to justify government production of outside money, even if they were valid, would justify a compulsory monopoly for government. There is no rationale for preventing attempts to produce a "public good" privately, or attempts to compete with a "natural monopoly." Should potential or actual competition make the real demand for government-produced outside money more sensitive to its depreciation, the real seigniorage yield for any given rate of monetary expansion would fall, reducing government's ability to tax money holders covertly through inflationary finance. In other words, open competition could erode the monopoly profit government currently enjoys in the production of outside money.[36]

Would it then be enough to allow private producers of outside money to compete with the Federal Reserve? Unfortunately, it most likely would not be. It is doubtful that a parallel monetary system could gain much of a foothold even in the absence of legal impediments, because of the natural tendency of money users in a region to converge on a common monetary unit. Each trader finds it most convenient to hold the money that he believes others will most likely accept in the near future, which normally is the money they have been accepting in the immediate past, even if that money is depreciating. Historical bouts with hyperinflation suggest that this momentum can carry an outside money at least through double-digit inflations. I hope that hyperinflation will not be necessary in the United States before competition in outside money can prevail.

If competition from alternative currencies would not be enough to neutralize the Federal Reserve's ability to do monetary damage, then the opening of competition must be supplemented by some policy for dealing with the supply of fiat dollars. A moderate policy would freeze the monetary base.[37] A more thorough policy would retire the stock of Federal Reserve notes and Treasury token coins via redemption for a potential commodity money. The commodity money could most plausibly be silver or gold. One advantage gold has over silver as a potential commodity money is that the federal government already has a large stockpile of gold that ought to be disgorged in any event. The advantages of silver are its greater circulability in coinage (a twenty-dollar gold piece at today's prices would be a very slight coin) and the greater geopolitical dispersion of silver mines. The point here is not to reestablish a link between government-issued money and a precious metal; it is to phase out government-issued money.[38] Given the market's tendency to evolve and sustain a payments system based on one and only one outside money, conversion to a precious-metal-based monetary system seems our best hope for a competitive supply of outside money.

Notes

1. Milton Friedman, *A Program for Monetary Stability* (New York: Fordham University Press, 1960), 4. While characterizing himself as "by no means convinced that the answer is indubitably in the negative," Friedman answers in the negative.
2. Compare Catherine England, "The Case for Banking Deregulation," Heritage Foundation *Backgrounder*, 26 March 1982, which mentions only the first three items. Privatizing of deposit insurance is advocated by Catherine England and John Palffy, "Replacing the FDIC: Private Insurance for Bank Deposits," Heritage Foundation *Backgrounder*, 2 December 1982.
3. *New York Times*, 16 November 1982, D14; *Wall Street Journal*, 16 November 1982, 2.
4. Milton Friedman, "Should There Be an Independent Monetary Authority?" in *In Search of a Monetary Constitution*, ed. Leland B. Yeager (Cambridge: Harvard University Press, 1962), 243. An identical statement appears in Friedman, *Capitalism and Freedom* (Chicago: Chicago University Press, 1962), 55.
5. Friedman, *A Program for Monetary Stability*, 108 n. 10. Though Friedman gave no citation, Becker's proposal is expounded in Gary S. Becker, "A Proposal for Free Banking" (manuscript, 1957).
6. Milton Friedman, "Monetary Policy for the 1980s," in *To Promote Prosperity*, ed. John H. Moore (Stanford: Hoover Insitution Press, 1984). The latter option has also been suggested by Richard H. Timberlake, Jr.,

"Monetization Practices and the Political Structure of the Federal Reserve System," Cato Institute *Policy Analysis,* 12 August 1981, 10–12.

7. Friedman, *A Program for Monetary Stability,* 6. I hope it is clear that I have no special animus against Friedman. Quite the contrary: I have singled out his statements for criticism only because our values are similar and, to his credit, his chains of reasoning on this topic are particularly clear and explicit. I also make these criticisms in *Free Banking in Britain* (Cambridge: Cambridge University Press, 1984), chap. 5, with special emphasis on the evidence from Scotland's free-banking experience. Friedman recently, in an article coauthored with Anna J. Schwartz, has explicitly reconsidered his earlier position on the rationale for government involvement in the monetary and banking system: Milton Friedman and Anna J. Schwartz, "Has Government Any Role in Money?," *Journal of Monetary Economics* 17 (January 1986): 37–62.

8. Arthur J. Rolnick and Warren E. Weber, "New Evidence on the Free Banking Era," *American Economic Review* 73 (December 1983): 1080–91; idem, "The Causes of Free Bank Failures: A Detailed Examination," *Journal of Monetary Economics* 14 (November 1984): 267–91. See also Hugh Rockoff, "The Free Banking Era: A Reexamination," *Journal of Money, Credit, and Banking,* 6 (May 1974): 141–67.

9. Arthur J. Rolnick and Warren E. Weber, "Free Banking, Wildcat Banking, and Shinplasters," Federal Reserve Bank of Minneapolis *Quarterly Review* 6 (Fall 1982): 10–19.

10. See White, *Free Banking in Britain,* chap. 2; Rondo Cameron, *Banking in the Early Stages of Industrialization* (New York: Oxford University Press, 1967), chap. 3; S. G. Checkland, *Scottish Banking: A History, 1695–1973* (Glasgow: Collins, 1975).

11. Adam Smith, *An Inquiry into the Nature and Causes of the Wealth of Nations,* ed. R. H. Campbell, A. S. Skinner, and W. B. Todd (Indianapolis: Liberty Classics, 1981), 313–17.

12. As Friedman recognized in *A Program for Monetary Stability,* 108 n. 10.

13. See Vera C. Smith, *A Rationale of Central Banking* (London: P. S. King & Son, 1936), 138–40.

14. Walter Bagehot, *Lombard Street: A Description of the Money Market* (London: Henry S. King & Co., 1873), 66–69, 100.

15. Eugene F. Fama, "Financial Intermediation and Price Level Control," *Journal of Monetary Economics* 12 (July 1983): 7–28, has adopted this position.

16. Murray N. Rothbard, "The Case of a 100 Percent Gold Dollar," in *In Search of a Monetary Constitution,* ed. Yeager, 113–20. Rothbard argues that a demand deposit should be treated in law as a warehouse receipt or bailment. But why should the law prohibit contracts that by mutual agreement do not treat demand deposits as bailments?

17. F. A. Hayek, *The Denationalisation of Money,* 2d ed. (London: Insitutute

of Economic Affairs, 1978). For an able survey of the literature on this topic see Pamela J. Brown, "Constitution or Competition? Alternative Views on Monetary Reform," *Literature of Liberty* 5 (Autumn 1982): 7–52.

18. F. A. Hayek, "Competition as a Discovery Procedure," in *New Studies in Philosophy, Politics, Economics and the History of Ideas* (Chicago: Chicago University Press, 1978), 179–90.

19. See F. A. Hayek, "The Future Unit of Value," in *Currency Competition and Monetary Union,* ed. Pascal Salin (The Hague: Mortinus Nijhoff, 1984).

20. F. A. Hayek, "Choice in Currency: A Way to Stop Inflation," in *New Studies,* 225. In this essay, written earlier than *Denationalisation of Money,* Hayek was willing (p. 227) to entertain the possibility that gold would prove to be the most popular currency.

21. Benjamin Klein, "The Competitive Supply of Money," *Journal of Money, Credit, and Banking* 6 (November 1974): 423–53.

22. Fischer Black, "Banking and Interest Rates in a World Without Money: The Effects of Uncontrolled Banking," *Journal of Bank Research* 1: (Autumn 1970): 9–20; Eugene F. Fama, "Banking in a Theory of Finance," *Journal of Monetary Economics* 6 (January 1980): 39–67; Robert L. Greenfield and Leland B. Yeager, "A Laissez-Faire Approach to Monetary Stability," *Journal of Money, Credit, and Banking* 15 (August 1983): 302–15. For criticism of the concept of a competitive payments system devoid of outside money, see Lawrence H. White, "Competitive Payments Systems and the Unit of Account," *American Economic Review* 74, no. 4 (September 1987): 699–712.

23. Lawrence H. White, "Free Banking as an Alternative Monetary System," in *Money in Crisis: The Federal Reserve, the Economy, and Monetary Reform,* ed. Barry N. Siegel (Cambridge, Mass.: Ballinger Publishing Co., 1984). Admittedly the emphasis there was on deregulation of inside money.

24. On the American experience, see Donald H. Kagin, *Private Gold Coins and Patterns of the United States* (New York: Arco Publishing, 1981).

25. For the first challenge see Tyler Cowen, "The Problem of Public Goods: A Preliminary Investigation" (manuscript, 1982); for the second see Robert Nozick, *Anarchy, the State, and Utopia* (New York: Basic Books, 1974), 95.

26. See Roland Vaubel, "The Government's Money Monopoly: Externalities or Natural Monopoly?," *Kyklos* 37, no. 1 (1984). After a thorough investigation Vaubel concludes (p. 45) that "externality theory fails to provide a convincing justification for the government's monopoly in the production of (base) money."

27. Carl Menger makes this argument in chap. 5 of his article "Geld," reprinted in *The Collected Works of Carl Menger,* ed. F. A. Hayek (London: London School of Economics and Political Science, 1936); unpublished

abridged English translation by Albert H. Zlabinger. The argument is also made by Karl Brunner and Allan H. Meltzer, "The Uses of Money: Money in a Theory of an Exchange Economy," *American Economic Review* 41 (December 1971): 801–2. It is cited and criticized by Vaubel, 30–31, n. 12. In particular, Brunner and Meltzer assert that the suppression of multiple issuers of bank notes in Britain by the Bank Charter Act of 1844 "raised economic welfare by reducing costs of acquiring information." Having studied the act and the circumstances surrounding it, I find this statement incredible.

28. Friedman, *A Program for Monetary Stability,* 75; Roland Vaubel, "Free Currency Competition," *Weltwirtschaftliches Archiv* 112 (1977): 437, 458.

29. Carl Menger, *Principles of Economics* (New York: New York University Press, 1981), chap. 8.

30. It cannot even be taken for granted that resource costs incidental to the system are higher under a gold standard than under a fiat standard. See White, *Free Banking in Britain,* 148–49; Roger Garrison, "The Costs of a Gold Standard," in *The Gold Standard: An Austrian Perspective,* ed. Llewellyn H. Rockwell, Jr. (Lexington, Mass.: Lexington Books, 1985); and Milton Friedman, "The Resource Cost of an Irredeemable Paper Money," *Journal of Political Economy* 94 (June 1986): 642–47.

31. As recognized by J. Huston McCulloch, *Money and Inflation: A Monetarist Approach,* 2d ed. (New York: Academic Press, 1982), 75–76. McCulloch makes an interesting case for silver as a better monetary metal than gold.

32. As noted by Phillip Cagan, "The Report of the Gold Commission (1982)," *Carnegie Rochester Conference Series on Public Policy* 20 (1984). On the U. S. Constitution's intended prohibition of fiat money, see Kenneth W. Dam, "The Legal Tender Cases," *Supreme Court Review* (1981): 381–82.

33. Friedman, *A Program for Monetary Stability,* 44, 100. On the other hand, Friedman, "Commodity-Reserve Currency," in *Essays in Positive Economics* (Chicago: University of Chicago Press, 1953), 218, endorses the holding of an ultimate reserve for a fractional-reserve banking system.

34. But for a contrary view see Charles Goodhart, *The Evolution of Central Banks* (London: London School of Economics and Political Science, 1985), 65 n. 2.

35. As evidence of this last barrier in practice, an experiment with privately issued indexed currency and deposits in New Hampshire between 1972 and 1974 was ended under legal pressure from the Securities and Exchange Commission. (Incidentally, the experiment was proving unprofitable.) See "Paying with Constants Instead of Dollars," *Business Week,* 4 May 1974, 29. On the other hand, the Secret Service found nothing illegal in the issue of gold-redeemable certificates by an individual in Maryland. See Irving Wallace et al., "Significa/The Money Maker," *Parade,* 21 February 1982, 20. Gold-coin-redeemable certificates are

currently being offered by the Gold Standard Corporation of Kansas City, Missouri.

36. David Glasner, "Seigniorage, Inflation, and Competition in the Supply of Money" (manuscript, February 1981).

37. See Friedman, "Monetary Policy for the 1980s," and Timberlake, "Monetization Practices." Timberlake adds that the gold in Fort Knox should be liberated to allow a private gold standard to emerge.

38. For further elaboration, see Lawrence H. White, "Gold, Dollars, and Private Currencies," Cato Institute *Policy Report* 3 (June 1981): 6–11, and White, "Free Banking and the Gold Standard," in *The Gold Standard*, ed. Rockwell.

3

Problems Inherent in Political Money Supply Regimes: Some Historical and Theoretical Lessons

Economists today generally recognize that stagflation and other aspects of contemporary monetary disorder are principally the results of the behavior of government monetary agencies. The behavior of government monetary agencies can only be understood as the result of the basic incentives and constraints facing their decision-makers. Yet the problems associated with government control over the quantity of basic money are often discussed as though they stem merely from the personalities of those in charge, or at worst from minor organizational design flaws, remediable by implementation of a new and improved operating blueprint for government management of the money supply. In particular, economists and political analysts have typically discussed programs for "depoliticizing" the supply of money without challenging government's monopoly control over the business of supplying basic money. These authors evidently believe it possible to take the "politics" out of money creation without taking money creation out of the province of government, or in other words, that a government authority for controlling the quantity of money can be run apolitically.

There is good cause for believing the opposite. However unpleasant the idea may be, the problem of political influence over money may not realistically be resolvable at a shallow level. This essay aims to elucidate the reasons why undesirable political influence may be

Reprinted, with permission, from *Political Business Cycles: The Political Economy of Money, Inflation, and Unemployment*, ed. Thomas D. Willett (Durham, N. C.: Duke University Press, 1988).

inherent in government supply of money. The reasons are clearly suggested by branches of economic theory, specifically by theories of seigniorage, bureaucracy, and the political business cycle. The relevant theories are critically examined below. The history of government monetary authorities or central banks may suggest reasons even more clearly. If the exercise of official influence over money was the purpose for which central banks were legislated into existence, then stripping them of their power would leave them without a rationale for government support. It seems extremely unlikely that monetary machinery erected to manipulate the money supply for reasons of state could be turned into the best apparatus for serving the public's interest simply by issuing the operator a new instruction manual, or even by tightening a few loose joints. Some pieces of relevant history are considered in the next section.

THE POLITICAL ORIGINS OF CENTRAL BANKS

Political influence over the supply of money, with its various features generally judged to be regrettable, is not new to the twentieth century. It has been present ever since ancient monarchs learned to raise revenue by monopolizing and then debasing the metallic coinage of their realms. In more recent times democratic bodies have passed legislation creating central banks for the purpose of exercising official influence over monetary and credit conditions. Considerations of state finance are crucial, though their influence is sometimes indirect, in explaining why governments have historically fostered the establishment of national monetary authorities and have arrogated to these monopoly agencies the production of a good—money—which the competitive market system readily supplies.

When central banks were established in the nineteenth and early twentieth centuries, it was certainly not for the purpose of manipulating macroeconomic variables according to the full-employment precepts of recent decades. The Keynesian notion of demand management did not yet exist. (Or more accurately, its nineteenth-century proponents had no influence and were dismissed as inflationist cranks.) [1] Nor were central banks invented for the purpose of generating seigniorage through simple additions to the stock of outside money. National economies were not yet on fiat monetary standards which allow the stock of outside money to be permanently expanded by means of the printing press or a central-bank balance-sheet entry. International gold and silver standards prevailed.

It is no accident that the emergence of central banks antedates the emergence of fiat money, for central banking is a precondition for fiat money. Fiat money cannot be established completely de novo because the acceptance of a money is a social convention that takes time to develop. The universal acceptance of gold and silver by the nineteenth century resulted from a long historical process of traders converging on them as the most marketable of all commodities.[2] Paper currencies and deposit monies made their initial appearance as claims to precious metal held by bankers.[3] The liabilities of central banks were initially of the redeemable sort too, as they would not otherwise have been accepted. Given a monopoly of the supply of bank note currency in a region, however, a central bank could terminate the region's gold standard and turn its own liabilities into the most basic money available by repudiating its obligation to redeem them for gold and silver. The Bank of England left the gold standard in 1797, returned in 1821, and abandoned it again in 1931. The Federal Reserve System was relieved of its redemption obligations toward domestic residents in 1933, and toward foreign central banks in 1971.

The Bank of England, the world's leading central bank during the era of the classical gold standard (up to 1914), was founded in 1694 purely as a conduit for government borrowing. King William III, his credit low, urgently needed funds to finance an ongoing war with France in defense of his throne. As a clever means of attracting funds, subscribers to a £1.2 million loan to the government were incorporated as the Governor and Company of the Bank of England. A "bank" with little but government debt as an asset, and little but equity and the government's working balances on the other side of the balance sheet, could hardly be apolitical. As Walter Bagehot wrote, it was a "Whig Finance company . . . founded by a Whig government . . . in desperate want of money. . . ."[4] Having created for itself a devoted pet bank, the English government found it easy and attractive to bestow exclusive privileges upon it. The exclusive possession of the government's balances, meager at first, later became a source of great prestige to the bank. In 1697 the bank's corporate charter was made exclusive: no other bank could be incorporated (given limited liability) while the Bank of England remained in operation. The field was left open to partnerships, but these were at a legal disadvantage. In 1708, as a quid pro quo for buying further government debt, Parliament delivered the decisive blow against the natural development of banking in England. It barred any bank of more than six partners from issuing bank notes, or any other negotiable securities dated shorter than six months, while the Bank of England existed. This was crucial in restricting competition with the Bank, because public holding of bank notes was the major source of bank funding in the eighteenth and nineteenth centuries.

As a result of political interventions, then, the Bank of England enjoyed a legal monopoly of note issue in London, Britain's financial center. For a long while it was the sole deposit banking corporation in England as well. Given its unnatural advantages, the Bank quite understandably acquired a special role in the monetary system, a role eventually identified by Bagehot and others as central banking. When other banks in the system came to hold Bank of England notes and deposits in place of gold reserves, the bank became sole holder of the nation's gold reserves. Bagehot himself incisively traced this development to the bank's legal privileges:

With so many advantages over all competitors, it is quite natural that the Bank of England should have far outstripped them all. Inevitably it became *the* bank in London; all the other bankers grouped themselves round it, and lodged their reserve with it. Thus our *one*-reserve system was not deliberately founded upon definite reasons; it was the gradual consequence of many singular events, and of an accumulation of legal privileges on a single bank which has not been altered, and which no one would now defend.[5]

It is certainly true, as Bagehot suggests, that no single mind designed in detail the institutional outcome of this process, nor could one have done so. Nonetheless, the sponsors of banking legislation were neither unaware of nor indifferent toward the centralizing tendency they were promoting. Sir Robert Peel, sponsor of the well-known Bank Charter Act of 1844 that finally clinched the Bank of England's central position, was candid as to his government's aim: "We think it of great importance to increase the controlling power of a single Bank of Issue."[6] A disinterested rationale for centralization was provided by the Currency School's business-cycle doctrines.

On closer inspection, however, it becomes evident that the weaknesses in the monetary system that the Currency School proposed to remedy by centralizing regulation were due to the centralizing regulations already in place. Fundamentally the act was designed to cement a close fiscal relationship between bank and state that had served both well and promised to continue doing so. The act's major provisions were in fact proposed to Peel by the two chief officers of the Bank of England.[7] The bank gained extended privileges, increased security of tenure, and greater opportunities to expand. The government could presumably look forward with even greater assurance to having a ready buyer for its debt in any circumstance that might arise.

The story behind the establishment of the Federal Reserve System as the central bank of the United States is similar in important respects to the account just given of the development of central banking in England. Key roles were played by the fiscal needs of the government and by the unintended consequences of interventionist measures designed to meet those needs. Unlike England, the United States had no continuously operating government-sponsored bank that was given a central-banking role as the banking industry developed. The Federal Reserve was established quite late in the game as an institution to supplement an already developed banking system. Nonetheless, the Federal Reserve Act of 1913 and the Banking Act of 1935 bear important parallels to Peel's Act of 1844. All were deliberate attempts to remedy by centralization the shortcomings of a banking industry whose dysfunctions arose from banking regulations designed to promote the sale of government debt.

Restrictions on entry into banking were imposed by state governments in America from the earliest days. The legislatures of several states extracted some of the monopoly rents thus created by requiring the purchase of state debt as a condition of obtaining a bank charter. The so-called free banking laws of the antebellum period regularized this system by granting the right to issue bank notes to all applicants who purchased approved bonds as collerateral and met other enumerated requirements.[8] The federal government appropriated the bond-collateral scheme in the National Bank Act of 1863, seeing it as a handy way to force-feed its Civil War debt to the banking system. In conjunction with a crushing tax on state bank notes, the act forced issuing banks to purchase federal government bonds to be held as collateral. The bond-collateral provision had an unintended consequence that eventually provided the prime motivation for the Federal Reserve Act fifty years later: it made the supply of circulating currency notoriously "inelastic." The proportion of the money stock taking the form of bank notes was not free to vary in response to public demand because the quantity of notes banks could circulate was governed instead by the inflexible stock of federal debt. Bank customers could not convert demand deposits into bank notes during those periods when many wanted currency rather than deposits. This may seem like a minor inconvenience. But it had a major ramification. Denied banknote currency, depositors instead withdrew the outside currency serving as bank reserves, which in turn reduced by a multiple the volume of deposits banks could maintain. Hence a simple demand that could have been met, absent the bond-collateral requirement, by an inconsequential change in the mix of bank liabilities gave rise to financial stringency and sometimes "panic" as the reserve drain pressured banks to contract their liabilities and assets.[9]

Some reformers, most notably the sponsors of the American Bankers Association's "Baltimore Plan" of 1894, recognized the principal root of the banking system's problems and called for an end to the bond-collateral restriction. A more influential group, however, proposed somewhat superficially to treat only the most visible symptom, namely the occurrence of systemwide reserve drains, by establishing an official institution for making additional reserves available to the banks in periods of heavy currency demand.[10] Rather than peel away restrictions, Congress chose to add the Federal Reserve System as an agency for "rational" management of banking crises under the aegis of the federal government. Initially the Fed's legislative mandate was merely to supplement the gold standard occasionally, and not to supersede it permanently, as a source of the nation's reserve money. Its capacity as a sponge for federal debt was rather limited. But with Franklin Roosevelt's executive order abrogating the domestic gold standard in 1933, and with the Banking Act of 1935 explicitly authorizing open-market operations and centralized control over the system, the Fed gained a mandate to accommodate the Treasury's borrowing needs and a virtually unconstrained capacity to do so.[11]

The vestigial remains of gold convertibility were finally eliminated in 1971.

THE POLITICAL INCENTIVES OF CENTRAL BANKS

The timing and institutional details of our arrival at the current monetary regime in America—a system of fiat money produced wholly at the discretion of an unconstrained government central bank—were in many respects the accidental outcome of a sequence of unique historical events. Yet is is not accidental that an ever-expanding federal government with ever-expanding revenue needs and macroeconomic designs has taken ever-increasing control over the creation of basic money. Today there is absolutely no tangible constraint on the Fed's capacity to expand the nominal stock of outside money (a.k.a. the monetary base or high-powered money, consisting of fiat currency plus commercial bank deposits at the Fed). The federal government can, through the Fed's open-market operations, create any nominal quantity of new outside money at will. (It can also destroy outside money, but the historical record shows a decided bias toward expansion.) This power can be used in pursuit of at least three different governmental objectives: (1) When the Fed purchases federal debt and rebates the Treasury's interest payments back to the Treasury ("monetizes" the debt), the federal government can expand its command over the economy's goods and services without increasing its effective debt obligations or explicit taxation. The greater the rate of creation of fiat money, up to a certain revenue-maximizing rate, the greater the transfer of wealth from the private sector to the government. Assuming the marginal resource cost of nominal base money creation to be essentially zero, the government gains $1 in seigniorage for each $1 of debt monetized during a given period.[12] The by now traditional theory of seigniorage elucidates the economic limits to government's profit from exploitation of this power.[13] (2) The Federal Reserve can expand its own command over goods and services, rather than the Treasury's wealth, by spending its interest earnings rather than rebating them. Economists have only recently begun to explore the implications and evidence for this bureaucratic discretionary profit-maximizing model of money creation. (3) The Federal Reserve can attempt to manipulate the money supply so as to influence macroeconomic conditions in timely and favorable fashion for the purpose of enhancing the political prospects of the Congress, the President, and itself. For the benefit of the Congress and the President this means stimulating the economy just prior to an election, creating a political business cycle. On its own account this means maintaining a credible public "posture" of "fighting" recession, inflation, high interest rates, appreciation (or depreciation) of the dollar, or whatever else a consensus of opinion ranks as the top policy priority.[14]

SEIGNIORAGE

The theory of seigniorage alerts us to expect systematic inflation under a regime of political money supply.[15] It has been plausibly argued that the United States government, unlike some other national governments, has not been pursuing a policy aimed single-mindedly at maximizing its seigniorage revenue from new money creation over the past three decades.[16] Even if correct, however, this finding would by no means make the broader theory of seigniorage irrelevant to an understanding of the Federal Reserve's behavior. It would be difficult to explain, without acknowledging the government's revenue from issuing additional base money, why the stock of base money and the price level have consistently risen quarter after quarter.[17] Political business cycle theory in its most general form does not indicate any such upward bias.[18]

The government's incentives in raising revenue by means of seigniorage may also give us some insight into why monetary expansion has been so irregular. The rate of base money growth has varied substantially from quarter to quarter and even from year to year. For example, the adjusted monetary base grew at 12.0 percent per annum during the first six months of 1983; at a 6.3 percent rate during the next six months; at 11.0 percent during the first six months of 1984; at 3.8 percent during the next six months; and at 10.0 percent during the first six months of 1985.[19] On a simple one-parameter theory of money demand this vacillation could reflect seigniorage maximization only if the Fed believed that the inflation-sensitivity (or nominal interest-rate elasticity) of base money demand were varying.[20] There is no obvious reason why it should have believed this. A more satisfactory explanation introduces the idea that money demand is positively related to the variability of inflation.[21] The government then raises the real demand for its base money, and hence its real seigniorage, for any given average inflation rate by gyrating the actual inflation rate above and below that average. It can cause these gyrations by varying the growth rate of the monetary base just as it did from 1983 through mid-1985.

It is moreover possible to supplement the traditional theory of seigniorage in various ways in order to explain why the government would aim at less than what is apparently the maximum available seigniorage. An obvious way is to assume that government is benevolent, so that it aims at a (model-defined) social welfare-optimizing rate of seigniorage rather than the maximum attainable rate. At least two problems undermine this approach, however. First, even if other distorting taxes are positive, the welfare-maximizing rate of seigniorage is zero in models where money is an intermediate good (a transaction cost-reducing medium of exchange). Second, even a benevolent monetary authority, if it has discretion to pursue inflationary finance (or to attempt temporary reductions in unemployment) through surprise inflation, may be driven to produce excessive inflations.[22] It is alternatively possible to explain actual monetary expansion less than the apparent maximum while retaining the less-question-begging assumption that government acts in its own pecuniary interest. Such an explanation continues to highlight the likelihood of systematic inflation under a discretionary fiat money regime.

In the traditional approach, as exemplified by Martin J. Bailey's classic contribution,[23] the seigniorage a government can raise depends on the scale of the real demand to hold the money it issues (this is its tax base) and on how sensitive this demand is to anticipated inflation (how quickly the tax base shrinks as the tax rate is raised). Attention is focused on steady states in which the known inflation rate is expected to persist indefinitely. We may supplement this by considering a stochastic setting. The sensitivity of real base money demand to an anticipated bout of inflation ought to be lower when periods of high inflation are expected to be followed by a reversion to low inflation, than when they are not. Individuals and firms will not readily invest in expensive cash-economizing devices or routines if high inflation is expected not to persist. Government's real seigniorage revenue from a period of inflation will therefore be greater if is expected to adhere to a policy of more moderate base money creation in the long run. The short-run (and measured) elasticity of real money demand will be less than the long-run (true steady-state) elasticity. A government recognizing this, and projecting that at any future date it might place an unusually high value on real seigniorage, for example because it might be at war, has a purely selfish incentive to pursue "moderate" money creation. This means abstaining during peacetime from expanding the monetary base at a rate as high as the apparent steady-state seigniorage-maximizing rate.

THE FEDERAL RESERVE AS MAXIMIZER OF ITS OWN INCOME

An alternative way to explain actual rates of monetary expansion, while retaining the assumption of rationally self-interested government, corresponds to the second possible objective for monetary expansion that we have identified: the enrichment of the Federal Reserve. This approach alerts us to the inflationary dangers of a politicized money supply stemming from a slightly different source than that identified by the traditional theory of seigniorage. In a model elaborated by Mark Toma, the management of the monetary authority aims to maximize its discretionary profits.[24] The Federal Reserve's profits are the difference between its "earnings" from holdings of Treasury bills (which it purchases by creating the new base money) and the minimal expenditures necessary to provide and maintain the stock of outside money.[25] Because Federal Reserve officials cannot directly pocket these earnings as dividends or profit-sharing bonuses, they can consume them only by padding expenditures. Unnecessary expenditures may take the form of high salaries, lavish offices and other amenities, travel budgets, vanity publications, or excessive numbers of employees.[26] The Fed would be unable to pad its budget in this way only if congressional monitoring of its consumption were costless. In fact, in the absence of competition, there is no way of knowing the minimum cost at which a product can be produced. Hence the Congress could never have a firm benchmark for judging unnecessary Fed expenditures.

The Federal Reserve rebates its earnings over and above its expenditures back to the Treasury.[27] It is sometimes concluded that the Fed has no incentive to expand the monetary base because its retained earnings from the marginal dollar of seigniorage must be zero. But this conclusion would follow only if monitoring of marginal Fed consumption were costless. If monitoring is costly at the margin of consumption, the Fed *is* in a position to "skim" some portion of the marginal seigniorage dollar into its own budget. Toma finds econometrically that in fact the Federal Reserve's expenditures have risen with its income, even after its service output and wage costs are taken into account, suggesting that a nonnegligible amount of "skimming" is going on.[28] The Fed then does have an incentive to promote monetary expansion on its own behalf.

Toma extends this model in an attempt to explain why the monetary authority may not aim for the maximum seigniorage apparently attainable.[29] He reasons that the current management of the authority may be constrained by potential competition from alternative management teams. Suppose that the next best team promises to produce base money with a total burden (welfare loss from its inflationary tax on cash balances plus its operating expenditures) just equal to the welfare burden of the seigniorage-maximizing rate of money creation. Suppose also that the current management is constrained to impose a burden on the public no heavier than the alternative team's, lest it be replaced. If the authority were to choose the seigniorage-maximizing rate of base money creation, it would then be constrained to zero expenditures, necessary or unnecessary. To maximize its discretionary profits (consumed through unnecessary expenditures) subject to the constraint, the authority must choose a rate of base money creation below the unconstrained revenue-maximizing rate. It can then pad its budget to an extent equal to the public's welfare gain from the reduced inflationary tax on cash balances, leaving the public no more (and no less) burdened than it would be under the alternative team.

The truth in this modification of the model is that the management of a monetary authority in a democracy may well be constrained in its monetary expansion and consumption by a fear of being generally perceived by the public as an engine of inflation and den of high living. Assuming that an alternative monetary regime were envisioned, this perception could indeed lead to popular demand for the termination of its tenure, as it did in Andrew Jackson's day.[30] At present, however, the Fed is clearly not tightly constrained by public, let alone by congressional, recognition of less burdensome alternative monetary regimes. After all, the regime of freezing the monetary base certainly exists as a viable alternative which could be operated with minimal administrative expense. If this were the benchmark the Fed had to meet, it would have to shrink the monetary base, providing the benefit of actual appreciation to holders of base money.

Given that efforts at monetary self-education and the exertion of political pressure for a less inflationary monetary regime have concentrated individual costs, while the benefits are diffuse and not fully appreciated, we should expect most citizens (and congressmen) to be understandably ignorant and unconcerned with monetary reform.[31] The Fed therefore enjoys a very long leash. Unusually high inflation may shorten the leash by awakening individuals to the possible benefits of altering the present monetary regime, and the Fed may therefore feel occasionally compelled to restore its honor by notching back the inflation rate, but the leash is dangerously long nonetheless. The long-term trend in the inflation rate since 1960, despite recent moderation, seems definitely upward.

POLITICAL BUSINESS CYCLES

Political business cycle theory alerts us to the possiblity that a politicized money supply regime poses not only the danger of secular inflation but also the danger of destabilization of real output and employment in pursuit of re-election. Early versions of the theory developed scenarios in which a government artfully slides the economy along long-run and short-run Phillips curves in order to attain for a fleeting pre-election moment the combination of unemployment and inflation rates most favored by voters.[32] These models rest on the assumption, which may or may not be borne out empirically, that voters myopically focus on the recent macroeconmic past when choosing between incumbents and challengers.[33] But the assumption deserving the most serious scrutiny is that the incumbent government has sufficient *control* and *knowledge* to move the economy off the long-run Phillips curve in the desired direction in a timely manner.

The ability of government in principle to control the economy so as to stimulate output and reduce unemployment every four years has been cogently challenged by proponents of "rational expectations" macroeconomics. In the expectations-augmented account of the Phillips curve, the ability of government to manufacture a boom through expansionary monetary policy depends upon its ability to create *surprisingly* high inflation. Underanticipated inflation distorts the output and hiring decisions of firms and the job-acceptance decisions of workers, and so initiates a reduction of unemployment below the natural rate. High inflation that is fully expected has no such effect. If the federal government were to methodically increase the inflation rate every fourth year, participants in output and labor markets would have to be somewhat dull-witted not to catch on to that policy and to revise their inflationary expectations accordingly. Once they have caught on, no systematic inflation surprises would occur, and no systematic increase in real output or reduction in unemployment would be produced by quadrennial jumps in the rates of monetary expansion and inflation.[34]

The government's policy strategy may, however, not be so methodical and transparent that market participants can see through it well enough to completely neutralize it. The strong form of the rational-expectations policy ineffectiveness proposition relies inter alia on the assumption that economic agents form their expectations using "the relevant theory." This "relevant theory" has to include knowledge of the monetary authority's decision rule and its perception of its own constraints. In the model of Robert J. Barro and David B. Gordon, for example, agents can form rational expectations of monetary expansion and inflation only because they know unambiguously the form and parameters of the misery function (defined over inflation and unemployment rates) that the monetary authority is trying to minimize, and know unambiguously the slope of the expectations-augmented Phillips trade-off that the monetary authority believes it faces.[35] To the extent that a monetary authority in the real world can successfully disguise or misrepresent its readiness to trade surprise inflation for temporarily lower unemployment, however, it can still exploit the short-run Phillips trade-off. Thus, if anyone takes its announcements seriously, the Fed has an incentive to *talk* a tougher anti-inflation line than it actually follows, to disclaim monetary aggregates when they indicate expansiveness in excess of its announced targets, and to insist that any disinflation that occurs is intentional while any acceleration of inflation is due to forces beyond its control.

It may take the public time to learn what to expect from the monetary authority, particularly when the latter changes its actual or announced [36] preferences, perceptions, or operating policies, so that an exploitable misanticipation of inflation may be created for a given pre-election year. The public is unlikely to see perfectly (at the margin) through the authority's smoke, especially if the authority does not accelerate monetary growth with perfect regularity prior to every election. If some incumbents fail to arrange an election-year boom through timely monetary expansion, this irregularity allows the public to be less than convinced that its inflationary expectations should be hiked as an election approaches, and so enhances the ability of other incumbents to exploit the relatively low inflationary expectations of an unsuspecting populace. [37]

Whereas the rational-expectations critique takes exploitable Phillips curve models of political business cycle theory to task for assuming the public to be implausibly dim, it is also possible to criticize those models for assuming the government to be implausibly clever and single-minded. For one thing, the requisite knowledge for a successful political business cycle includes at least a rough ability to forecast the lags with which innovations in monetary growth impinge on real output, unemployment, and inflation. Past forecasts by the United States federal government have been no better than *very* rough. [38] The argument that the monetary authority may lack the knowledge required to create a successful political business cycle is, of course, basically an extension of the familiar argument that the authority lacks the knowledge necessary to dampen business fluctuations of nonmonetary origin, i.e., to fine-tune the economy. The size and timing of monetary injections that will maximize electability is no less difficult to estimate than the size and timing of those that will minimize discrepancies between the stock of base money and the shifting quantity of base money demanded.

Even keen awareness of its own forecasting inaccuracy, however, cannot be relied upon to prevent an administration from *trying* to generate a favorably timed business cycle. It may intelligently perceive that the expected vote-maximizing policy lies *in the direction* of speeding up monetary growth at *some* point, say ten quarters before the election day, but it may not know precisely by how much and when.[39] If the public has come to anticipate this acceleration of the money supply, the policy becomes all the more necessary in order to avoid a negative monetary surprise. Inaccurate forecasts may help account for the failure of some recent presidents to successfully engineer their own re-election.

A significant modification of political business cycle theory, also arising from a more skeptical view of the central government's cleverness, consists in recognizing that not all cycles attributable to monetary surprises need to be the result of an intentional macroeconomic policy. A particular business cycle may instead be the *unintended* consequence of an innovation in monetary policy that happens to disturb macroeconomoic equilibrium. A jump in the rate of monetary expansion may, for example, be produced by the pursuit of greater short-run seigniorage. Richard E. Wagner has suggested that variations in the price level may be "merely [a] by-product of political efforts designed to modify the structure of relative prices,"[40] i.e., designed to redistribute wealth and buy votes through targeted expenditure of seigniorage revenues. When attempts at redistribution are concentrated near election time, macroeconomic discoordination would then be synchronized with elections. As redistributive spending intensifies, inflationary finance through monetary expansion intensifies. Newly created money, injected by government spending into specifically favored sectors, stimulates economic activity in a temporary and definitely lopsided way. The historical applicability of this model remains a topic for future research. But its immediate plausibility, owing to its consistency with the incentives and powers of a modern democratic government with a ready apparatus for money creation, makes the model a cogent addition to the reasons for believing that political money supply regimes are radically flawed.

CONCLUSION

This essay has tried to bring together a number of relevant points about the history and theory of central banks as government agencies. History (as exemplified by British and U.S. experience) indicates that central banks did not emerge for "natural" economic reasons, but instead for reasons of state. A monopoly historically created by political intervention, and today thoroughly harnessed to the central government, should not surprise us when it serves political ends. Economic theory suggests what those ends may be, and how a central bank can serve them. It can help finance government spending by creating new batches of money year after year, and will be all the happier to do so if it can spend some of this money on its own perquisites. It can try to help reelect incumbents by timing the creation of money in accordance with approaching elections, either to bend macroeconomic variables or to finance special-interest spending. In pursuing any of these ends the central bank is being used as a tool by those holding political power and is not serving the interests of the citizens compelled to use government-issued money.

Notes

I am indebted to King Banaian, Gregory Christainsen, Milton Friedman, Thomas Willett, and members of the research department of the Federal Reserve Bank of St. Louis for comments and discussion. The C. V. Starr Center for Applied Economics provided clerical support.

1. These proponents in Great Britain included Thomas Attwood and Sir John Sinclair. On Attwood as a proto-Keynesian whose policy proposals were uninfluential see Frank W. Fetter, *The Development of British Monetary Orthodoxy 1797–1975* (Cambridge: Harvard University Press, 1965), 74–77.
2. The classic theoretical account of this process is Carl Menger, "On the Origin of Money," *Economic Journal* 2 (June 1892): 239–55.
3. See George A. Selgin and Lawrence H. White, "The Evolution of a Free Banking System," *Economic Inquiry* 25 (July 1987): 439–57.
4. Walter Bagehot, *Lombard Street: A Description of the Money Market* (London: Henry S. King, 1873), 94.
5. Ibid., 99–100.
6. Speech of May 6, 1844, in *Hansard Parliamentary Debates*, 3d ser., vol. 74 (London: T. C. Hansard, 1844), col. 742.
7. John Clapham, *The Bank of England*, 2 vols. (New York: Macmillan, 1945), 2:178–79. On Currency School doctrines and the weakness in the English monetary system see Lawrence H. White, *Free Banking in Britain* (Cambridge: Cambridge University Press, 1984), 38–54.

8. However, many states allowed a broad range of collateral in addition to home state bonds. See Arthur J. Rolnick and Warren E. Weber, "Inherent Instability in Banking: The Free Banking Experience," *Cato Journal* 5 (Winter 1986): 877–90.

9. See Alexander Dana Noyes, *History of the National-Bank Currency* (Washington, D.C.: Government Printing Office, 1910), and Milton Friedman and Anna J. Schwartz, *A Monetary History of the United States, 1867–1960* (Princeton: Princeton University Press, 1963), 168–69. Evidence that the public wanted currency in general rather than outside currency in particular may be found in the ready public acceptance of currency issued (illegally) by clearinghouse associations during the panics of 1873, 1884, 1890, 1893, and 1907. See Richard H. Timberlake, Jr., "The Central Banking Role of Clearinghouse Associations," *Journal of Money, Credit, and Banking* 16 (February 1984): 1–15.

10. Timberlake, "Central Banking," p. 14; Vera C. Smith, *The Rationale of Central Banking* (London: P. S. King, 1936), 133–46.

11. On Fed accomodation of Treasury needs, see Robert J. Shapiro, "Politics and the Federal Reserve," *Public Interest* 66 (Winter 1982): 119–39.

12. Here seigniorage is defined as the *profit* to government from *additions* to the stock of base money. Contrast this to the definition used by some economists, which identifies seigniorage as an *implicit stream* of interest savings to government from the *existing* stock of its non-interest-bearing liabilities outstanding. The former definition is appropriate where the central bank issues irredeemable (fiat) money, because such issues are permanent and are not really liabilities. Under this definition no seigniorage is captured during a period in which the stock of base money remains constant.

13. Martin J. Bailey, "The Welfare Cost of Inflationary Finance," *Journal of Political Economy* (April 1956): 93–110; David Chappell, "On the Revenue Maximizing Rate of Inflation," *Journal of Money, Credit, and Banking* 13 (August 1981): 391–92. The real revenue-maximizing limit is established, as with other taxes, where the shrinkage of the tax base (here, real demand to hold fiat money) begins more than to offset the increasing tax rate (rate of monetary expansion or inflation).

14. On the "number one evil" syndrome, see William Poole, "Monetary Control and the Political Business Cycle," *Cato Journal* 5 (Winter 1986): 685–99.

15. See especially H. Geoffrey Brennan and James M. Buchanan, *Monopoly in Money and Inflation* (London: Institute of Economic Affairs, 1981).

16. See J. Harold McClure, Jr., and Thomas D. Willett, "The Inflation Tax," in *Political Business Cycles: The Political Economy of Money, Inflation, and Unemployment* (Durham, N.C.: Duke University Press, 1988). J. Harold McClure, Jr., and Thomas D. Willett, "Inflation Uncertainty and the Optimal Inflation Tax," Claremont Center for Economic Policy Studies

Working Paper (Claremont, Calif.: Claremont Graduate School, 1987), show that taking into account plausible negative effects of inflation on output, due to inflation uncertainty, dramatically lowers estimates of the revenue-maximizing rate of inflation.

17. Explanations resting on the assumption that prices are nowadays inflexible downwards entirely beg the question.

18. In fact, with a stable long-run Phillips curve, an adaptively shifting short-run Phillips curve,, and an election-day voter preference map centering on zero current inflation and current unemployment below the natural rate (for models with this structure, see note 32 below), the vote-maximizing strategy over the electoral cycle entails *deflation* on average. In that way the stage is set for moving, just prior to the election, "northwest" along a short-run Phillips curve adapted to deflation, to a point combining zero inflation with unemployment as far below the natural rate as desired.

19. Courtenay C. Stone, untitled note, Federal Reserve Bank of St. Louis *U.S. Financial Data* (5 July 1985), 1.

20. In the Bailey model the seigniorage-maximizing rate of monetary expansion does *not* vary with the *scale* of real money demand, contrary to what has been suggested by at least one author, but only with its sensitivity to the inflation rate (which varies percentage point for percentage point with the rate of monetary expansion).

21. Such a positive relationship is found empirically by Benjamin Klein, "Our New Monetary Standard: The Measurement and Effects of Price Uncertainty 1880–1973," *Economics Inquiry* 13 (December 1975): 461–84. The result can be theoretically derived if the demand for money is properly specified as a function of the expected real rate of return on money rather than the expected rate of inflation, because the expected real rate of return on money is greater for a more variable rate of inflation (holding the mean constant). For example, inflation at 25 percent every period means a real rate of return on money of 0.80, whereas inflation at 50 percent half the time and zero the other half (averaging the same 25 percent) means an average real rate of return of 0.83 (the average of 0.67 and 1.00), a payoff more than 4 percent higher. See Benjamin Eden, "On the Specification of the Demand for Money: The Real Rate of Return versus the Rate of Inflation," *Journal of Political Economy* 84 (December 1976): 1353–59.

22. The first point is made by Kent P. Kimbrough, "Inflation, Employment, and Welfare in the Presence of Transaction Costs," *Journal of Money, Credit, and Banking* 18 (May 1986): 127–40. The second is made by Robert J. Barro, "Inflationary Finance under Discretion and Rules," *Canadian Journal of Economics* 16 (February 1983): 1–16. This is an application of the general point that period-by-period decisions by a government authority may easily lead to a suboptimal equilibrium,

made by Finn E. Kydland and Edward C. Prescott, "Rules Rather Than Discretion: The Inconsistency of Optimal Plans," *Journal of Political Economy* 85 (June 1977): 473–91.

23. Bailey, "Welfare Cost."
24. Mark Toma, "Inflationary Bias of the Federal Reserve System: A Bureaucratic Perspective," *Journal of Monetary Economics* 10 (September 1982): 163–90.
25. The Federal Reserve and the Internal Revenue Service are the only two profit-making agencies of the federal government. The Fed "makes money" by literally making money.
26. See William F. Shughart II and Robert D. Tollison, "Preliminary Evidence on the Use of Inputs by the Federal Reserve System," *American Economic Review* 73 (June 1983): 291–304. One Federal Reserve economist I have communicated with argues to the contrary that Fed salaries and amenities are "notoriously" below those available in the private sector.
27. Toma, "Inflationary Bias," 166–67, explains the origin of this arrangement.
28. Ibid., 185–88.
29. Ibid., 170–71.
30. One Jacksonian theorist who called for abolition of the Bank of the United States because he saw it as a source of monetary instability and corruption, and because he had the alternative regime of free banking clearly in mind, was William Leggett. See Leggett in *Democratick Editorials: Essays in Jacksonian Political Economy*, ed. Lawrence H. White (Indianapolis: Liberty Press, 1984), 63–188.
31. On the costs of inflation and the failure of economists to understand them, see Axel Leijonhufvud, *Information and Coordination* (New York: Oxford University Press, 1981), 227–89. The same "free rider" problem applies to the individual congressman as to the rationally ignorant citizen because his district would capture very little of the benefit were he to incur the costs of monitoring the Fed more closely.
32. William D. Nordhaus, "The Political Business Cycle," *Review of Economic Studies* 42 (April 1975): 169–90; C. Duncan MacRae, "A Political Model of the Business Cycle," *Journal of Political Economy* 85 (April 1977): 239–63.
33. See Friedrich Schneider and Bruno S. Frey, "Politico-Economic Models of Macro-economic Policy," in *Political Business Cycles: The Political Economy of Money, Inflation, and Unemployment*, ed. Thomas D. Willett (Durham, N.C.: Duke University Press, 1988).
34. Bennet T. McCallum, "The Political Business Cycle: An Empirical Test," *Southern Economic Journal* 44 (January 1978): 504–15, tests for correlation between unemployment and phase of the U.S. electoral cycle by adding variously constructed electoral proxies to regressions of unem-

ployment on three lagged unemployment terms using quarterly data. His results are unfavorable to the Nordhaus hypothesis that an electoral unemployment cycle exists. Nordhaus had found an unemployment cycle analyzing annual U.S. data in a nonparametric way. Daniel J. Richards, "Unanticipated Money and the Political Business Cycle," *Journal of Money, Credit, and Banking* 18 (November 1986): 447−57, regresses unanticipated money (M_1) growth proxies on an electoral timing dummy variable, and finds that polical business cycle-type monetary policy appears to have existed in the period 1960−74 but not in 1975−84.

35. Robert J. Barro and David B. Gordon, "A Positive Theory of Monetary Policy in a Natural Rate Model," *Journal of Political Economy* 91 (August 1983): 589−610. But where the public remains in the dark about how monetary policy is formed period by period, and the monetary authority lacks a model of how the public forms its expectations, there may be no rational-expectations equilibrium to the game in which the monetary authority tries to outwit the public while the public tries to guess how expansive the authority will be. See Roman Frydman, Gerald P. O'Driscoll, Jr., and Andrew Schotter, "Rational Expectations of Government Policy: An Application of Newcomb's Problem," *Southern Economic Journal* 49 (October 1982): 311−19.

36. In the Barro-Gordon model it would be irrational for people to take seriously what the monetary authority *says* about its own policies, because they already know what it is really up to. Perhaps in our world people should likewise totally discount Federal Reserve statements. Nonetheless, many people apparently do not.

37. Growth in the aggregate M_1 was slightly lower in the third year than in the first year of the presidential terms of Gerald Ford and Jimmy Carter (by 0.6 and 0.8 percentage points, respectively). Both were defeated in bidding for a second term. Richard Nixon and Ronald Reagan, by contrast, enjoyed third-year M_1 growth 3.1 and 4.1 points higher than first-year growth. Both were reelected. Data from Allen R. Thompson, *Economics* (Reading, Mass.: Addison-Wesley, 1985), 848, 854, 864.

38. It would be surprising, after all, for the government's forecasters to be better than those in the private sector.

39. For a journalist's historical account of election-timed presidential manipulation of U.S. money growth, see Maxwell Newton, *The Fed* (New York: Times Books, 1983). Kevin B. Grier, "Presidential Elections and Federal Reserve Policy: An Empirical Test," *Southern Economic Journal* 65 (October 1987): 475−86, has adduced econometric evidence for the existence of a cyclical pattern in U.S. monetary growth consistent with political business cycle theory. The pattern shows reduction of money growth in the seven quarters after a presidential election, followed by increasing growth rates up to the next election. The pattern is not explained away by fiscal policy variables.

40. Richard E. Wagner, "Economic Manipulation for Political Profit: Macroeconomic Consequences and Constitutional Implications," *Kyklos* 30 (Fall 1977): 395–410. See also Gerald P. O'Driscoll, Jr., "Rational Expectations, Politics, and Stagflation," in *Time, Uncertainty, and Disequilibrium,* ed. Mario J. Rizzo (Lexington, Mass.: Lexington Books, 1979).

4

Depoliticizing the Supply of Money

Recognition of the dangers posed by the political incentives of government monetary authorities has prompted a wide array of proposals for partial or full depoliticization of the money supply process. This chapter evaluates these proposals. The next two sections examine the question, raised by programs for partial depoliticization through central bank independence or legislated monetary rules, of whether any government money-creating agency can really be sealed off from internal and external political agendas. If not—if an apolitical government monetary authority is chimerical—then a nongovernmental monetary system clearly demands consideration. Accordingly, the third section inquires into the feasibility of free-market monetary arrangements, and finds that public-goods and natural-monopoly arguments made against competitive private provision of money are not compelling. The concluding section suggests that if the choice between governmental and market monetary institutions turns on the question of which sort of institution can more credibly be bound by contract to perform as desired, then market institutions have the advantage.

AN "INDEPENDENT" CENTRAL BANK

Perhaps the mildest of proposals for monetary regime change is the suggestion that the central bank should enjoy greater "independence" from the direct control of elected officials. Independence is supposed to enable the central bank to resist the partisan demands

Reprinted, with permission, from *Political Business Cycles: The Political Economy of Money, Inflation, and Unemployment*, ed. Thomas D. Willett (Durham: N. C.: Duke University Press, 1988).

of the legislative and executive branches of government for inflationary finance and for election-year monetary stimulus. If this were true, however, it would also mean that the management of an independent monetary authority is able to resist all other demands, e.g., those of the public (to whatever limited extent it could discover and obey them). Being directly answerable to no one is certainly a comfortable situation. For this reason the officials of any central bank are themselves likely to be found in the forefront of those advocating independence for the agency. As Edward R. Tufte has commented, "The rhetoric of depoliticization [in the sense of independence] is itself a political weapon, inspired by agencies seeking to prevent external political control and to permit them quietly to serve the interests of their own constituencies."[1] An independent central bank's private constituency—presumably the large commercial banks—will generally have a private agenda which is not identical with the preferences of the common holders of money. The supposed influence of commercial banks over the Federal Reserve System, through their nominal ownership of the regional reserve banks, has been offered as an explanation of the Fed's continual emphasis on current credit-market conditions (e.g., the use of interest-rate targets) in the making of short-term policy decisions.[2] It is difficult to separate commercial bank influence from Treasury influence here, however, given that the Treasury is continually concerned with marketing interest-bearing debt. In any event, the prospect of a central bank beholden to the commercial banks is not much cheerier than that of a central bank beholden to Congress.

The degree to which a government-sponsored central bank in a democracy can ever be independent from the control of the legislative and executive branches of government is, of course, severely limited. Congress created the Federal Reserve System, and can rewrite its mandate at any time as it has in the past. Knowing this, the Federal Reserve's management cannot afford to be unresponsive to congressional pressures. The same is undoubtedly true of any other legislatively created central bank. The managers of a government monetary agency, particularly when they are political appointees like the governors of the Federal Reserve, may well lack even the conception that their own objectives might properly differ from the legislature's or the administration's objectives. Much less have they any strong incentive to resist political pressures (which may simply appear to be helpful suggestions) from these sources.

CONSTRAINING THE CENTRAL BANK BY A MONETARY RULE

Numerous reform proposals more far-reaching than "independence" for the central bank, and more likely to make a perceptible difference, have been made under the rubric of monetary "rules" or a "monetary constitution." These proposals would not eliminate a government monetary role, but would limit the monetary authority to the robotlike administration of a fully specified set of instructions for the creation of base money. The best-known plan of this sort at present is undoubtedly still Milton Friedman's 1959 program for adhering permanently to a prespecified steady and low growth path in the M_1 or M_2 measure of the stock of money.[3] Other writers have recommended more complex plans whereby the authority would adjust the target path in response to realized shifts in the growth rate of real national income or velocity, so that demand-induced deviations in the purchasing power of money would be counteracted. Still others have variously suggested that some index of purchasing power should be the explicit target on which the authority's sights are trained, with a feedback rule governing weekly base money creation.[4]

It would be impossible in the space available here to consider critically the technical aspects of each of these plans in any adequate detail. Instead, I have singled out a generic feature of these plans: the notion that the mind of man can design a government bureau which, once off the drawing board and staffed with real self-interested residents of the nation's capital, will function more or less as planned and will generate sufficient political support for its own perpetuation. In other words, each designer must tacitly assume that his plan represents a roughly stable political-economic equilibrium in the face of internal and external pressures for piecemeal modifications. The attempt to design a pressure-proof agency confronts at least three difficulties. It must be possible to specify the bureau's routine tightly enough for its mandate to require little interpretation, since extensive interpretation could serve as a means of subverting the rule in the interests of the staff itself, the legislature, the executive branch, or a private constituency. The operation of the rule must leave no interest group wanting and able to revise it through a plausible appeal to a later session of the legislature. And it must be possible to establish a disciplinary mechanism which will effectively prevent departures from the legislated instructions, whether intentional or due merely to innocent error.

The hypothesis that all these conditions can indeed be satisfied by the legislated version of a given rule cannot be empirically falsified, of course, without trying the experiment. (It cannot be decisively falsified even then. It could always be argued that the rule failed only because the effort to implement it wasn't sincere enough.) Perhaps with enough academic input the legislative or constitutional amendment process really can give birth to a single-mindedly apolitical government agency for controlling something as consequential as the money supply. But the logic of bureaucracy does not offer much encouragement. Nor does history offer a single apparent precedent.[5]

The power of money creation is so extremely tempting for government to exploit that continual public vigilance (incurring of monitoring and enforcement costs, in other words) would be necessary to hold a government agency possessing that power to a prescribed routine. There is a free-rider problem here, which is more pronounced the more costly the rule is to monitor, in that most members of the public will rationally choose to let others bear the burden of keeping well informed about the conduct of the monetary agency. Keeping well informed would be all the more difficult because a monetary agency that naturally wanted to escape tight constraints on its behavior in order to pursue its own agenda would have an incentive to pollute the available information on its conduct, making public accounting more difficult. So long as an expert agency existed to administer the monetary rule, the public would have to be well informed enough to see through all of the superficially plausible rationalizations the agency might offer for deviations from the monetary rule, such as, the deviation is really just a measurement error, or due to a distortion in the aggregate being measured, or is really not a deviation from the *spirit* of the rule, or is justified by events unforeseen by the framers of the rule. To arrive at an informed opinion on each separate case is implausibly costly for many members of the public to undertake.

To be economically monitored and enforced, and hence workable, a monetary rule must be so plain and straightforward that violations are transparent. Once in operation, the simpler the rule, the less the public needs to know to detect violations. A solid public consensus must hold "dogmatically" that the rule is never to be violated as a matter of principle. Such a consensus would not be easy to form in any case, but it would be less difficult to form the simpler and more clear-cut the rule. For these reasons a no-feedback rule stands a better chance for effectiveness than a price-level feedback rule or a velocity shift-adjusted money growth rule. A zero money growth rule stands a better chance than a fixed positive-growth rule, and a rule of freezing the monetary base stands a better chance than one of freezing a wider monetary aggregate.[6]

Freezing the monetary base would be uniquely easy to enforce because it is the only "monetary rule" which, like the First Amendment to the U.S. Constitution, does not direct government to perform any positive task. It merely proscribes what the federal government shall *not* do: it shall not expand the stock of monetary instruments issued by itself. Because no positive money-creation power is assigned, no money-creating agency whatsoever is needed. The Federal Reserve System could readily be eliminated as a branch of growth once its open-market desk was closed down and its rediscount window shuttered.[7] The Fed's bank-regulatory activities could either be terminated or transferred to another federal agency. Its check-clearing and wire-transfer facilities could be privatized quite practicably. Check-clearing operations were entirely private before the advent of the Fed, are in large part privately run in the United States today, and are entirely private in Canada and other nations. Privatization would require only that the stock of member banks in the twelve district reserve banks be treated as genuine ownership shares. The Bureau of Engraving and Printing might be allowed the job of replacing worn currency, or a plan might be devised to allow currency issued by private banks to displace government currency, so that the stock of high-powered money would come to be held exclusively as bank reserves.[8]

Any monetary rule less strict than freezing the monetary base quite obviously allows open-market operations to continue, and therefore allows some government monetary agency to carry on the function of altering the stock of base money. Under any growth rule for a wider monetary aggregate the agency is charged with offsetting changes in the relevant money multiplier; under any positive-money-growth rule it is charged with adding regularly to the stock of base money. The dynamics of government growth give good reason to fear that the very existence of a government money-creation agency, no matter how circumscribed its initial activities, represents the thin edge of a very powerfully propelled wedge. The agency's officials can lend the weight of their expert opinion to the case for giving them greater powers to perform functions which only they, purportedly, truly understand.[9] The modification of an existing agency's operating routine is certainly less likely to encounter pitched public resistance than the creation of an entirely new agency.

This "thin edge" problem—the worrisome potential for degeneration of any legislated barriers against discretionary behavior by an existing monetary authority—cannot be dismissed by saying that we need not worry about attempts to erode the barriers until they occur. One fundamental benefit promised by a monetary rule is the assured environment it would provide, by *precommitting* the monetary authority to a predictable path of behavior, for private planning based on firmly held inflation-rate expectations.[10] The transitional drawbacks of disinflation, for example, are generally understood by economists to be less severe the more credible is the monetary authority's commitment to a disinflationary path, because greater credibility allows prudent agents more promptly to moderate the nominal prices and wages they demand in long-term contracts. If the public widely considers a particular legislatable monetary rule to be fragile and unreliable because they perceive that it may not survive political and bureaucratic pressures, then the adoption of the rule will not provide the benefit of a credible precommitment. It may even be worse than no rule. The pursuit of a low-inflation policy rule in a setting where the public cynically expects high inflation is a recipe for unnaturally high unemployment and depressed real output.

There is a second respect in which a legislated monetary rule will fail to provide its advertised benefits if its long-term political survival is not sufficiently credible. A common argument for adopting a fiat money regime governed by some designed rule constraining growth in the stock of fiat money, rather than adopting a commodity-based regime (e.g., a gold-coin standard) governed by demand and supply conditions in the market or the money commodity, is that rule-constrained fiat money can provide an equivalent nominal anchor at a lower resource cost.[11] Fiat money provides a social windfall, so the argument goes, by freeing the existing stock of monetary gold to be used for industrial and consumptive purposes and by releasing resources devoted to augmenting the stock of monetary gold through mining and prospecting to be used for other industries. These events require, however, that the relative price of gold be lower under the fiat money regime than under the gold coin standard. During our current experiment with fiat money this has not happened. The relative price of gold is higher, apparently due to the demand to hold gold coins and bullion as a hedge against fiat money inflation, implying that industrial and consumptive uses are more restricted and that mining and prospecting activities are greater.[12] Whether the relative price of gold would be lower under a *rule-constrained* fiat money regime depends on whether the political survival of the rule is credible enough to discourage substantial speculative holdings of gold. In view of the "thin edge" problem, it may unfortunately be the case that no rule whose administration requires the existence of a government monetary agency can achieve the requisite survival credibility.

Taking the logic of the "thin edge" problem a bit further, it is possible to doubt that even freezing the monetary base removes the power of money creation far enough from the hands of government to constitute a politically stable arrangement. Freezing the base establishes an "authorized issue" for the central government. At a later date it might plausibly be argued that since the level is arbitrary, there is no reason for not raising it to meet some pressing government expense. As a historical illustration, the second batch of fiat greenbacks issued to finance the U. S. Civil War met with less opposition than the first (which Congress had promised would be the only batch). The first batch was itself justified by reference to the precedent of the moneylike Treasury notes issued in the previous decades.[13]

A slightly outlandish analogy may make the point even more

clearly.[14] The approach to monetary reform that consists of giving a discretionary monetary authority unsolicited advice for better policy is like the approach of a team of Wild West railroad detectives who, confronting a gun-toting gang in the midst of robbing a train, attempt to persuade the gang through reason that they really should be using their guns in a less threatening manner. Success is unlikely given the other side's incentives.[15] Advocacy of a legislated rule for monetary growth is like demanding that the gang holster its guns and promise to leave them holstered. This arrangement is a bit better, but still not nearly as reassuring to the train passengers as the natural solution, familiar from old Westerns, of demanding that the gang drop it guns. Leaving the loaded guns within easy reach makes it all too easy for the train robbers to seize an opportunity to break their promise, so that extremely vigilant attention to their behavior remains necessary. The strongest form of a monetary rule, freezing the monetary base, might be likened (at the expense of stretching the analogy even further) to a policy of allowing the outlaws to keep their guns provided that they throw down their bullets. That arrangement certainly promises greater stability than the weaker gun-holstering rule, but arguably it may not go far enough toward removing the ultimate threat and reassuring the passengers.

A FREE MARKET MONETARY SYSTEM

The analogue of the drop-your-guns approach in monetary reform is the proposal that government remove itself completely from the business of supplying money. In its place a free-market monetary system would prevail, shaped and disciplined not by a legislated blueprint but by rivalrous competition among money producers for consumer patronage. The money's spendability and purchasing power would be secured by contractually guaranteed redeemability into a standard basic asset, either a commodity money or an equivalently acceptable privately produced asset held by all banks and used as a clearing medium among them.[16] Because it represents depoliticization of the money supply in the most thorough conceivable form, this system merits consideration by anyone who recognizes the drawbacks of a political monetary regime. Unless a free-market monetary system somehow inherently fails to provide money with the generally desired features that a legislatively designed system clearly would provide, competition among private suppliers may be the best means of meeting the preferences of moneys users. In fact this conclusion should not be surprising, given that the virtues of competitive markets are widely recognized when the supply of other private goods and services is at issue.

It has been argued in several ways that a free-market monetary system may inherently fail to perform in a desirable fashion. These arguments have often been made on a purely theoretical level, with their proponents neglecting to examine the historical evidence on market freedom in monetary institutions in order to see whether the projected ill effects really did occur. The available evidence that is most relevant is taken from the clearest episode of monetary freedom on record, namely Scotland's twelve-plus decades of experience with free banking from 1716 to 1844 (which ended when the Parliament in London moved to assimilate Scottish banking to the English central banking system by barring the entry of new currency-issuing banks). The evidence shows that a banking system can succeed rather dramatically in the absence of significant government intervention.[17] The so-called free banking era in the United States appears, in the light of recent revisionist economic history, to have been an era of decentralized but by no means unregulated currency supply. While the era was not as chaotic as previously believed, it was marked by undeniable shortcomings which can be attributed to state-imposed regulations, particularly bond-collateral restrictions on bank note issues and barriers to branch banking.[18]

Theoretical arguments for "market failure" in the provision of money generally fall into one of two categories: (1) arguments claiming that money, or some aspect of money, is a public good or a source of nonappropriable external effects; or (2) arguments proposing that the supplying of money is a natural monopoly due to economies of scale in production. (Some authors have pointed to "social economies of scale" in the *use* of money, but these economies are more appropriately considered to fall into the category of external effects.) Both sets of arguments have been examined by Roland Vaubel, who concludes that neither of them makes a valid case for exclusive government provision of money. In Vaubel's words, "externality theory fails to provide a convincing justification for the government's monopoly in the production of (base) money," and "since, finally, we cannot even be sure that money or the currency unit is a natural monopoly, the case against restrictions of entry is overwhelming."[19] The even stronger conclusion is warranted, however, that no convincing case for the necessity or social desirability of *any* government involvement has been made.

The public-good or externality argument is rather obviously not applicable to money as a medium of exchange, since the liquidity or ready spendability services of money accrue exclusively to its owner and not to others. Nonetheless, it might be argued that an individual's use of a *common* medium of exchange confers nonappropriable external benefits to others who can now trade with him more cheaply, and that therefore a free-market monetary system will underproduce the quality characteristic of commonness or general acceptability in exchange media. This argument runs up against the historical fact that the market did *not* fail to produce commonly accepted media of exchange prior to government involvement in money. Gold and silver emerged spontaneously as nearly universal monies because of strong *private* incentives for individuals to use as exchange media the commodities that other traders most readily accept.[20] If we assume that some fraction of the transactions cost savings accomplished through use of a common money are enjoyed by the marginal user, the remainder being enjoyed by those with whom he transacts, then there is no divergence between what is privately optimal and what is "socially optimal" in the choice among exchange media.[21]

The most that could be argued on grounds of transaction-cost externality is that the market's convergence on a common money may occur too slowly because each trader has limited information about which exchange media are being accepted by the other traders.[22] If this argument went through, it might be used to make a utilitarian case for collective subsidy of convergence-speeding information additional to the information that would be privately produced. It could not be used to justify government imposition of a monetary standard by edict, however, because an unbiased market process is necessary in order to discover what type of money traders will find most suitable. To enhance "social utility," of course, government would have to know (how would it?) what information was in fact socially valued more than its cost of production even in the absence of any revealed willingness to pay for it, and would have to spend less (what would limit it?) on its production than the information was worth. But even if that were possible, government's limited publicity role would disappear entirely once the economy had fully converged on a common money. Private provision of money suffers no informational externality problems once a monetary standard has emerged.[23]

On the other hand, it might be argued that informational problems do not entirely disappear with convergence on a monetary standard. There are two cases to consider. The first case involves the transition away from the current government fiat monetary system toward a system allowing private competition in the supply of outside money. There is a strong utilitarian case to be made for minimizing calculational and transactional confusion during the transition by having the government, as it disengages from production of fiat dollars, take minimally interventionist steps to favor a particular new standard upon which the market economy could then rapidly converge. Obvious steps the government could take include announcing its intention to use a particular new unit for its own accounting and transactions.[24] If a precious-metal standard is to be established, fiat dollars could be made redeemable for the metal, so that an initial stock of the new outside money is made immediately available. This transitional step, by absorbing and retiring fiat dollars, solves the problem of a collapsing demand for Federal Reserve notes that might otherwise penalize their holders.[25]

The second case involves an economy that is already on a monetary standard allowing private production of outside money. The question of establishing a new standard may arise if the purchasing power of the existing monetary unit begins to fluctuate considerably or deteriorate rapidly. (Presumably this would be an unanticipated development, because instability would militate against a standard's adoption in the first place.) The market's tendency to stick with an existing standard, each individual waiting for others to go first in getting a new system off the ground, may prevent the expeditious emergence of a new money.[26] For plausible private monetary standards, however, the hypothesized problem may well never arise. For an indexed or commodity-basket standard, purchasing-power instability is virtually ruled out by definition. For a more pedestrian gold or other single-commodity standard, there are both theoretical and historical reasons for having confidence in the stability of the monetary unit. The theory of commodity money demonstrates that potential changes in the purchasing power of the monetary unit are dampened by the price elasticity of supply and nonmonetary demand for the money commodity. A fall in the purchasing power (relative price) of gold, for instance, whether due to a fortuitous discovery of gold or a fall in the demand for outside money, is impeded by the reduced quantity of gold that will be mined and the increased quantity that will be demanded for nonmonetary purposes at any lower price. An ongoing fall in the value of gold due to continually greater cost reductions in gold mining than in other industries is fairly implausible, and so is a nonrecurring but sharp fall in the modern world where there is little prospect of a purely fortuitous major gold discovery. For a nonrenewable resource whose reserves are known, economic theory suggests that under competitive conditions the relative price of the resource will rise over time at a rate somewhat less than the real rate of interest (the difference depends on the marginal cost of extraction). The gold standard automatically generates an approximation of the "optimum quantity of money," as holders of gold-denominated money may thereby enjoy a mild ongoing appreciation in the value of their cash balances. The history of the classical gold standard may contain some noteworthy episodes of variation in the purchasing power of the monetary unit, but the overall picture from 1821 to 1914 is indeed one of mild secular appreciation in the value of money, with deviations from trend strikingly smaller than under subsequent monetary systems.[27]

The argument that money production is a natural monopoly is sometimes based on a confusion between the market tendency to converge on a single monetary *standard* and the prevalence under natural monopoly of a single *producer*. In a setting of competition among *noncommodity* monies, if each producer's brand of money were to constitute its own standard, the tendency to converge on a single standard might well favor the survival of a single producer of outside money for reasons quite distinct from natural monopoly in the usual sense of unlimited economies of scale. This result does not occur, however, where market forces lead producers to denominate their monies according to the same standard, as should be expected even in the case of irredeemable monies.[28] Where a commodity money unit constitutes the monetary standard, it is clearly feasible to have multiple producers of money unless there are genuine natural-monopoly characteristics present. Many competing mines can produce the same precious metal, many competing mints can produce standardized coins from that metal, and many competing banks can offer bank notes and checkable deposits redeemable for those coins. It would seem to be a historical question whether unlimited economies of scale operate at any of these levels of money production, and the historical evidence indicates that they do not.[29]

It has been argued on various theoretical grounds, however, that natural monopoly must be present in money production. For one, stochastic economies of scale have been identified in banking (declining inside-money "production" costs).[30] These economies undoubtedly do exist, but beyond some point they are evidently swamped by diseconomies of coordinating a large banking firm or of "selling" inside money balances. More provocatively, Michael Melvin, drawing on the work of Benjamin Klein, has deduced natural monopoly in money from the belief that the costs of creating consumer confidence in the trustworthiness of the issuer, necessary in order to "sell" real money balances, are largely fixed costs.[31] In Melvin's own framework, however, it is natural to believe that these costs are *not* fixed, but rise with the quantity of real balances to be sold. The "confidence capital" an issuer must acquire, in order to convince the public that he will not find it profitable to cheat them through overexpansion, would seem to be proportional to the real money balances he has in circulation, because his potential gain from cheating is proportional to his existing circulation. If so, then confidence-bolstering expenditures are not a fixed cost, no natural monopoly exists on this account, and no case has been made for government over private provision.[32]

Melvin makes a related argument for government provision that also deserves to be considered here. He argues that "the costs of individually contracting for privately produced high-quality money are prohibitive," i.e., performance contracts between issuer and money holder cannot be cheaply written and enforced. To achieve a stable private money, therefore, a large premium (in the form of zero interest on cash balances and steady erosion of purchasing power through inflation) would have to be continually paid to a private money issuer, a sort of "protection money" fee, to make it relatively unprofitable for the issuer to take the one-shot gain available from a surprising flood of money production. This large premium then "suggests that quality is realized more cheaply through government production."[33] Even granted the initial premises, however, the comparative cheapness of government production does not follow unless it can be shown that an equally large protection premium does not have to be paid to a government producer to assure quality. If the government has an uncertain tenure and therefore a shorter time horizon or higher discount rate than a private firm, as Klein has noted to be the case,[34] then the quality-assuring premium necessary for stability with government production of money would be even higher than the premium necessary with private production, assuming effective performance contracts to be prohibitively expensive in both cases. Melvin seems to believe that the money-holding public as a body can relatively cheaply contract or "vertically integrate" with government for good performance so that a high premium can be avoided. But on this belief it would appear quite puzzling that in fact no constitutional "contract" currently limits the U.S. government's monetary behavior, which in recent years has been far from good. Our discussion above concerning the difficulties inherent in monitoring, enforcing, and preserving an explicit rule binding a government monetary agency suggests that explicit performance contracting costs with government may indeed be prohibitive.

Fortunately the initial premise that Melvin adopts, that "the costs of individually contracting for privately produced high-quality money are prohibitive," is empirically false. Redemption contracts, as carried on the faces of privately issued bank notes during historical episodes of free banking in such words as "the ABC Bank will pay to the bearer on demand one pound sterling," are cheap to write and to enforce. A note holder denied redemption can simply be granted a lien against the issuing bank.[35] Swift and certain enforcement of redemption ensures that bank notes are high-quality money, their purchasing power equal to that of the specie or other assets to which they are claims. Accordingly, de facto redeemability of private money into specie makes Melvin's analysis irrelevant. Bank note issuers on a gold standard do not, contrary to what Melvin asserts, have to "maintain large stocks of gold in order to build confidence in their money" directly; note holders have no need to observe the size of the gold reserve so long as they feel assured of continued redeemability.[36] The reserve is instead held to meet stochastic redemption outflows as they occur, and thereby indirectly (through a good track record) to help provide quality assurance. Though some expenditures are necessary to convince the public that a bank is not a fly-by-night affair, convertibility eliminates the need for confidence capital of the Klein-Melvin sort. Convertible private money therefore does not require that money holders bear a high cost in the form of a protection premium paid to money issuers. In fact, the opportunity cost of holding currency was definitely lower under historical gold-standard free-banking regimes than it is today, because lower inflation made for lower nominal interest rates on alternative assets.[37]

CONCLUSION

Chapter 3 of this volume explored the incentives of a political money issuer unbound by an enforceable performance rule. The first half of the present chapter examined the question of whether any durable and credible rule could be fastened onto a political money supplier. Finally, in considering the feasibility of private production of money, we have been led to ask a similar question about private issuers: Can they be effectively contractually bound to good performance? Our conclusion turns out to be one of skepticism toward the potential for enforcing any explicit rule (other than freezing the money base) for properly "depoliticized" monetary behavior by the central government. There is, after all, little or no precedent for such a thing, at least under fiat money regimes. (It remains to be understood why some central banks are less mischevious than others today.) On the other hand, we find that there exists at least one effectively enforceable contractual arrangement—convertibility—which makes desirable monetary behavior quite credible for competitive private issuers of money. The road away from political business cycles and the political economy of stagflation toward a depoliticized and responsible set of money institutions would therefore seem to point rather clearly in the direction of private contractual arrangements for the supply of money. It is simply too difficult to believe that a government can be more easily held to its promises than a private firm in a competitive environment.

Notes

I am indebted to King Banaian, Gregory Christainsen, Roger Garrison, John R. Lott, Jr., Milton Friedman, Anna J. Schwartz, Thomas Willett, and members of the Austrian Colloquium at New York University for comments and discussion, and to the C. V. Starr Center for Applied Economics for clerical support.

1. Edward R. Tufte, *Political Control of the Economy* (Princeton: Princeton University Press, 1978), 139.
2. See Milton Friedman, "Should There Be an Independent Monetary Authority?" in *In Search of a Monetary Constitution*, ed. Leland B. Yeager (Cambridge: Harvard University Press, 1963), 238.
3. Milton Friedman, *A Program for Monetary Stability* (New York: Fordham University Press, 1960), esp. chap. 4. Recently, Friedman has progressed to the advocacy of zero growth in the stock of base money, abolition of the Fed, and thorough deregulation of banking, as "the best real cure" for the instability of the current monetary regime. See idem, "Monetary Policy for the 1980's," in *To Promote Prosperity*, ed. John H. Moore (Stanford: Hoover Institution Press, 1984), 40–54.
4. See the discussion of such proposals in Pamela Brown, "Constitution or Competition: Alternative Approaches to Monetary Reform," *Literature of Liberty* 5 (Autumn 1982): 17–18. The set of rules focusing on purchasing-power index targets includes recent "supply-side" proposals for linking open market operations to the price of gold.
5. The principal "rule of the game" under the international gold standard, i.e., convertibility at a fixed parity, was not the creature of legislative design. Central banks empowered to deviate from that rule were not free from political influence. Conversely, the durability and credibility of the classical gold standard was enhanced, I would hypothesize, by the fact that the Bank of England was privately owned.
6. See Friedman, "Monetary Policy," 48–50, for a base freeze proposal and the argument that "zero growth has a special appeal on political grounds that is not shared by any other number."
7. The desk-closing would require an end to the pointless (after a base freeze) activity of rolling over Treasury securities in the Fed's portfolio as they mature. This could be accomplished by a simple bookkeeping change involving the Treasury.
8. For such a plan, see G. A. Selgin, *The Case for Free Banking: Then and*

Now, Cato Institute Policy Analysis series, no. 60 (21 October 1985). Privatization of the district Federal Reserve banks has long been advocated by Richard H. Timberlake.

9. Richard H. Timberlake, "Legislative Construction of the Monetary Control Act of 1980," *American Economic Review* 75 (May 1985): 101–2, provides a case study of this process in action: "Fed officials in their testimony to congressional committees persistently and doggedly advanced one major theme: the Fed had to have more power. . . . By misdirection and subterfuge, the Fed inveigled an unwary Congress into doing its bidding."

10. On monetary rules as precommitments, see Robert J. Barro and David B. Gordon, "A Positive Theory of Monetary Policy in a Natural Rate Model," *Journal of Political Economy* 91 (August 1983): 589–610.

11. The best-known estimate of the resource costs of a commodity standard is probably Milton Friedman's figure of 2.5 percent of annual net national product (*Program for Monetary Stability,* 5). That estimate assumes mandatory 100 percent reserves against all of M2, however. With historically reasonable fractional reserve ratios the figure falls to about one one-hundredth of Friedman's, namely, 0.014 to 0.028 percent (depending on assumptions about the secular trend in velocity). See Lawrence H. White, *Free Banking in Britain* (Cambridge: Cambridge University Press, 1984), 148.

12. This point is made by Roger W. Garrison, "The 'Costs' of a Gold Standard," in *The Gold Standard: An Austrian Perspective,* ed. Llewellyn H. Rockwell, Jr. (Lexington, Mass.: D. C. Heath, 1985). As this is being proofed the dollar price of gold is about $400 per troy ounce. Deflating by the GNP deflator, this is equivalent to about $120 per ounce at 1967 prices, at which time the official price of gold was $35 per ounce, and about $50 per ounce in 1929 terms, at which time gold was $20.67 per ounce.

13. For excerpts from the congressional debate over the initial issue of greenbacks, see Herman E. Krooss, ed., *Documentary History of Banking and Currency in the United States,* 4 vols. (New York: Chelsea House/McGraw-Hill, 1977), 2:1267–1321. On Treasury notes as a precedent for greenbacks, see Richard H. Timberlake, *The Origins of Central Banking in the United States* (Cambridge: Harvard University Press, 1978), 85–86.

14. The analogy is due to Roger W. Garrison, "Gold: A Standard and an Institution," *Cato Journal* 3 (Spring 1983): 236, though he may wish to disclaim the extensions made here.

15. Robert J. Barro, "United States Inflation and the Choice of Monetary Standard," in *Inflation: Causes and Effects,* ed. Robert E. Hall (Chicago: University of Chicago Press for the National Bureau of Economic Research, 1982), 109, aptly comments: "Telling the Federal Reserve to

select substantially different values—usually lower values—for monetary growth seems similar to urging firms and households to choose different numbers for prices, unemployment, production, and so on. As in the private sector, it is reasonable to view the Fed's monetary decisions as emerging from a given structure of constraints and rewards." This is the point of the analogy. It is *not* intended to suggest that Federal Reserve officials are personally malicious characters.

16. For some of the present author's previous writings on this topic, see Lawrence H. White, "Competitive Money, Inside and Out," in *The Search for Stable Money*, ed. James A. Dorn and Anna J. Schwartz (Chicago: University of Chicago Press, 1987); and idem, "Free Banking as an Alternative Monetary System," in *Money in Crisis*, ed. Barry N. Siegel (San Francisco: Pacific Institute for Public Policy Research, 1984). See also George A. Selgin, *The Theory of Free Banking* (Totowa, N.J.: Rowman and Littlefield, 1988). For a somewhat different perspective that nonetheless may fit within the institutional pattern predicted here, see Robert L. Greenfield and Leland B. Yeager, "A Laissez-Faire Approach to Monetary Stability," *Journal of Money, Credit, and Banking* 15 (August 1983): 302–15.

17. See White, *Free Banking in Britain*, chaps. 2, 5. For earlier accounts see Rondo Cameron, *Banking in the Early Stages of Industrialization* (New York: Oxford University Press, 1967), chap. 3; and Vera C. Smith, *The Rationale of Central Banking* (London: P. S. King, 1936), chap. 2.

18. The chief contributions to this new scholarship are Hugh Rockoff, "The Free Banking Era: A Reexamination," *Journal of Money, Credit, and Banking* 6 (May 1974): 141–67; Arthur J. Rolnick and Warren E. Weber, "Free Banking, Wildcat Banking, and Shinplasters," Federal Reserve Bank of Minneapolis *Quarterly Review* 6 (Fall 1982): 10–19; idem, "New Evidence on the Free Banking Era," *American Economic Review* 73 (December 1983): 1080–91; idem, "The Causes of Free Bank Failures: A Detailed Examination," *Journal of Monetary Economics* 14 (November 1984): 267–91; idem, "Instability in Banking: Lessons from the Free Banking Era," *Cato Journal* 6 (Winter 1986): 877–90; and Robert G. King, "On the Economics of Private Money," *Journal of Monetary Economics* 12 (July 1983): 127–58.

19. Roland Vaubel, "The Government's Money Monopoly: Externalities or Natural Monopoly?" *Kyklos* 37 (1984): 45, 47. Vaubel does, however, leave open the possibilities that peripheral forms of government intervention (deposit insurance, lender of last resort, subsidization of marginal bank accounts in undermonetized economies) might be justifiable, and that government ought to be allowed to compete as a money supplier. The case for a completely free market monetary system would need to rebut these arguments as well.

20. The classic account of the convergence process set in motion by the

discovery of these incentives is Carl Menger, "On the Origin of Money," *Economic Journal* 2 (June 1892): 234–55.

21. Vaubel's argument to this effect regarding choice among established monies ("Government's Money Monopoly," 41–44) applies equally to choice among premonetary media of exchange, at least to the extent that we can view these choices statically.

22. This argument has, indeed, been made by Stephen O. Morell, "Exchange, Money, and the State: An Essay on the Limits of Government Involvement in Monetary Affairs" (typescript, Auburn University, 1983).

23. Vaubel, "Government's Money Monopoly," 41, draws a similar conclusion: "However, where, like in the industrial countries, all economic agents do use money, transaction cost externalities of using money cannot be Pareto-relevant."

24. Leland B. Yeager has argued for these steps in "Stable Money and Free-Market Currencies," *Cato Journal* 3 (Spring 1983): 319, 324. Yeager calls them a "non-coercive nudge," but it is doubtful that a measure which would presumably require payment of taxes in a particular form should be called "non-coercive."

25. Leland Yeager, "Deregulation and Monetary Reform," *American Economic Review* 75 (May 1985): 105, sees "no satisfactory answer" to the collapsing dollar problem in a transition to the non-commodity-money competitive payments system he favors.

26. I am indebted to Gregory Christainsen for bringing this problem to my attention.

27. For graphical evidence on the historical behavior of the purchasing power of gold see Michael David Bordo, "The Gold Standard: Myths and Realities," in *Money in Crisis,* ed. Siegel, 212, 213, 215. For elaboration of the depletable resource theory of a gold standard, see Michael David Bordo and Richard Wayne Ellson, "A Model of the Classical Gold Standard with Depletion," *Journal of Monetary Economics* 16 (July 1985): 109–20. On both the theory and the history, see Hugh Rockoff, "Some Evidence on the Real Price of Gold, Its Costs of Production, and Commodity Prices," in *A Retrospective on the Classical Gold Standard, 1821–1931,* ed. Michael D. Bordo and Anna J. Schwartz (Chicago: University of Chicago Press for the National Bureau of Economic Research, 1984), 613–49, esp. 619–20.

28. F. A. Hayek, *Denationalisation of Money,* 2d ed. (London: Institute of Economic Affairs, 1978), 123–24, imagines that the typical private producer of irredeemable money will promise to stabilize its purchasing power in terms of a particular index, so that other producers could easily adopt the same "standard" by targeting the same index. In the Greenfield-Yeager system the unit of account (or payment "standard") is divorced from the media of exchange, so that a single standard is clearly compatible with a plurality of issuers.

29. Vaubel, "Government's Money Monopoly," 47 n. 37, cites several relevant studies and concludes: "Historically, competition has not tended to destroy itself in the money-producing industry." For evidence on competitive private mints, see Donald H. Kagin, *Private Gold Coins and Patterns of the United States* (New York: Arco, 1981); for evidence on competitive bank note issuers, see White, *Free Banking in Britain*, 23–49, 146.

30. See Ernst Baltensperger, "Economies of Scale, Firm Size, and Concentration in Banking," *Journal of Money, Credit, and Banking* 4 (August 1972): 467–88.

31. Benjamin Klein, "The Competitive Supply of Money," *Journal of Money, Credit, and Banking* 6 (November 1974): 447–49; Michael Melvin, "Monetary Confidence, Privately Produced Monies, and Domestic and International Monetary Reform," in *Political Business Cycles: The Political Economy of Money, Inflation, and Unemployment*, ed. Thomas D. Willett (Durham, N. C.: Duke University Press, 1988).

32. I am indebted to John R. Lott, Jr., for discussion on this point. The tenability of Klein's confidence-capital equilibrium has been cast into sharp doubt by Bart Taub, "Private Fiat Money with Many Suppliers," *Journal of Monetary Economics* 16 (September 1985): 195–208.

33. Melvin, "Monetary Confidence," in Willett ed., 446.

34. Klein, "Competitive Supply of Money," 449–50.

35. In the Scottish system this was known as the note holder's right of "summary diligence." See S. C. Checkland, *Scottish Banking: A History, 1695–1973* (Glasgow: Collins, 1975), 121. During the United States' so-called free banking era, state legislatures sometimes legalized suspensions of gold redemption, but that is quite different from inherently costly enforcement.

36. The competing Scottish banks did not find it necessary to advertise the size of their gold reserves. Having unlimited shareholder liability for their debts, which was both enforceable and enforced, however, new banks did advertise the names of their wealthy shareholders.

37. Even in American "free banking," in which redemption was not so easily enforced in practice, the average note holder loss from bank suspensions and failures amounted to less than the loss from a 2 percent inflation rate (Rockoff, "Free Banking Era," 151).

5

Privatization of Financial Institutions in Developing Countries

The degree to which a modern economy's financial sector functions properly in large measure determines the economy's degree of success in real per capita growth and income over the long term. The financial sector plays two crucial roles. First, the financial system determines allocation of income between present and future (consumption today versus more consumption tomorrow through savings, investment, and capital formation) and allocation of current investment funds among various competing projects. Its second role is the administration of the payment system in the economy. Financial development—the emergence of sophisticated and efficient institutions for coordinating payments and investment decisions—has gone hand in hand with real per capita economic growth throughout economic history.[1]

The development of intermediary institutions fosters growth because it improves coordination between potential savers and investors, both nationally and internationally. It thereby increases the size of flows from savings into capital formation. Simultaneously and just as importantly, it improves the effectiveness of the process of allocation whereby investable funds are distributed among projects, increasing the useful capital-formation payoff from any given outlay of funds. Development of techniques of payment, which begins with monetization of the economy, allows increased coordination between specialist producers and potential buyers, expanding the possibilities for the division of labor.

Reprinted, with permission, from *Privatization and Development*, ed. Steve H. Hanke (San Francisco: Institute for Contemporary Studies Press, 1987).

Historical evidence indicates that financial institutions develop more strongly and efficiently when left to the private sector, primarily because the flexibility of private ownership promotes effective specialization among varieties of institutions. The profit motive channels financial entrepreneurs into the niches where their personal expertise operates most effectively to cultivate supplies of investable funds, to evaluate investment projects as worthy borrowers of funds, or to combine these two activities. The historical development of specialized financial market institutions in the economically advanced countries of the world—institutions such as stock and bond markets, brokerage houses, mutual funds, investment banks, and consumer banks—took place in a largely market-directed environment. This does not mean that an identical set of institutions is necessarily appropriate to develop countries today, or even constitutes a goal for the future. Different financial technologies are appropriate to different cultures, stages of development, and eras of history. The point is not the outcome of evolution elsewhere but the framework for the process: the private market framework allows the financial system to adapt itself best over time to the evolving desires of a developing society.

The chief social advantages of a market system of private and deregulated financial intermediaries over a nonmarket system of state-operated or state-controlled enterprises come from its use of market price signals and the profit motive rather than arbitrary bureaucratic criteria to attract an appropriate volume of savings and to allocate the scarce pool of savings in society to its most productive uses. Market institutions can attract an appropriate volume of savings by establishing an interest rate paid to savers that accurately reflects the balance between perceived present and future wants in society. Interest is a reward paid for relinquishing present income in favor of future income. In developing countries where present wants are relatively urgent and where capital (the pool of resources for producing future income) is relatively scarce, high real interest rates will naturally prevail in the market. These attractive rates will persuade urban and rural income earners to provide adequate additions to the pool of capital in the economy. No compulsion or expropriation of income (from the agricultural sector to feed the industrial sector, for example) is necessary. Nor is it desirable if the process of growth is to respect the preferences of the public.

Unfortunately, state-owned financial institutions in developing countries have shown a tendency to try to suppress the knowledge that capital is scarce by holding interest rates below market-clearing figures. A shortage of loanable funds naturally arises as potential savings are inhibited while the demand to finance investment projects—especially capital-intensive and long-range projects—swells at artificially low rates of interest. Official credit must be rationed by some mechanism other than price. An unofficial market for funds springs up outside the banking sector, but intermediaries in this unsanctioned market typically cannot offer savers much security. Borrowers must therefore pay higher rate so that the intermediaries can offer the premium necessary to attract savings in the face of the risk of default. As a result, the imposition of an artificially low official interest rate, contrary to its ostensible aim, makes credit more expensive to all but a few borrowers.[2]

In private markets, the profit motive, guided by prices, effectively penalizes substandard performance in the allocation of loanable funds. The motive begins with individual savers, who seek the highest (risk-considered) yield. They will shift funds away from bankers who make too many loans to uncreditworthy borrowers or low-yield projects—and who consequently cannot pay much interest—toward better bankers who offer a higher yield on deposits. Bankers thus find that they must approve only those loans that give the best indication of genuine profitability (they are also subject to pressure exerted in this direction by their shareholders). The pursuit of profitability has the result (although it is not part of the banker's calculation) of steering loans toward projects with the highest potential for adding to aggregate wealth measured at market prices.[3] It also results in vesting responsibility for direction of resources in the country's most promising entrepreneurs. If banks and entrepreneurs are both guided by unmanipulated market prices, the investment projects selected will be appropriate to the country's wants and resource endowments as reflected in its relative prices for outputs and for labor, capital equipment, and raw materials. Unfortunately, many developing countries routinely manipulate the prices of consumer goods—through marketing boards, for example—and the prices of labor and capital goods. The continuation of nonmarket pricing policies in these areas would, of course, severely constrain the benefits of financial liberalization. Conversely, elimination of price distortions would be highly complementary to privatization of the financial sector.

Tax-funded government-sector financial institutions, in contrast to private banks, are not held continuously accountable for misallocations. They may continuously squander scarce social capital on loans that yield little or no return, and yet not be penalized by any reduction in the quantity of funds made available to them. In Bangladesh, for example, the repayment rate on loans from the government's development banks has been only 14 percent, with little or no penalty being placed on borrowers for loan delinquency.[4] Such "banks" are in practice making outright grants rather than loans. They are wasting scarce funds, and the real resources purchased with them, on projects that give no evidence of profitability. Because the recipients can nonetheless profit personally, scarce resources are also dissipated in lobbying efforts to obtain gratuitous loans. Where economic profitability is not a criterion, ample opportunity exists for favoritism in directing loans to politically well-connected individuals, firms (particularly state-owned enterprises), industries, and regions. The same opportunity exists in a rationed credit market where government banks grant loans at below-market interest rates. The dreary spectacle of government favoritism and recipient lobbying is not, of course, unfamiliar to taxpayers in developed countries.

A third social advantage of private financial intermediaries is that they operate at lower cost, due to concern for their own profitability. State banks generally incur high overhead costs because of overstaffing and bureaucratization in addition to the large costs of writing off bad loans. Low rates of repayment sometimes prompt overmonitoring of loan recipients. A World Bank report on Indonesia estimated that its state banks' intermediation costs consumed 7 to 8 percentage points of interest rates charged.[5] Such a large wedge between loan rates and the rates payable to savers is a wasteful obstacle to intermediation. Long delays in service are another burden associated with state-run banking: loan decisions take an average of twelve months in Bangladesh,[6] and India's government-owned banks require five weeks to clear checks between Bombay and Calcutta.

CONDITIONS

The privatization of the financial sector entails, first and foremost, transferring the assets of government-owned banks to the private sector. In a developing country the banking system typically dominates the financial sector, and in many cases provides practically the only formal market for intermediation (securities markets are generally of minor scope and importance). For a private banking system to thrive and make good use of assets, the following conditions are important:

Enforceable Contract Law

Lenders must be able to enforce collection of payments contractually due from borrowers. Borrowers must recognize that the failure of a project means the loss not only of borrowed funds but of pledged collateral, such as previously acquired equity. Government must not prevent the liquidation of insolvent firms.

Freedom from Interest Rate Controls

Freedom of banks to set loan rates is crucial to the efficient placement of scarce loanable funds.[7] Complex interest rate structures that arbitrarily impose dozens of different lending rates for different classes of borrowers are particularly invidious. The Greek government, for example, sets one rate for small business and agricultural loans, one for long-term investment projects, one for working capital, and one for housing mortgages.[8] These rate structures, if they are at all binding, not only repress intermediation generally but also distort allocation by denying funds to sectors that are more productive at the margin than others. Freedom to set bank deposit rates, on the other side of the balance sheet, is crucial for bringing the savings of the nonwealthy out of hoarding, and perhaps even some of the savings of the wealthy elite back from overseas into the domestic financial system.

Open Entry into Banking

Transferring a highly concentrated banking system from government to private ownership may simply replace a state cartel with a nominally private cartel unless entry of new banks into the system is also permitted. Open entry is vital and, in banking (where cornering the market is a practical impossibility), generally sufficient for competitive pricing and other conditions to prevail. The optimal scale of banking firms and the individuals best suited to run them can be discovered only under these conditions.

Furthermore, open entry offers the most successful entrepreneurs in the informal financial sector of a developing economy—moneylenders, pawnbrokers, shopkeepers, middlemen—the opportunity to develop and expand their traditional lending practices within banking structures as formal as they find appropriate. It makes the most effective use of their unique knowledge of local borrowers and circumstances. The transition from traditional to modern finance can be made most smoothly if traditional lenders are free to open formal banks. Native institutions that evolve in this way would seem to hold out the highest promise of mobilizing domestic savings economically and funneling them to the small rural and urban entrepreneurs who in many countries have been denied access to organized sources of financing.[9] Although it is independent of privatization, open entry for foreign banks is also desirable as an element of financial liberalization.

Nonregulation of Bank Portfolios

The following common political practices are for obvious reasons inimical to a thriving private banking industry: (1) forcing banks to hold stipulated quantities of government bonds or large quantities of the central bank's deposits; (2) requiring that certain proportions of bank assets be devoted to domestic investments or to specified classes of borrowers; (3) requiring bank borrowers to conform to arbitrary financial criteria. Privatization under rigid regulations such as these, or under conditions of discretionary official guidance along similar lines, is largely a mockery.

TYPES OF INSTITUTIONS

The privatization of banks potentially encompasses a number of types of institutions. Different types may call for different privatization strategies. We will focus on two broad groups.

State development and investment banks are not prime candidates for having their equity sold to private investors because their net worth is likely to be negative. "Recapitalizing" insolvent development banks would simply pour more taxpayer funds down the drain. The portfolios of such institutions can be privatized by selling their assets in secondary markets or by auction, to the extent that they consist of marketable forms, such as bonds and equity shares. Long-term loans to state enterprises that may themselves be in the process of being auctioned off can be converted into marketable bonds. Short-term loans, if any, may be allowed to run to maturity, at which point creditworthy borrowers can refinance with private bank loans. Costa Rica has begun to liquidate the portfolio of its insolvent state devel-opment bank. The brick-and-mortal capital of development banks is generally negligible, as by definition these banks do no consumer banking, so that finding new tenants should not be a major difficulty. This recommendation to liquidate state development banks is not intended to suggest that private development banks are impossible or undesirable; there are a number of examples to the contrary. But private development banks are probably better begun from scratch than from an attempt at radial conversion of an institution accustomed to continual tax infusions and considered more of a soft touch than a stern moneylender.

Consumer and commercial banks owned by the government are more likely to be solvent, and therefore are candidates for privatization by an open auction of their equity. Bangladesh has denationalized two of its commercial banks by sale of equity to the public, with both sales being oversubscribed. Such a sale would naturally have to be preceded by an independent audit of balance sheet assets. One possible obstacle to straightforward application of this method arises when the scale of a state-owned banking enterprise is far too large for economical operations in its intended market (for example, the National Bank of Greece alone holds 60 percent of domestic bank deposits, almost nine times the sum held by its largest private competitor). The "optimal" scale of the new enterprise cannot be known in advance with much assurance. But it would seem reasonable to limit any newly privatized bank to an initial market share of 25 percent or less, so that at least four banks initially occupy the new market. Subsequent growth and mergers—which may be necessary to capture economies of larger scale—need not be discouraged. When entry is free, fears of monopoly powers are unfounded. A well-planned division of assets both financial and physical will be necessary where a large state-owned bank is to be subdivided into two or more independent potential competitors.

ADDITIONAL STEPS

Privatizing the commercial and consumer banks that issue checking accounts is already an important step toward privatizing the payments mechanism. But there is a case for going at least two steps further, particularly for developing countries.

The first additional step is privatization of the international payments system; in other words, the foreign-exchange market. This measure requires the elimination of the all-too-common system whereby the central bank fixes an official conversion rate of local to international currency but refuses to abide by it, pursuing instead an independent monetary policy. The central bank overexpands the stock of domestic currency and then refuses or finds itself unable to accommodate all demands to exchange local for foreign currency. By this strategy combined with credit controls, the central bank becomes a monopolist in a rationed foreign-exchange market.

One alternative is a cleanly floating exchange rate. But for most developing economies this option is rendered infeasible by their smallness, specialized output, and resulting dependence on international trade and cross-border contracts. The other, more feasible alternative is monetary unification with one or more larger trading partners. In this arrangement, as practiced most consistently by Liberia and Panama, the monetary unit used domestically is one of the major internationally traded currency units, although it may carry a different local name. The advantages are straightforward: exchange risk is entirely eliminated for domestic and foreign firms trading within the unified currency area, and loans and investments from transnational banks and corporations are unobstructed by actual or feared exchange controls and the rationing of credit. Under complete monetary unification and financial liberalization, domestic banks can use foreign currency directly as reserves, accepting deposits and making loans denominated in that currency. The cost of market unification is sacrificing the opportunity for an independent national market policy. This is not a great loss and is probably a substantial gain for the citizens of most developing countries, whose monetary policies have brought high rates of inflation and have not been noticeably effective at dampening business cycles.

The second recommended step in privatization of payments consists of recognizing the right of private domestic banks to issue redeemable currency. The currency would be redeemable for central bank deposit liabilities or, if currency unification is undertaken, for widely accepted assets denominated in the internationally traded currency (such as actual pieces of a foreign currency).[10] In the latter case the domestic central bank has no role whatsoever to play as a liability issuer. The inter bank clearing system can be run by a private clearinghouse, as in Canada and many other developed nations. Systems of this kind proved successful in promoting the growth and industrialization of Scotland, the United States, Canada, and other Western nations in the last century before being shunted aside by central bank monopolization of currency issue. The primary advantage of a private bank currency system for a developing economy is that it sets the profit motive to work in promoting thorough monetization, which remains to be achieved in many developing areas. Competition for the profits from issuing currency leads banks to open branch agencies in comparatively remote areas, to provide services to customers and potential customers, and to otherwise encourage the use of money in place of barter.

OBSTACLES TO FINANCIAL PRIVATIZATION

The potential obstacles to a policy of privatizing state-owned financial institutions can be divided into two categories: interests and beliefs. Interests provoke the opposition of persons and agencies who fear a loss of power or income from the policy. Beliefs, mistaken or not, lead people and institutions not directly interested to support the status quo of state ownership.

The most obvious loss of income threatened by financial privatization is the central government's loss of revenue from "seigniorage," i.e., from printing new money and spending it into circulation. Where currency and bank reserves are privatized and the central bank is removed from the issue of high-powered money, the elimination of revenue from seigniorage is direct. But even a more modest policy of commercial bank privatization can, by making check payments a more attractive alternative to currency, reduce the real demand for and market value of central bank liabilities, and therefore indirectly reduce the real seigniorage income from any given rate of money creation. To overcome this obstacle, it will be necessary to convince governments either that substitute methods of raising revenue are preferable, or that spending should be reduced. The former is perhaps more likely, though the latter is possible.

A strong case can be made for the idea that high rates of monetary expansion are actually counterproductive as a means of raising revenue. First, they severely disrupt the organized economy so that activity in normally taxed channels (such as imports, exports, production, and sales) is constricted, bringing down tax yields. The economy is depressed below its potential volume of output, and a larger share of the remaining activity is diverted into informal channels (such as barter) that are difficult to tax. Second, at the high rates of price inflation accompanying rapid monetary expansion, increases in nominal tax receipts tend to lag behind increases in prices, so that real (inflation-adjusted) tax receipts shrink. In several Latin American nations this shrinkage has been found to be dramatic. When a government attempts to make up its revenue shortfall by stepping up monetary expansion even higher, the economy is headed toward a hyperinflation crack-up. Forswearing inflationary finance by privatizing the issuing of money is a credible method of keeping the economy from going down that path.

The income and prestige of officials in state-run development banks and other institutions are naturally threatened by privatization. It can be pointed out to such officials that the opportunity to administer private banks will reward them more lucratively. If they demur, they admit that they are not really skilled at evaluating the profitability of projects proposed by borrowers. But the real obstacle is that these officials are in fact likely to be skilled at cultivating constituencies of favored borrowers. These constituencies may be highly organized. They know the game of wrangling loans from the state banks on concessionary terms, but may fear strongly—and often for good reason—that private banks will be less accommodating. The large number of entrepreneurs and members of the public who will benefit from an open and competitive loan market may not be easy for anyone to identify before privatization. In countries that have successfully liberalized their financial sectors (such as Indonesia and South Korea), it has been necessary to form a broad-based consensus that the change will be good for all, however much inconvenience it may cause for some in the short run.

The beliefs inimical to privatization held by those not pecuniarily interested are sometimes outgrowths of a lack of appreciation for the virtues of decentralized markets; that is, for letting individuals make decisions for themselves. In the financial sector the principal fear seems to be that private banks will not choose to make the "right" sorts of loans. But private banks have every incentive to seek out and make loans to projects that look to be profitable—projects that promise to add to total wealth—since these are the ones to combine relatively low-valued resources into higher-valued products. It is difficult to see what is "wrong" about this criterion.

It might be argued that the judgments of banks concerning the profitability of various investment projects do not incorporate the social benefits of the projects (their valued spillover effects) and that government therefore has a role to play in providing subsidized loans to deserving areas of the economy neglected by the private financial system. But what are these supposed social benefits? One development economics text accounts for subsidized loans to heavy industry by noting that "it is industrial development that is expected [by governments] to bring desired employment opportunities and technological advances to complement local programmes of education and generally to conform with the aspirations of development plans."[11] In some developing countries, agriculture is expected to bring such benefits. The benefits, in other words, consist of twisting the economy in a direction preferred by central planners or the politically favored, not of producing effects generally valued by members of the public. The "desired employment opportunities" for some come at the expense of denied opportunities for many in the sectors passed over by the political allocation of loans. Even if there were valid arguments for subsidization of some projects (and criticism of the argument for subsidy based on the notion of social benefits or positive externality is obviously beyond the scope of this discussion), the mixing of subsidy decisions with bona fide loan decisions in state development banks is a recipe for contaminating the lending process with grant-seeking, with all the disadvantageous consequences that can readily be predicted.

Extreme skepticism is likewise warranted toward assertions that private banks will make too few loans to projects that are small in scale, high in risk, or located in certain areas. If loans to these projects appear at least to some banks to be profitable (and at an interest rate that incorporates an appropriate risk premium they should so appear), it is hard to see why all banks would shun them. If they do not appear to any bank to be profitable, it is difficult to understand why it would be improper for the banks to shun them. There is no obvious reason for believing that a project is entitled to subsidy simply by virtue of its small scale, high risk, or location.

People who regard privatization as a process for handing over state-owned enterprises to nominally private associates of authoritarian rulers, such as Ferdinand Marcos of the Philippines, understandably look on private banking with a certain diffidence. No oligarchic policy of this sort is being advocated or excused here. Instead, privatization of the financial sector is proposed as part of the agenda for genuine liberalization, decentralization, and separation of economic affairs from political power.

Notes

Helpful comments have been received from Martin J. Anderson, Jerry Jenkins, Arthur Seldon, Robert Slighton, Michael Todaro, Bernard Wasow, and participants in the USAID International Conference on Privatization. A version of this essay appeared in *Economic Affairs* 6 (August/September 1986): 38–42.

1. The standard reference here is R. W. Goldsmith, *Financial Structure and Development* (New Haven: Yale University Press, 1969). See also P. J. Drake, *Money, Finance and Development* (New York: John Wiley & Sons, 1980), chap. 3. A recent study is Woo S. Jung, "Financial Development and Economic Growth: International Evidence," *Economic Development and Cultural Change* 34 (January 1986): 333–48.
2. See Ronald I. McKinnon, "Financial Policies," in *Policies for Industrial Progress in Developing Countries,* ed. John Cody et al. (London: Oxford University Press, 1980).
3. This point will be familiar to readers of Adam Smith, *An Inquiry into the Nature and Causes of the Wealth of Nations,* ed. R. H. Campbell, A. S. Skinner, and W. B. Todd (1776; Indianapolis: Liberty Classics, 1981), 456.
4. This figure is for 1981–82. As of June 1982, only 6 percent of loans were being repaid on schedule. B. Wasow and B. Rahman, "Industrial Finance Policy" (Paper prepared for the Bangladesh Investment Incentives Study Unit, June 1985).
5. Cited by Chris Sherwell, "Indonesia's Successful Banking Reforms," *The Banker* (August 1985), 28.
6. Wasow and Rahman, "Industrial Finance Policy."
7. This has been stressed by Ronald I. McKinnon, *Money and Capital in Economic Development* (Washington, D.C.: Brookings Institution, 1973).
8. Michael Blanden, "Bringing Greek Banking up to Date," *The Banker* (June 1985), 33–34. Until recently the government dictated hundreds of different rates for different categories of loans.
9. See Drake, *Money, Finance, and Development,* 152, 221.
10. Had Panama allowed private currency issue, it could have avoided the currancy shortage caused by U.S. authorities cutting off shipments of dollar bills.
11. Drake, *Money, Finance, and Development,* 181.

II

The Question of
the Monetary Standard

6

Gold, Dollars, and Private Currencies

The Federal Reserve System has quite properly come under heavy criticism in recent years for its instrumental role in creating both the chronic inflation and the wild macroeconomic fluctuations from which the American economy suffers. This criticism has begun to take the form of a ground-level reconsideration of the theory of central banking. It is about time: A rethinking of the fundamental doctrines of monetary policy is long overdue.

The most basic of the issues at hand is not whether the monetary authority should be compelled to follow some set of "rules" or should have discretionary control over the nation's money. It is not "this constitution" (one set of rules) versus "that constitution" (an alternative set of rules); it is not gold versus paper money. The fundamental issue is national monetary authority versus unhampered competitive market provision of currency. The idea of currency competition used to be called "free banking." It has recently been revived by F. A. Hayek under the name "denationalization of money."[1] Free banking was the leading topic of monetary controversy in Britain, the United States, and several European nations in the de:ades before national central banks, through political means, consolidated their positions as monopoly suppliers of base money.[2] The time is ripe for raising the question of competitive currencies.

There are at least three streams of thought on monetary policy.[3] There are (1) those who, like Milton Friedman,[4] would bind the monetary authority by means of an artificially designed set of rules of conduct, usually called by its proponents a "monetary constitution"; and (2) those who, like Keynesian writers, would allow the monetary authority practically unlimited discretionary power. Then

Reprinted, with permission, from *Policy Report*, vol. 3, no. 6 (June 1981).

there are (3) those who, like Hayek, would do away with the monetary authority altogether and allow a market order to prevail in the monetary arena. Ludwig von Mises also belonged to this third tradition, the free-banking tradition.[5]

ADVANTAGES OF COMPETITION

The case for a competitive currency system is akin to the case for competitive market provision of oil or any other commodity. It rests on the fact that a market system has two advantages over government monopoly: a price system for coordination and a profitability test for discipline. By means of an unhampered market-price system a society can best turn the knowledge and initiatives of millions of individuals to the satisfaction of consumer wants. A free market in privately issued currency would mean provision of the most desirable sorts of money from the consumer's perspective. There is every reason to believe that market currency would be the most convenient for transactions purposes, the most trustworthy, and—what makes it especially attractive—the most stable and likely to increase in purchasing power. An irresponsible issuer—one who inflated as much as the Fed has of late—would lose customers to his rivals. The Federal Reserve Board faces no such discipline.

Delegating control over the supply of currency to a monetary authority subjects us to the combined shortcomings of monopoly provision and central planning for the currency market: low-quality product and unpredictable supply conditions from which there is no escape. Closing down the Federal Reserve System would yield benefits similar to those to be gained by closing down the Department of Energy. (Not that the Fed has never produced a dollar, in the same way that the DOE has never produced a drop of oil—quite the contrary. The Fed is more like a DOE that diluted the nation's gasoline in unpredictable ways.) Just as the best government energy policy is *no* energy policy, the best government monetary policy is *no monetary policy.*

Economists searching through the years for a "sound monetary policy" have been pursuing a chimera. "Sound monetary policy" is impossible in the same way that "sound central planning" is impossible. Hayek argues insightfully to the effect that central banking is a form of central planning: "A single monopolistic government agency can neither possess the information which should govern the supply of money nor would it, if it knew what it ought to do in the general interest, usually be in a position to act in that manner."[6] The proper volume and distribution of money for an entire nation can never be known to a single planning authority. The attempt by some economists to design a simple set of rules for optimal currency supply rests on enormous intellectual conceit. Only competition, to quote a nineteenth-century writer, can provide "the nice adjustment of the currency to the wants of the people."[7]

Many thoughtful persons considering an end to the Federal Reserve fiat money system, either because of a principled adherence to a free society or because of an empirical recognition of the disruptive character of the system, have embraced the gold standard as a superior and viable alternative. They sometimes make the claim that the gold standard alone represents a "free-market" monetary system or is alone consistent with a free society. It is therefore supposed to be incumbent on supporters of an unhampered market economy to call for redefinition of the dollar as so many grams of gold.

GOLD AND THE MARKET

Certainly an attractive feature of a gold-based monetary system is that it does not presuppose a monetary authority. The historical evidence indicates that the system works quite well without one. Competitive issue of gold-convertible bank currency generates a stable and self-regulating monetary order.[8] The question of whether gold can justly claim today to be *the* free-market money, so that anyone calling for denationalization of money must be committed to gold, is worth examining. Discussion of such a question must by the nature of the case be conducted at a somewhat speculative level.

The free-market argument for gold runs something like this: (1) Gold spontaneously emerged as money in the Western world and persisted as money in the United States until its death at the hands of Franklin Delano Roosevelt in 1933; (2) the factors important for the emergence and persistence of gold are timeless; (3) therefore even today gold would spontaneously emerge as money in a competitive market setting. Any shortcomings in this argument must lie in claims (1) and (2). The trouble with (1) is that the historical record is not entirely lopsided on gold's behalf. The problem with (2) is that more than 50 years of being off the gold standard cannot be shrugged off. The past status of gold is not sufficient to guarantee its reestablishment as money.

The historical record is complicated by the fact that silver emerged and persisted as money jointly with gold. The triumph of gold over silver came at the hands of deliberate government policies or non-deliberate government price-fixing of the terms of trade between coins in the two metals. (The incidental fact that government mints monopolized the supply of coinage services does not, however, further weaken the market-chosen money status of the precious metals. The mints merely coined what the market process had already converged upon as media of exchange.)

The case for silver is strong enough that those who would have the market determine the monetary standard must be committed at least to allowing private issuers of gold and silver currencies to compete for patronage. They cannot preemptively enthrone gold. Once a competition among standards begins, however, there is no reason to limit the field to two candidates. The currency systems that private issuers might offer are mány: (a) gold and gold-convertible currency; (b) silver and silver-convertible currency; (c) "symmetallic" currency, wherein the currency unit is convertible into so many grams of gold plus so many grams of silver; (d) currency convertible into some nonmetallic commodity or basket of commodities, with token coinage; (e) convertible currency whose purchasing power is stabilized by indexation of the conversion rate, as envisioned by Irving Fisher;[9] (f) inconvertible currencies, perhaps purchasing-power-stabilized in the manner envisioned by F. A. Hayek;[10] (g) currency convertible into foreign government fiat currencies; and (h–z) as many others as monetary entrepreneurs might convince the public to hold.

Advocates of gold as free-market money must presume that gold would emerge from a competition among standards as the single predominant standard—else why advocate gold as such? Here we confront their argument's second shortcoming. The handicap that gold faces in the competition is that today, after decades of not being money, it is more or less just another metal. The "more" is what remains of its old reputation ("mystique" to those who don't understand it) as sound money. The "less" is its new reputation as a commodity whose purchasing power is subject to violent and erratic fluctuation.

It is true that gold still has the usefulness and particular physical properties that enabled it (with silver) to emerge out of a state of barter as a universal medium of exchange, via the market process.[11] Gold coins are still portable, which is to say that they have a high ratio of purchasing power to bulk and weight, though today that ratio may be too high to make a full-bodied gold coinage convenient. They are nontarnishable and attractive and can be easily verified as genuine, though not so easily by today's populace as by that of the nineteenth century. But the question is not what would happen upon a return to a primitive premonetary situation. The arrow of time is irreversible. The question today is whether gold would outcompete other full-blown currencies. It is a question that cannot be answered until another question is settled: What becomes of the fiat dollar?

For any commodity to have become money—the most salable of commodities—it must have had prior exchange value. This is as true of the dollar bill as it was of gold. Before transactors began accepting it generally, they must have had reason to accept it at all. Gold was originally demanded for its ornamental value. The dollar bill derived its initial exchange value from its being a secure claim for—convertible into—gold. Only when paper currency became generally accepted in exchange was it possible for its issuer to suspend convertibility permanently and still retain the paper's exchange value.[12] Once the paper dollar became a general medium of exchange, its universal acceptance generated the self-reinforcing expectation-fulfillment process whereby it continued to circulate even after convertibility was suspended. Each individual continued to accept dollars in the belief, ratified by experience so long as enough others acted likewise, that his dollars would be accepted elsewhere the next day.

Clearly, neither gold nor inconvertible private currencies will emerge as money under present circumstances. Each transactor pursuing his or her own self-interest finds it far too convenient to deal in a single standard for purposes of accounting and (so long as others are doing so) currency transactions. The persistence of the paper mark during the German hyperinflation between the wars seems to indicate that inflation much reach mindboggling proportions before alternative currencies can gain a foothold. It should be noted that the previously existing legal barrier to contracting in gold or other alternative currencies in the United States, the "Gold Clause" Joint Congressional Resolution of 5 June 1933, was removed by the Helms Amendment of October 1977.[13]

THE TRANSITION PROBLEM

A thorny question thus arises for those who would denationalize the American currency industry: How to make the transition away from the dollar standard? The dollar must initially be linked to any new standard, so that an unbiased competition among alternative new standards hardly seems possible. The route to a predetermined new commodity standard is straightforward: Have the Treasury lay in a stock of the commodity, establish convertibility of dollars into the commodity, withdraw Federal Reserve notes and token Treasury coins from circulation via conversion, and open the market to private issuers of coin and convertible bank notes. The route to a system of competing private inconvertible currencies is less clear. One way might be to do to the Federal Reserve note what Roosevelt did to gold: Have banks issue their own dollar-convertible hand-to-hand currency (these would be just like traveler's checks without the signatory bother and refundability) and coins, then suspend convertibility of these and other bank-issued near-monies (checking- and savings-account deposits, savings certificates, and so on) into Federal Reserve notes and confiscate the Federal Reserve notes in private hands. In any case some resolution would have to be found to an important problem that troubled American free-banking advocates in the 1830s, that of discovering a means by which the federal government could avoid favoritism among privately issued currencies in its own fiscal dealings.

Were the first route taken and a new metallic or commodity standard initially adopted, it is no more likely that privately issued inconvertible currencies could gain a footing than it is that they can gain a footing against the fiat dollar. While the commodity serving as the new standard would have been chosen outside the market, as it were, competition from other commodities would not be fore-closed. It is not implausible to postulate that another metallic standard might eventually supplant the metallic standard initially chosen. Full-bodied coins of different metals might well circulate in parallel, it being convenient for portability reasons to mint coins of lower purchasing power from less precious metals. It might then be possible for different banks to market notes convertible into the different metals, whose exchange-values would float against one another. Out of that situation the market process might converge on notes convertible into a single metal as the general medium of exchange; the metal need not be the one into which the old Federal Reserve notes were converted. It is also conceivable that parallel standards would persist.

Were the second route taken and inconvertible currencies initially adopted, it is similarly unlikely that commodity-convertible currency would gain a footing against them. Since an issuer offering convertibility would not be able to pay interest on currency and deposits quite as high as that paid by competitive issuers of inconvertible money—he has to hold commodity reserves where they hold only earnings assets—he would have to attract customers on the basis of superior purchasing-power reliability. His notes would fluctuate in value, however, with the relative price of the commodity to which they were claims. Until that commodity became the monetary standard, it would not enjoy the stable demand facing a monetary commodity. Nor could the issuer vary supply at will so as to offset the impact of demand changes on price. His notes would therefore probably not be reliable for purchasing-power stability.

Bank-issued private currencies would float against one another unless convertibility into some common medium, or purchasing-power stabilization in terms of some common commodity basket, were adopted. A pegged exchange rate system among rival issuers would clearly be in no issuer's self-interest under inconvertibility. A bank pledged to trade its rival's inconvertible notes at par could be forced to accumulate them ad infinitum by a more expansive rival, and in any event would have to hold costly reserves.

A joint-float arrangement might nonetheless emerge via an invisible hand or market process of the following sort. Each issuing bank would most likely find that it did better business by accepting the notes of other issuers at market value (rather than refusing them) from customers making deposits or repaying loans. A pair of issuers might then discover that both did better business by accepting one another's notes at a fixed parity, thereby sparing their mutual customers calculational difficulty and exchange risk.[14] Other issuing banks might later join them. These issuers would at the same time have to enter into a mutual clearing arrangement for settlement of accumulated balances of one another's liabilities. Each member bank would have to pledge to honor its liabilities at a rate fixed in terms of some common medium, so as to obviate the forced-accumulation problem.[15] Adverse clearing balances would be liquidated by transfer of the clearing medium, loss of which would automatically signal to the relatively expansive issuer the need for restraint. In this day and age, it is not obvious that gold would be chosen as the principal clearing medium. Treasury bills, or some other low-risk earning asset that virtually all banks held to begin with, would likely be used.[16]

THE POSSIBILITY OF INFLATION

It might be urged against a system of inconvertible private currencies that it leaves the money stock "unanchored," making any rate of inflation possible. It is true that the adverse clearing mechanism within a joint-float arrangement would not, in and of itself, check whatever rate of growth in nominal money stock was common to all issuers. Neither would issuers anywhere within a system of private inconvertible currencies be legally bound to a noninflationary issuing policy. This problem in fact arises in *any* inconvertible currency system. It is with us under the Federal Reserve System. The nominal money stock in the United States today is "anchored" only by whatever constrains the Fed from expanding the monetary base. A commodity-convertible currency system, by contrast, restrains the expansion of base money. Still, there may be periods of upward price-level drift due to changes in supply conditions that allow relatively rapid growth in the stock of the base-money commodity. If the base money is metallic, for example, there may be fortuitous ore field discoveries or breakthroughs in mining technology.

Under any standard, the ultimate safeguard against chronic inflation is competition or potential competition from noninflationary alternative standards. An open-entry system of private issue, whether of convertible or inconvertible currencies, offers the widest scope for competition among standards. This is true even though the choice of a transitional path away from the dollar will determine the standard likely to prevail for some time. The present system of *preemptive state fiat issue,* by contrast, leaves us nowhere to turn while the purchasing power of the dollar is progressively diluted.

The overriding goal of modern monetary reform, then, should be privatization of currency. To shine the spotlight on gold would be to divert attention from the primary issue. Reestablishment of gold convertibility for the U.S. dollar is neither a necessary condition for denationalization of money in the United States nor—if the most enthusiastic gold advocates be believed—a necessary condition for reemergence of the gold standard. That it is nowhere near a sufficient reform hardly needs arguing. To link currency to gold is not yet to divorce currency from the state. If the issue of currency is left as a monopoly in the hands of the national monetary authority, there remains much power for mischief despite the golden handcuffs. The historical record of the gold standard indicates that while it does provide a long-run check on the inflationary powers of a central bank, it does not prevent the central bank from engineering short-run expansions sufficient to generate severe business cycles. The long-run check, moreover, is only as good as the central bank's commitment to conversion at the traditional parity. State-sponsored central banks have been notoriously fickle in that regard, especially when confronted with state demands for wartime inflationary finance.

A gold standard, like any other standard, realizes its full potential for supporting a self-regulating monetary order only when coupled with a free-banking system. A return to gold without an end to the monopoly of currency issue would at best be no more than half a victory. At worst it might foreclose the opportunity for full-fledged reform.

Notes

1. F. A. Hayek, *Denationalisation of Money,* 2d ed. (London: Institute of Economic Affairs, 1978); idem, "Toward Free Market Money," *Wall Street Journal,* 19 August 1977.

2. Lawrence H. White, *Free Banking in Britain: Theory, Experience, and Debate, 1800–45.* (Cambridge: Cambridge University Press, 1984), chaps. 3–4; Vera C. Smith, *The Rationale of Central Banking* (London: P. S. King & Son, 1936).

3. Compare John Hicks, "Monetary Theory and History—An Attempt at Perspective," in *Critical Essays in Monetary Theory* (Oxford: Clarendon Press, 1967), who sees only two streams of monetary thought.

4. Milton Friedman, *A Program for Monetary Stability* (New York: Fordham University Press, 1960).

5. Ludwig von Mises, *The Theory of Money and Credit,* trans. H. E. Batson rev. ed. (Irvington-on-Hudson, N.Y.: Foundation for Economic Education, 1971), 312; idem, "Monetary Stabilization and Cyclical Policy," in *On the Manipulation of Money and Credit,* trans. Bettina Bien Greaves (Dobbs Ferry, N.Y.: Free Market Books, 1978).

6. Hayek, *Denationalisation of Money,* 98.

7. Samuel Bailey, *A Defence of Joint-Stock Banks and Country Issues* (London: James Ridgway, 1840), 99.

8. Lawrence H. White, *Free Banking in Britain,* chaps. 1, 2, 5.

9. Irving Fisher, *Stabilizing the Dollar* (New York: Macmillan, 1920).

10. Hayek, *Denationalisation of Money,* 55–62.

11. Carl Menger, *Problems of Economics and Sociology,* ed. Louis Schneider (Urbana: University of Illinois Press, 1963).

12. Note that under a system of plural competitive issuers of gold-convertible currency no one issuer can suspend convertibility and yet keep his paper in circulation. Any suspension is, moreover, an actionable breach of contract.

13. See J. Huston McCulloch, "The Ban on Indexed Bonds, 1933–77," *American Economic Review* 70 (December 1980): 1018–21.

14. Suggestive of this possibility is the fact that the major U.S. airlines voluntarily accept one another's tickets at face value.

15. This process may explain the emergence of Boston's Suffolk Bank System for note-clearing in the early nineteenth century.

16. Exchequer Bills were used to settle the bulk of note-exchange balances during the free-banking era in Scotland.

7

Fix or Float? The International Monetary Dilemma

The esoteric topic of international monetary relations has recently spilled from the business sections onto the front pages of the nation's newspapers. At least since the Williamsburg economic summit conference of May 1983 brought together the leaders of the seven largest industrial nations (the United States, West Germany, Japan, Britain, France, Canada, Italy), international currency questions have been highly prominent. Particularly at issue are the alleged "overvaluation" of the dollar on foreign-exchange markets and the volatility of exchange rates. President François Mitterand of France has attracted attention by calling for a new international exchange-rate-fixing scheme. And former West German Chancellor Helmut Schmidt has been widely quoted for writing that "the present 'world monetary system' does not deserve the name. At best, it is an unstable constellation."

An odd coalition of the exponents of supply-side and Keynesian economics, both groups opposed to floating exchange rates, has been trumpeting loudly for reform of the current system. Supply-siders Robert Mundell of Columbia University and Representative Jack Kemp (R-N.Y.) staged a "Pre-Williamsburg" conference-and-media-event in Washington, D.C., bringing academics together with past, present, and would-be members of government to debate the question of fixed versus floating exchange rates. Kemp and economic analyst Jude Wanniski have published opinion pieces with titles like "A Floating Dollar Costs Us Jobs" and "A Floating Dollar Does Nothing for Trade." Meanwhile, the Keynesian economist C. Fred

Reprinted, with permission, from *Inquiry*, vol. 6, no. 12 (November 1983).

Bergsten, a former Treasury official under Jimmy Carter who heads the Institute for International Economics in Washington, has been cited by the *New York Times* and other newspapers for pronouncing the dollar to be "overvalued" by some 20 percent. Both Bergsten and economist Robert Triffin, a former professor at Yale University, are promoting schemes for exchange-rate pegging by the government. Monetarist economists, on the other hand, continue to defend the present system of floating exchange rates among national fiat currencies.

In contrast to all this publicity about the monetary relations between the United States and other sovereign nations, the monetary relations between California (or any state) and the rest of the United States have not occasioned any concern. No one frets over California's "balance of payments" being in surplus or in deficit. No one argues grimly that California employment suffers from "overvaluation" of its monetary unit, so that imported Detroit autos are "underpriced." The value of California's currency does not vary unpredictably relative to the value of other states' currencies, frustrating long-term investment across state borders. Neither does California's monetary system face the problem of having to rely for the stability of its currency's value on reserves of interstate currency that alternately pile up excessively and run dangerously low, depending on which way the trade balance is running.

How is California able to avoid those monetary problems that bedevil European economies? The answer is simple: California has no distinct state currency. So it has no state governmental monetary authority with power over its money supply. California, in relation to the rest of the United States, is part of what economists call a "unified currency area." When Californians purchase goods from the rest of the country, the dollars they pay are transferred directly to out-of-state sellers without the intervention of a currency exchange. The regional distribution of dollar holdings within the United States changes smoothly and without alarming complications.

If international monetary relations are more complex and less harmonious than this, the reason may simply be that the creation of national monetary authorities and distinct national monies has made them so. In the absence of central banks and other agencies fostered by national legislatures throughout the world, the entire globe certainly could and perhaps naturally would become a fully unified currency area.

WHY NATIONAL MONIES?

To gain perspective on the international aspects of monetary policy, it is useful to ask: Why have a national monetary policy at all? Why have the provision of money subject to the control of a national government or central bank? Does this make any more sense than state or local government control? The debate between proponents of fixed exchange rates and proponents of floating exchange rates focuses on the questions of how our central bank should interact with foreign central banks and how our national currency should relate to theirs. Both schools take it for granted that we *should* have a central bank and a distinct national currency. Curiously, few have called for California and other American states each to have its own central bank and currency.

The analogy between California's participation in the American monetary system and the United States' participation in a world monetary system may be misleading or unhelpful in an important respect. It may seem that California can easily do without its own distinct currency and central bank only because it is part of a national central banking system, the Federal Reserve System. On this interpretation, the United States could forgo monetary policy only by subjugating itself to a world central bank. From where else could a world money come? The answer is readily apparent to anyone with the slightest inkling of monetary history. The international silver and gold standards prevailing in the centuries before World War I came close to providing the ideal of a homogeneous global monetary system, though the nationalistic activities of mints and central banks ultimately prevented the precious metals from completely realizing their potential. The precious metals spontaneously emerged as international monies through the choices of market traders, without the intervention of any world monetary authority. Metallic money can be produced entirely without government involvement where private mines and private mints (these flourished during the American gold rushes) are permitted.

The simplest sort of international specie standard we can imagine is a purely metallic currency system in which only specie (coined precious metal) circulates as money, without banking institutions and paper money. No one seriously advocates this, of course, but an understanding of its workings helps us to understand more complex systems. Under a purely metallic currency system, any region, whether a nation, province, city, neighborhood, or household, pays for its purchases from the rest of the world with gold or silver. It gets this money in the first place (unless it has a mine) by selling goods and services to the rest of the world, or by borrowing.

Obviously, a single household can spend more than its income plus borrowing over any period *only* by reducing the amount of money it holds. The same principle applies to any group of households in relation to the rest of the world (transactions between households within the group "cancel out" for this accounting purpose). If the money spent on imports exceeds the money earned through export sales plus money borrowed from outside, there must be an outflow of money from the group. In the jargon of international trade this is a "balance-of-payments deficit." A regional group of households that does the opposite, accumulating money by earning and borrowing more than it spends, is said to run a balance-of-payments surplus.

By watching the changes in money holdings, we can see that a region will run a deficit when the people within it desire on average to reduce the amount of money they have on hand. Running a surplus is how the region can add to its aggregate money holdings. A flow of money out of or into the region is usually the symptom of, and the cure for, a discrepancy between the amount of money on hand and the amount of money people wish to have on hand. Each ounce of gold that is paid to persons outside the region reduces some resident's money holdings, and thereby the region's money stock, by one ounce. (Each ounce that flows in must increase the money supply by one ounce.) Net outflows or inflows continue until the discrepancy is eliminated, at which point they cease. Under an international specie standard, the flows of gold between nations are self-limiting. They have no life of their own, but continue only as long as not-yet-satisfied people continue to make the adjustments that constitute the money flows.

Contrary to what the headlines lead us to think, there is no cause for alarm at the international money flows or resulting trade "deficits" and "surpluses" in a world of purely metallic currency. Indeed, there is no special reason even to keep track of national aggregates. One might as well keep track of net money shipments from left-handed to right-handed persons. Money moves across national borders as easily and inconsequentially as it moves from one side of Main Street to the other. The concept of a national money supply is irrelevant, because the world's money is homogeneous.

The introduction of banking institutions and bank-issued forms of money need not upset the essential homogeneity of the world's money. Were banks transnational, paying a foreigner by check would present no more difficulty to the monetary system than paying a neighbor. But historically this has not been the case. International monetary relations became troublesome in the nineteenth century, when European central banks began regulating monetary affairs along national lines. The United States joined the movement toward "monetary nationalism," as F. A. Hayek has termed it with Congress's creation of the Federal Reserve System in 1913.[1] This movement has reached its logical conclusion in the system of utterly independent and distinct national currencies that has prevailed since 1973.

THE ROAD TO MONETARY NATIONALISM

It is worth reviewing briefly the route taken to the present jumbled system of national fiat monies in order to see the difficulties introduced at each step. The first step governments took favoring monetary nationalism was the establishment of national mints. But these mints had little impact on the movement of money as long as one nation's coins could readily be circulated in other nations according to their bullion content, or could be melted down, shipped as bullion, and restruck at the initiative of gold owners. The national mints were more important for establishing the precedent of government's involvement with money. This precedent was often invoked in the nineteenth century by those favoring the establishment of central banks.

The importance of central banking within an international specie standard lies in the fact that the central bank monopolizes the holding of a nation's gold reserves. The pressure of supplying gold to meet a national balance-of-payments deficit is thus concentrated on a single institution rather than being spread across a dozen or more large banks. The nation's monetary system under central banking is often compared to a giant inverted pyramid resting on a single point, with all bank notes and bank deposits depending for their redeemability on a single ultimate reserve of gold. Under "the natural system," as Victorian banking theorist Walter Bagehot called it,[2] where each bank holds its own reserves, the monetary system is more like a multilegged stool. The contrast in stability should be obvious.

In a plural banking system on the gold standard, the miscalculations of any single bank have largely local consequences, which are rapidly felt and easily corrected. The miscalculations of a central bank can devastate a nation. The central bank's monopoly position gives it influence in the short run over the nation's money and credit supplies (in the long run it is restrained by its obligations to the gold standard), and with this influence comes the power to generate business cycles by expansive and contractionary policies. In a typical cycle of the gold-standard era, overexpansion by a central bank like the Bank of England created a false boom in business that generated, as a consequence of the excessive supply of money, an outflow of gold in purchases from abroad. The drain of gold from the central bank's vault could not be allowed to continue indefinitely. At some point the bank would reverse policy suddenly to protect its dwindling reserve, contracting credit sharply. Interest rates would seesaw from an artificially low level to an artificially high level, and the business boom would be choked off.

The occasional need to contract money and credit in order to safeguard its gold reserves, or, in other words, the requirement that the central bank subordinate itself to the demands of the domestic and foreign users of money, is the much-discussed "discipline" that a gold standard imposes on central banks. It is readily apparent why central bankers were eager to eliminate the international gold standard in the twentieth century. The gold standard restrained them from pursuing the discretionary monetary policies that became so alluring with the advent of Keynesian economics. Perhaps more importantly, it prevented them from creating the practically unlimited amount of paper money needed to buy back and retire the massive debts their governments piled up in the two world wars.

The road between the international gold-coin standard and today's floating fiat currencies was not traveled in one day. The elimination of gold from many nations' coinage and domestic transactions moved those nations onto what is called a gold-exchange standard. But this development did not remove them from the international gold standard that prevailed up to World War I. As long as central banks redeemed their notes at par for gold bullion, national currency units continued to signify definite quantities of gold. But the gold-exchange standard made possible the next step, the development between the two world wars of what economist Ludwig von Mises called "the flexible standard."[3]

Under the flexible standard, the central bank or some other government body could change the gold value (or "parity") of the domestic monetary unit whenever convenient. In practice, central banks almost always used this power to reduce the amount of gold with which they were obliged to redeem their liabilities, an action termed "devaluation" of the currency. The nation's gold debtor, in other words, had the power to scale down its debts unilaterally. The policy of devaluation was especially convenient when gold reserves were dwindling and the central bank or government did not wish to contract credit. Devaluation shatters the stability of the monetary unit's value in terms of gold and gold-defined currencies, and introduces a new risk into foreign-exchange transactions.

In the polite circles of international monetary bureaucracies, as Mises noted, one never speaks of "redeeming" a domestic currency for gold or another currency at a certain parity, since that would suggest a binding contractual commitment. Instead, one speaks of "pegging" the external value of the domestic currency or the "price of gold." In fact, the only way a central bank can "peg" a currency's value at a certain rate of exchange against another money is to stand ready to buy and sell any amounts offered or demanded at that rate, exactly the policy entailed in honoring a commitment to "redeem" at that rate. Perhaps the terminology is preferred because it seems eminently reasonable that a "peg" should be "adjusted" periodically, whereas a change in a redemption rate seems suspicious.

BRETTON WOODS AND BEYOND

The next important stop along the road—important for how long it lasted—was the Bretton Woods international monetary system. Hatched out of a conference of politicians, bureaucrats, lawyers, and economists from forty-four nations, assembled at Bretton Woods, New Hampshire, in 1944, the system provided indirectly for pegged exchange rates among the world's currencies and gold. Only the United States undertook to buy and sell gold at a fixed rate of exchange in transactions with foreign monetary authorities. (The official price of $35 per ounce reflected Franklin Roosevelt's 59 percent devaluation of the dollar in 1934. The price corresponding to the earlier gold definition of the dollar had been $20.67 per ounce.) Other countries pegged the dollar values of their currencies by buying and selling against dollars in foreign-exchange markets. The International Monetary Fund was established as an agency for cushioning the discipline of fixed exchange rates by lending funds to nations running low on foreign-exchange reserves. Devaluation was to be allowed only in cases of "fundamental disequilibrium," which in practice meant when a country's monetary authority had been so much more expansionary than the United States' that its dollar reserves were depleted. Correction through contraction in such cases was judged too unpleasant a prospect.

The United Kingdom was the most important nation to develop the problem of severely declining dollar reserves, culminating in devaluation in 1967. For other nations the opposite problem occurred: The United States in the 1950s and 1960s gradually flooded the world with dollars to the point where the U.S. Treasury could no longer honor its commitment to redeem dollars for gold at $35 per ounce. This dollar expansion was no accident. It makes perfect sense from the point of view of the U.S. government to finance some of its welfare and military spending not by explicitly taxing its citizens but by printing money. Monetary expansion covertly taxes holders of existing dollars by diluting the purchasing power of their holdings. In a fiat money system, this opposition's attractiveness is limited by the public's outrage at the price inflation the excess dollars bring about. But under Bretton Woods, the excess dollars did not all have to remain at home to bid up domestic prices; many were exported to buy European goods. Thus the bill for U.S. government spending in the Vietnam War era was partially footed by European monetary authorities that obligingly accumulated dollars and paid the implicit tax on cash balances. Economist Benjamin Klein has suggested that the stationing of U.S. troops in Europe was the principal quid pro quo for the Europeans' willingness to bear this arrangement.[4] (At times the bargain with Germany was stated fairly explicitly.) It is perhaps no accident, then, that the French government both dropped out of NATO in the sixties and was the government most insistent on redeeming large batches of excess dollars for gold over U.S. government objections. This insistence was the final straw prompting President Nixon in 1971 to "close the gold window," that is, to renege officially on the convertibility of the dollar. By then, the U.S. government's monetary gold stock had fallen, after years of decline, to less than one-sixth of its total liquid liabilities to foreigners. Before 1960 its gold stock had exceeded such liabilities.

With the gold window closed, foreign central banks had no outlet for their excess dollars but to sell them on the foreign-exchange markets for whatever they would bring, which meant they were no longer pegging their exchange rates against the dollar. Official attempts to reestablish rates pegged to the dollar, but without gold convertibility, were unworkable and were finally abandoned in March 1973. These attempts were doomed because no monetary authority, sensibly enough, wanted to bear the burden of accumulating indefinitely the currencies being supplied most promiscuously or being abandoned by speculators fearing devaluation.

Since 1973 the world's major currencies have traded against one another at unpegged or "floating" rates determined by the supplies and demands impinging on foreign-exchange markets. The Western European central banks have ostensibly been making an effort to peg the exchange rates among their currencies, but "realignments" have been so frequent that the exercise is something of a joke. Viewed from a monetarist perspective, the final abandonment of pegged exchange rates means the end to price-fixing attempts in foreign-exchange markets and the arrival of unhampered freedom to control the growth of the national money stock. It is certainly true that fixing the dollar's exchange rate is incompatible with predetermining the number of dollars in circulation. As we have seen, pegging the rate means passively supplying dollars whenever they are demanded, and absorbing dollars whenever they are offered at that rate of exchange. The central bank, as a currency monopolist, is like any other monopolist: it can fix the selling price, or it can fix the quantity sold, but it cannot fix both together.

The major disadvantage of floating exchange rates, which has recently become fairly obvious as exchange rates have moved beyond historical ranges, is the extraneous risk that floating rates introduce into international business. The profitability of a plan to produce goods for a foreign market can be wiped out in a matter of minutes by a swing in the exchange rate. Complete hedging of this risk is often very costly or impossible. As a result, fewer such plans are initiated. So the international division of labor is hampered to an extent that can never be known.

Calls for merely "greater stability" of fiat-money exchange rates, however, are either empty, if they don't specify a plan for intervening in foreign-exchange markets, or foolish, if they do. Occasional Treasury interventions to counter or slow movements in market exchange rates but not seriously to peg them, such as the actions taken during the Reagan administration, accomplish nothing but the enrichment of foreign-exchange traders at the expense of the U.S. taxpayer. They involve selling a currency whose price is rising in order to stockpile another currency whose price is falling. Economist Dean Taylor has estimated that the U.S. government's foreign-exchange interventions between 1973 and 1980 resulted in net losses of over $2.3 billion.[5] The notion that Treasury bureaucrats know better than the market where exchange rates "should" be in a floating-rate world is absurd. Recent opinions to the effect that the dollar is "overvalued," usually based on aggregate price-level indices, are similarly presumptuous if they are meant to suggest that the market price is somehow out of kilter and needs to be moved to a level determined by expert judgment.

It indeed makes sense to denounce as price fixing any attempt to peg the exchange rate between two distinct national fiat currencies being independently supplied, or between a fiat dollar and a nonmonetary commodity. But price fixing between independent monies is not the real alternative to floating rates and the disruptive impact they have on international trade. The genuine alternative is international currency unification. This is difficult to envision without the renunciation of fiat money and the restoration of a money outside the control of political authorities.

We return, then, to the question posed earlier: Why central banking and political control over money? Endless words can be spent quibbling over the technical advantages of guiding central bank policy by a monetarist "quantity rule" versus a fixed-exchange-rate "price rule." Efforts at international monetary reform would be better spent in reexamining critically why we should have central banking and nationalized monies in the first place.

Notes

1. F. A. Hayek, *Monetary Nationalism and International Stability*, reprint (New York: Augustus M. Kelley, 1971).
2. Walter Bagehot, *Lombard Street: A Description of the Money Market* (London: Henry S. King, 1873), 329.
3. Ludwig von Mises, *The Theory of Money and Credit*, new enl. ed. (Irvington-on-Hudson, N.Y.: Foundation for Economic Education, 1971), 429–30.
4. Benjamin Klein, "Competing Monies, European Monetary Union, and the Dollar," in *One Money for Europe*, ed. Michele Fratianni and Theo Peeters (London: Macmillan, 1978), 91 hr. n. 36.
5. Dean Taylor, "Official Intervention in the Foreign Exchange Market; or, Bet Against the Central Bank," *Journal of Political Economy* 90 (April 1982): 356–68.

8

Free Banking and the Gold Standard

The conjunction of "free banking" with "the gold standard" in the title of this chapter suggests to me two questions: Is free banking necessary to the success of the gold standard? And, conversely, is a gold standard necessary to the success of free banking? My aim in what follows will be to see how much of a natural affinity can be found between the principles of the gold standard and the principles of a freely competitive monetary order, or to put it metaphorically, to see whether gold and free banking are really warp and woof of the fabric of a successful monetary system.

Focusing the chapter in this way may leave it with little to say to those who find neither free currency competition nor commodity money attractive or interesting. Its concerns will likely seem idle to those who find the current national systems of banking regulation cum fiat money part of the best of all possible worlds. There is encouraging evidence, however, that serious interest in alternative monetary systems, particularly the gold standard and various proposals for a laissez-faire approach to money, is on the rise both within academic circles and among participants in political affairs.

THE CRITERIA FOR MONETARY SUCCESS

Posing the question of how essential free banking is to the successful working of a gold-based monetary order obviously raises another question: What are the proper criteria for success in a monetary system? The answer to this second question is not obvious. Nor is it

Reprinted, with permission, from *The Gold Standard: An Austrian Perspective*, ed. Llewellyn H. Rockwell (Lexington, Mass.: Lexington Books, 1985).

obvious by what method an economist can best go about developing an answer, if there is one. One approach that seems clearly inadequate is worth mentioning and criticizing because it is so popular: the method of sheer presumption. Too often economic analysts begin with what Gerald P. O'Driscoll, Jr., has aptly characterized as "a long 'laundry list' of macroeconomic goals to be achieved by a monetary standard."[1] The desirability of these goals is usually taken for granted by those who propose them. Worse, it is assumed without a second thought that the way to achieve a desirable monetary system is to use the political means to create institutions that can be programmed to generate the behavior in macroeconomic aggregates called for by the goals. Monetary institutions are viewed in purely macroinstrumental terms, as tools that government policymakers may design or redesign. The relative goodness of various institutional arrangements is to be judged solely by comparing the various statistical time series they generate. A "desirable" monetary system, according to this view, is one that produces the outcomes presumed desirable by the analyst.

One alternative to the macroinstrumental approach for judging monetary systems is what we might call the microsovereignty (for "microeconomic" and "individual sovereignty") approach. It asks: How well does a particular system serve the interests of money users as they themselves see their interests? Does it leave individuals desiring feasible alternative arrangements, yet block them from making the changes they desire? "Feasible" in this context means not just technologically feasible, but potentially achieving consent from all those traders whose participation is desired. The question, in more technical terms, is whether a monetary system leaves Pareto improvements uncaptured.

The microsovereignty approach is, of course, the approach most economists take when evaluating the success of arrangements for supplying virtually every good other than money. A "monetary system" is simply a set of institutions for supplying the economic good we call "money." No proper economist, speaking as an economist, would presume to judge the goodness of the current American playing card (or, for that matter, baseball card) system by contrasting its characteristics to a list of characteristics he thought desirable. None would fault the system for the possible unpredictability of the purchasing power or relative price of cards from year to year, or for the possible nonuniformity of cards from producer to producer. A proper economist would instead ask whether there existed any reason to suppose that card users were not getting the kinds of cards they wanted (that is, any kinds for which they were willing to pay cost-covering prices). He would not try to second guess consumers' preferences.

Why is money treated differently? It is probably because few economist are accustomed to thinking of money as a private good. Government provision of money has come to be taken for granted, especially so in this century of government fiat monies. *Given* the institution of state-issued fiat money, there clearly must be some definite government policy for regulating the quantity issued. *Given* the inescapability of monetary policy under a fiat regime, government clearly needs expert opinion regarding the desirable goals to be pursued by monetary policy and the technical means to pursue those goals effectively. Unlike a private firm producing playing cards in a competitive environment, a government producing money is not automatically guided by the profit-and-loss system toward meeting consumer wants. Government monetary authorities have no bottom line for which they are accountable. That of course is a major part of the explanation for their poor performance (poor by almost anyone's standards) over the past decades.

The possibility of free banking, if it means nothing else, means that government provision of money ought *not* be taken for granted. The fact that monetary policy becomes necessary when government produces money is no more an argument for treating money differently than other goods than is the fact that a playing card policy becomes necessary when government produces cards. The provision of all forms of money, like the provision of cards, can be left to the marketplace. If the microsovereignty approach is respected, then to argue that either good ought to be brought within the province of government requires one to make a case that free-market provision leaves some subset of individuals frustrated in their attempts to reach mutually preferred arrangements. This case must rely on more than just sheer presumption regarding the content of consumer preferences. It is one thing to attribute concrete preferences to consumers (for example, risk-averse preferences for low variance in aggregate nominal income[2] for the sake of particular modeling exercises (the value of such exercises is questionable, especially when individual preference functions are defined over economywide aggregates that no individual confronts directly). It is quite another thing to claim policy relevance for these models on the implicit assumption that consumers in the real world have the stipulated preferences. Some evidence of this ought to be provided, namely by reference to the preferences actually demonstrated by money users.

The gold standard in particular is often evaluated on the basis of whether it produces relative stability or predictability in the purchasing power of money (which operationally means zero mean or low variance in the first differences of a price index). On the microsovereignty approach these would be among the proper criteria only if they were among the criteria money users themselves consulted in choosing among monetary standards.[3]

Certainly advocates of the gold standard need not view it purely in macroinstrumental terms as a device for producing approximate price-level stability. Few are likely to view it in such a way. For one thing, price-level stability may be arrived at through alternative routes, namely, various quantity-rule or price-index-rule devices for manipulation of the quantity of fiat money which do not command much enthusiasm among those who value a gold-coin standard. From the perspective that takes departures from the gold-coin (specie) standard to be compromises of the gold standard ideal, the enthusiasm shown by some supply-siders for a fiat-money "price rule" looks more like a variant of (early) monetarism than like a wing of the traditional gold-standard camp. The same applies to Fisherian "compensated dollar" schemes with or without gold trappings.[4] Second, the "dishonesty" of fiat money criticized by gold's partisans seems to be not so much its purchasing-power behavior as its potential for inflationary finance—that is, for covert taxation through expansion of the monetary base. Even under a fiat-money policy that stabilizes the price level, cash balances are taxed at a rate equal to the difference between zero and the rate of appreciation of purchasing power that would be generated by fixing the monetary base. This corresponds to the rate of base growth necessary to offset secular growth in real demand for base money. In historical experience, of course, inflationary finance has been much greater.

The following statement by Phillip Cagan, though it shows a greater effort to understand the pro-gold position than other monetarists have made, nonetheless misinterprets the position of many in the gold camp:

Stripped of its rhetoric, however, the position of the gold advocates is really a plea for a stable purchasing power of money, with as close to a guarantee of stability as one can obtain in this uncertain world. There is no logical basis for their opposition to any monetary system that provides a reasonable promise of a stable value of the currency. Why then do advocates of gold not support monetarism which shares the same goal?

As far as I can see, the opposition is not over principle but rather over technique.[5]

There is every reason indeed for gold-standard advocates who personally value stability in the purchasing power of money to prefer monetarism (that is, slow and steady growth in the money supply) within the context of a fiat-money regime, to the sort of discretionary policy seen in the last decade. But again, price-level stability is not, or need not be, the point of advocating a gold-based monetary system. The point may instead be minimization of avoidable interferences with provision of the types of money individuals desire to use. The historical record certainly makes it possible to believe that gold and gold-redeemable instruments came to assume a monetary role precisely because they were the kinds of money people wanted to use. If so, the forced transition to fiat money was a contravention of individual sovereignty that ought to be reversed.

FREE BANKING AND INDIVIDUAL SOVEREIGNTY

If the rationale for a gold standard lies in a microeconomic or individual sovereignty approach, then free banking clearly *is* necessary for the success of the system. Individual sovereignty in economic affairs amounts to the freedom of potential buyers and sellers to make their own bargains, unimpeded by third-party impositions or barriers.[6] It amounts, in other words, to free trade. A system of free banking entails free trade in the market for inside money (demand liabilities of banks), particularly for bank notes. No legislative barriers are placed in the way of exchanges of bank notes or demand deposits between potential issuers and money users. Individuals are free to accept or reject the liabilities of particular banks as they see fit. Banks are free to pursue whatever policies they find advantageous in the issuing of liabilities and the holding of asset portfolios, subject only to the general legal prohibition against fraud or breach of contract.[7]

Demand liabilities of banks under any monetary standard constitute sight claims to the economy's most basic money. Under a gold-coin standard the most basic form of money is by definition coined precious metal or specie. Mintage can be performed exclusively by competing private firms, and the ethic of free trade would suggest that they ought to be provided competitively rather than by government monopoly. Only under open competition are there market forces tending to ensure that consumers get coins having the attributes they demand, for example having the denominations (sizes) they find most convenient.[8] This question is independent, however, of the operation of the bank system.

Claims to specie issued by banks serve as money when transactors generally accept payments in the form of transfers of claims which they in turn transfer in payments to others. Titles to specie can then change hands without any physical transfer of specie. Early in history, bankers and their customers discovered mutual advantage in the transfer of deposit balances by book entries, sparing the need for cumbersome withdrawals, transfers, and redeposits of gold. The personal check emerged as a means of signaling banks to perform such transfers. Later the bank note, payable to the bearer on demand, emerged as a means for transferring claims to specie without the involvement of the bank.[9] For particular purposes one or the other form of redeemable claim on bank specie is more convenient to use than actual specie. The ability of these claims to function as money —their general acceptability as means of payment—of course depends on their being regarded as actually redeemable for basic money at par on demand.[10] This feature fixes the exchange value of notes and demand deposits equal to that of the specie to which they are claims, enabling them to serve as substitutes for coin.

Under free banking individuals may choose among the notes of a plurality of private issuers. They are not limited to using the notes of a privileged central bank. Monopolization of note issue is a defining characteristic of central banking, and a characteristic that has always emerged from legislative intervention. There is no evidence of a tendency toward natural monopoly in the issue of bank notes.[11] Open competition in issue ensures that banks will provide notes with the characteristics note holders demand. The quality dimensions along which notes may differ include ease of redemption, reputability of issuer (this is a combination of trustworthiness and renown), and proof against counterfeiting. All of these will affect a note's most important characteristic, its ability to circulate. Competition among issuers of bank notes is in many respects similar to the competition we see today among issuers of credit cards and traveler's checks, as well as to the competition among banks for checking-account customers.[12] Respect for microeconomic criteria and individual sovereignty requires that government not limit consumers' choices by interfering with competition among potential bank-note issuers.

One argument sometimes made against competitive issue of bank notes (and which presumably also could be made against competitive issue of checking accounts, traveler's checks, and credit cards, though it rarely is) runs as follows: The reason people use money is to lower the information or transactions costs of accomplishing desired trades. Dealing with numerous brands of hand-to-hand currency implies bearing high information or transactions costs. Suppressing the number of issuers therefore improves economic welfare. I have elsewhere offered the rebuttal that this argument is paternalistic; it amounts to saying that too much choice makes life difficult for people and should be eliminated by letting the government choose for them. If valid in the case of bank notes, this argument would be valid against brand proliferation in any industry.[13] Here I wish to elaborate on that rebuttal. Consider an initial situation with only a single brand of bank notes. What is the case against allowing a second brand? Individuals (for example, shopkeepers) who do not wish to be bothered with the new brand can refuse to deal with it. If they do choose to deal with it (accept it), presumably they consider the information and transactions costs worth bearing in light of the benefits they expect. If the costs are generally considered not worth bearing, the market will not support a second brand. This reasoning holds for $n+1$ brands as well as for two. The rationale of open competition among multiple brands of bank notes (as among brands of anything else) is the freedom to discover which brands and how many brands best suit consumer preferences. The central bank's monopoly of note issue eliminates the chance for individuals to accept other brands of notes, even when the benefit exceeds the cost.

FREE BANKING AND FRACTIONAL RESERVES

Discussion of free banking usually focuses on the liability side of banks' balance sheets, particularly on the freedom to issue bank notes. But freedom on the asset side is also controversial. The alternative assets banks on a gold standard choose among, when permitted, can be divided most simply into two categories: specie reserves and interest-earning assets such as loans and securities. A bank holds specie reserves to honor its contractual obligation to redeem on demand its notes and deposits. The size of the reserve it chooses to hold reflects its perception of the risk of sudden redemption outflows. The bank holds interest-earning assets having varying degrees of ready marketability, with the readiest serving as a "secondary reserve" that can be sold for gold to replenish the specie reserve on short notice.

Each category of assets has been historically subjected to government regulation. Restrictions on the choice of interest-earning assets were part and parcel of so-called free banking legislation enacted by midnineteenth-century American states. Banks issuing notes were required to own, and to place in the possession of state regulators, certain types of assets, most notably state government bonds. Restrictions on reserve-holding choices, namely "reserve requirements," were imposed by several states before the Civil War. They have been part of federal regulation since the National Bank Act of 1863.[14] Both categories of asset regulation prevent consumers from freely choosing among banks with alternative portfolio policies and hence with alternative risk-return characteristics. They prevent banks from achieving desired risk-return performance most efficiently. The function of bank notes as hand-to-hand currency suggests that consumers will prefer the notes of issuers who present close to zero illiquidity and insolvency risk.[15] It also suggests that bank notes will generally be non-interest-bearing. The forces of competitive selection shaping banks' asset portfolios will hence focus primarily on the methods of producing consumer confidence in bank notes and deposits (exemplary past redemption performance, which depends on adequate reserves, being the chief method) and on the rates of return paid on deposits (these rates depend on bank holdings of interest-bearing assets). Under competitive conditions banks are compelled to act in compliance with consumer preferences in balancing the benefits of additional specie reserves (lesser chance of illiquidity) against the alternative benefit of additional interest-bearing assets (higher returns on deposits).

Some gold-standard advocates, most notably Murray N. Rothbard, have argued for 100 percent reserve requirements against demand deposits and bank notes. Rothbard urges this position not as a paternalistic intervention into the market for inside money, but on the grounds that the holding of less than 100 percent reserves against demand liabilities is per se fraudulent. This argument is more jurisprudential than economic. He has recently written: "It should be clear that modern fractional reserve banking is a shell game, a Ponzi scheme, a fraud in which false warehouse receipts are issued and circulate as equivalent to the cash supposedly represented by the receipts." And in rebuttal to the argument that banker hardly needs 100 percent reserves in order to meet all the redemption demands that will in fact confront him at any one time, he writes: "But holders of warehouse receipts to money emphatically *do have* . . . a claim, even in modern banking law, to their own property any time they choose to redeem it. But the legal claims issued by the bank must then be fraudulent, since the bank could not possibly meet them all."[16] Rothbard's view that bank notes are the legal equivalent of warehouse receipts is based on what he thinks legal practice *ought* to be, not on the interpretation courts have actually made of the contractual obligations incurred by the issuers of bank notes.[17]

It is difficult to see why an analyst committed to the ethic of individual sovereignty, as Rothbard elsewhere clearly is, would wish to prevent banks and their customers from making whatever sorts of contractual arrangements are mutually agreeable. The British Court decisions cited and criticized by Rothbard, to the effect that bank notes do not contractually bind their issuers to holding 100 percent reserves, seem eminently reasonable given the inscription actually found on the face of a typical British bank note: The Bank of XYZ "promise to pay the bearer on demand one pound sterling."[18] There is no promise made about reserve-holding behavior. There is nothing to indicate that the note constitutes a warehouse receipt or establishes a bailment contract. But ought it do so? According to the individual sovereignty approach, that would depend on the contractual arrangement to which a bank and its customer mutually consent. Nothing in a free banking system prevents an individual who desires 100 percent-reserve banking from explicitly contracting for it. In fact, safety deposit boxes have commonly been offered by banks for those who wish their money held as a bailment, who wish, in other words, to retain unconditional title to it. It would be silly to suggest that bank notes and demand deposits gained acceptance historically only when their holders were fraudulently misled by the misrepresentation of bank demand liabilities as unconditional warehouse receipts. It is in fact evident that most individuals will voluntarily accept nonbailment bank note and demand deposits.

According to the title-transfer of contracts, a bank note payable to the bearer on demand, with no stipulation of the reserves to be held, constitutes a *conditional* title to bank-held specie, conditional on presentation for redemption.[19] In a title-transfer regime, prevention of breach of contract by banks issuing such notes requires only that any obligation to redeem on demand be satisfied for all customers who actually present notes and deposits for redemption. Fractional reserves do not constitute breach of contract. Furthermore, consistent with title transfer, a bank may insert a clause into note and deposit contracts reserving to itself the option of delaying redemption. Historically the Scottish banks did this for notes before the practice was outlawed, and American banks have more recently incorporated option clauses into NOW checking accounts.[20] Such option clauses mean that a sudden redemption outflow from a bank can be headed off without breach of contract. In practice an issuer will not likely exercise the option to defer redemption, except in an emergency, because an expectation by the public that the option will be used would impair the circulability of the issuer's notes and hence would reduce the demand to hold those notes.

FREE BANKING AND MACROECONOMIC PERFORMANCE

The case to be made for free banking on macroinstrumental grounds is this: The aggregate performance of an economy on a gold standard is likely to be better under free banking than under central banking. A large body of theoretical and historical work in economics identifies errors in money supply as a significant source of business cycle disturbances.[21] The advantage of free banking is that a plurality of issuers minimizes the chances for large-scale errors in the money supply. One reason is readily apparent: No single issuer controls a large share of the circulation. Equally important, the plurality of issuers brings with it, in the form of the interbank clearinghouse for bank notes (and checks), an automatic mechanism for preventing major money supply errors by any single bank. The clearinghouse gives each issuer both the information to detect, and the incentive to correct promptly, any deviation of the quantity of inside money it supplies from the quantity of its inside money that the public desires to hold. This process of negative feedback is absent from a central banking system, where the supply of bank notes is monopolized and the liabilities of the central bank are held as reserves by commercial banks. Only with free banking is the operation of the gold standard fully self-regulating.

The contrast between free banking and central banking with regard to the mechanisms regulating the money stock can be spelled out here in somewhat greater detail.[22] The public's demand to hold the demand liabilities (notes or demand deposits) of any particular bank is a definitely limited magnitude (in nominal as well as real terms given that the purchasing power of notes and demand deposits is fixed by their redeemability for specie). Suppose a single bank in a multi-issuer system issues too many notes or deposits, "too many" being more than the public desires to hold. People who find themselves holding excess notes or deposits will get rid of them largely by depositing them in checking or savings accounts at their own banks, or by spending them away to persons who will deposit them. Given that our single bank is relatively small, all but a small fraction of the excess notes or deposits will wind up as deposits in rival banks. The rival banks that accept these deposits will quickly turn around and demand redemption of the first bank's liabilities through the interbank clearing system. The overexpansive bank will discover that its specie reserves are draining away, a situation it cannot let persist. Reserve losses signal to the bank the need to correct its course to prevent complete illiquidity. The negative feedback is rapid enough that any disturbance to the credit market or aggregate spending will likely be quite minor.

A central bank, by contrast, faces no rival for the circulation of its notes. Both its notes and its demand deposits may serve as reserves for commercial banks, displacing specie from that role. Hence an overexpansion of central bank liabilities, supposing one to occur, will not find its way into the clearing mechanism and thereby rapidly reveal its presence. Instead, commercial banks that come to hold extra liabilities of the central bank will be impelled by their swollen reserves to expand their own liabilities. The resulting overexpansion of the entire system will be revealed only through a relatively slow and drawn-out process. An excess stock of money stimulates greater spending as individuals adjust their wealth portfolios. This leads to an "adverse" balance of trade with other nations, that is, an excess of imports over exports, both directly as the excess stock of money prompts greater spending on imports as well as on domestic goods, and indirectly as increased spending on domestic goods bids up their prices and makes imports more attractive. The excess of imports over exports must be paid in international currency, namely gold. Settlement of the balance then drains gold from the central bank's vault. The signal to reverse its course finally appears to the central bank. But in the meantime the economy may have been driven through an artificial credit boom of major proportions which must be painfully reversed when the central bank contracts credit to stanch its reserve losses.

Even under a gold standard, then, a central bank may have sufficient leeway to issue sharp monetary shocks and thereby to generate severe business cycles. Much work remains to be done by modern historians in exploring the applicability of this theory to business cycles actually experienced, particularly in Britain under the gold standard managed by the Bank of England after 1821 and in America under the Second Bank of the United States. There is no question that many sophisticated contemporary observers of the Bank of England under the classical gold standard blamed it for creating or aggravating business cycles through improper issuing policies. It is for this reason that the program of the well-known Currency School called for restriction of the Bank of England's discretionary power of issuing notes. Such a restriction was embodied in Peel's Bank Charter

Act of 1844. The Free-Banking School of the same era argued more perceptively and radically for an end to the legal privileges that bestowed on the Bank of England its central banking powers.[23] In the United States, the Jacksonian case against the Second Bank of the United States, providing the rationale for the veto of its recharter in 1832, rested in part on the argument that its mismanagement of the currency had sent the economy through boom-and-bust cycles.[24]

The policy of free banking gained Ludwig von Mises' endorsement as an essential barrier against business fluctuations driven by over-expansionary central-bank policies. Wrote Mises:

Free banking is the only method available for the prevention of the dangers inherent in credit expansion. It would, it is true, not hinder a slow credit expansion, kept within very narrow limits, on the part of cautious banks which provide the public with all information required about their financial status. But under free banking it would have been impossible for credit expansion with all its inevitable consequences to have developed into a regular—one is tempted to say normal—feature of the economic system. Only free banking would have rendered the market economy secure against crises and depressions.[25]

The overwhelming source of the cyclical macroeconomic difficulties of recent years has clearly been the money-supply shocks emanating from monetary authorities presiding over national fiat money regimes. A major threat to long-term planning is that the purchasing power of money has become impossible to predict with any accuracy more than a few quarters into the future, because the nominal quantity of money is anchored to nothing more than the discretion of a monetary bureaucracy. In this environment, the gold standard, which Keynes once derided as a ''barbarous relic,'' has attracted new attention as a device for limiting the discretion of central banks. There is no question that a commitment to a fixed gold definition of the dollar would anchor the nominal quantity of money, make its purchasing power more predictable, and thereby promote coordination of long-term plans. But as far as damming the source of cyclical monetary disturbances, the gold standard is inadequate without free banking. A central bank tied to gold at a fixed parity can no longer inflate without limit in the long run, but it *can* manipulate in the short run the quantity of high-powered money, and thereby can subject the economy to monetary disruption—to what Mises calls "credit expansion with all its inevitable consequences."

A central bank that has the power to cause monetary disturbances inevitably will cause them. Central bankers, like central economic planners in general, typically lack the incentives and inevitably lack the information that would be necessary for them to perform as skillfully as a market system in matching supplies with demands. The incentive structure surrounding the monetary authorities is important because inflation and recession may often be the by-product of intentional policy actions. The public-choice approach to government agencies suggests that government policymakers who are entrusted with control over money should be expected to succumb to the temptations of easy money.[26] The information problems of the monetary authorities are at least as important as these incentive problems. Even a "virtuous" central bank on a gold standard must make money supply errors because it lacks any timely and reliable signal of excess supply or demand for its liabilities. It is limited to such macroeconomic indicators as price indexes, interest rates, exchange-rate movements within the gold points, and international gold flows. The information they give is either ambiguous or obvious only after an excess has already had its discoordinating effects, for example after an external drain has begun.[27]

IS GOLD NECESSARY TO FREE BANKING?

If we take "free banking" to indicate a monetary system free not only from government regulation of the issue of inside money but also from government control over outside money, the field of potential outside monies is circumscribed only by the exclusion of actively issued government fiat money. It is conceivable then that free banking could be established with an outside money other than gold. Silver is an obvious alternative to gold. Supposing that bank liabilities are claims redeemable for silver coin rather than gold coin alters none of the analytical properties of a free banking system. Several sorts of nonfiat currencies beside gold and silver have been proposed in the past and are still advocated today. A third candidate for potential free-market outside money is "symmetallic" currency (or the vermeil standard, if you will), where the monetary unit is defined as so many grams of gold plus so many grams of silver. A fourth is currency redeemable for some nonmetallic (and nonmonetary) commodity or basket of commodities. A fifth is redeemable currency whose redemption rate is indexed to provide for stable purchasing power of the monetary unit. A sixth is inconvertible but privately issued currency.[28] Two further theoretical possibilities for elimination of government control over the quantity of outside currency also present themselves. The first of these is to freeze the stock of fiat money or the monetary base. The second is to have a payments system that makes no use of outside money.[29]

From the microsovereignty perspective, all the candidate monetary standards (with the exception of gold and silver) ought to be regarded as untried entrepreneurial ideas. To discover which one(s) money users would actually prefer to use, potential suppliers of the various currencies should be allowed to compete. This would require lifting any prohibitions, taxes, regulations, and legislated accounting rules that could serve as barriers to entry of alternative outside monies. The belief that none of the alternatives would lead to voluntary abandonment of an established precious-metal standard seems warranted by historical experience. But the choice, given a microsovereignty ethic, ought not to be foreclosed by anticompetitive policies.

The burden of outcompeting an established standard is significant. The persistence of a single monetary standard, like the emergence of money in the first place, can be explained by the personal convenience of using a medium of exchange most readily accepted by other traders.[30] It is therefore difficult to convince any individual in a monetized economy to accept as a medium of exchange an asset that is neither a claim to something nor itself something that other individuals already accept as readily as money. In pondering the transition to open competition among monetary standards there is of course no a priori reason to consider gold or silver, rather than government fiat paper, vermeil, or plywood, as the proper initial monetary standard. The reason must instead be historical: gold and silver emerged as money in advanced nations out of an invisible-hand convergence process driven by individual preferences. Gold and silver were chosen as money before governments got into the act of restricting monetary options. They gradually displaced other standards, presumably because they represented superior monies in the eyes of money users in areas that came into trading contact with specie-using areas.[31] Neither gold nor silver is logically necessary to free banking, but respect for historically demonstrated consumer preferences suggests that a specie standard is the natural place to start.

Notes

1. Gerald P. O'Driscoll, Jr., "A Free-Market Money: Comment on Yeager," *Cato Journal* 3 (Spring 1983): 327.
2. This example is taken from Allan H. Meltzer, "Monetary Reform in an Uncertain Environment," *Cato Journal* 3 (Spring 1983): 97–105. Other examples of preferences attributed (without evidence) to consumers by monetary reformers would be preferences for higher real gross national product, more stable purchasing power of the monetary unit, and uniformity of money across producers.
3. In fact the relative instability and unpredictability of silver's purchasing power may have contributed to its abandonment in favor of gold during the nineteenth century. One would like to have a thorough interpretation of the historical evidence on this question, as governments' interests rather than individuals' preferences may have ben responsible for switches from silver to gold.
4. The "compensated dollar" was the brainchild of Irving Fisher, who revived the quantity theory of money early in this century. See Irving Fisher, *Stabilizing the Dollar* (New York: Macmillan, 1920).
5. Phillip Cagan, "A Review of the Report of the Gold Commission and Some Thoughts on Convertible Monetary Systems" (manuscript, Columbia University, October 1982), 4.
6. To use the terminology of Murray N. Rothbard, *Power and Market* (Menlo Park, Calif.: Institute for Humane Studies, 1970), complete individual sovereignty in the market requires the absence of triangular intervention. See also Donald C. Lavoie, "The Development of the Misesian Theory of Interventionism" in *Method, Process, and Austrian Economics*, ed. Israel M. Kirzner (Lexington, Mass.: Lexington Books, 1982), 178–79, where Lavoie points out that certain forms of taxes constitute triangular intervention.
7. It should perhaps be noted explicitly that the so-called free banking systems in several American states between 1837 and 1863 did not meet these conditions. For a recent account of New York State's free-banking experience see Robert G. King, "On the Economics of Private Money," *Journal of Monetary Economics* 12 (July 1983): 139–56.

8. For American experience with private mints in the Appalachian and Californian gold-producing regions, see Donald H. Kagin, *Private Gold Coins and Patterns of the United States* (New York: Arco, 1981). For an early free trade defense of exclusively private coinage, see Thomas Hodgskin, *Popular Political Economy* (London: Charles Tait, 1827; reprint, New York: Augustus M. Kelley, 1966), 190–96. For a recent defense, see Rothbard, *Power and Market*, 59–60, where Rothbard points out that only competitive private coinage can be presumed to give consumers the denominations of coins they want.

9. For an evolutionary perspective on monetary institutions, see Lawrence H. White, "Competitive Payments Systems and the Unit of Account," *American Economic Review* 74 (September 1984): 699–712. On the early history of European banking see Raymond de Roover, *Business, Banking, and Economic Thought in Late Medieval and Early Modern Europe* (Chicago: University of Chicago Press, 1956), chap. 5. See also Ludwig von Mises, *The Theory of Money and Credit,* trans. H. E. Batson, new ed. (Irvington-on-Hudson, N.Y.: Foundation for Economic Education, 1971), 278–80.

10. See Mises, *Theory of Money and Credit,* 50–53.

11. King, "On the Economics of Private Money," 154, affirms this conclusion for New York State's experience; Lawrence H. White *Free Banking in Britain* (Cambridge, England: Cambridge University Press, 1984), 146, affirms it for Scotland's experience with free banking.

12. See White, *Free Banking in Britain,* 7–8.

13. Lawrence H. White, "Competitive Money, Inside and Out," *Cato Journal* 3 (Spring 1983): 292. I am grateful to David Price for bringing this question to my attention.

14. See Milton Friedman and Anna Jacobson Schwartz, *A Monetary History of the United States, 1867–1960* (Princeton, N.J.: Princeton University Press, 1963), 56n.

15. Ludwig von Mises, *Human Action,* 3d ed. (Chicago: Henry Regnery, 1966), 445–47.

16. Murray N. Rothbard, *The Mystery of Banking* (New York: Richardson and Snyder, 1983), 97, 100.

17. Ibid., 93–94, briefly relates the legal precedents on this question.

18. Specimens of Scottish banknotes may be found in S. G. Checkland, *Scottish Banking: A History, 1695–1973* (Glasgow: Collins, 1975), 32, 67, 98, 105, 185, 383, 546–48.

19. On the title-transfer model, see Williamson M. Evers, "Toward Reformulation of the Law of Contracts," *Journal of Libertarian Studies* 1 (Winter 1977): 3–13. I would argue that the title-transfer view is uniquely compatible with an ethic of individual sovereignty.

20. On the option clause in early Scotland, see Checkland, *Scottish Banking,* 67–68, 82, 110. The law banning them in 1765 met with Adam Smith's

approval: see *An Inquiry into the Nature and Causes of the Wealth of Nations*, ed. R.H. Campbell, A.S. Skinner, and W.B. Todd (1776; reprint, Indianapolis: Liberty Classics, 1981), 325–26, 329. It should be noted that the option clauses in Scottish banknotes specified an interest yield (5 percent per annum) in case of deferred redemption, and specified the period of deferral (six months). A representative "optional" note read: "The Royal Bank of Scotland . . . is hereby obliged to pay to————or the Bearer, one pound sterling on demand, or, in the Option of the Directors, one pound six pence sterling at the End of Six Months after the day of the demand. . . ." Checkland, *Scottish Banking*, 67, provides a specimen. This interest penalty, imposed by competition, further discouraged banks from exercising the option.

21. Comprehensive referencing of this literature would take a long article by itself. On the early nineteenth-century literature, see White, *Free Banking in Britain*, chaps. 3, 4. Classic works in the Austrian monetary theory of the business cycle include Ludwig von Mises, *On the Manipulation of Money and Credit* (Dobbs Ferry, N.Y.: Free Market Books, 1978) and F.A. Hayek, *Prices and Production*, 2d ed. (New York: Augustus M. Kelley, 1967). Important works in the Monetarist tradition include Friedman and Schwartz, *A Monetary History of the United States, 1867–1960*, and Robert E. Lucas, Jr., *Studies in Business Cycle Theory* (Cambridge, Mass.: MIT Press, 1981).

22. This and the following paragraph draw upon White, *Free Banking in Britain*, 14–19.

23. Ibid., chap. 3 and chap. 4, sec. 3.

24. For an example of fairly sophisticated argument along these lines by a leading Jacksonian theoretician see William Leggett, "Bank of the United States" in *Democratick Editorials*, ed. Lawrence H. White (Indianapolis: Liberty Press, 1984), 63–70.

25. Mises, *Human Action*, 443.

26. Ibid. Mises quite bluntly blamed actual central bank overexpansions either on deliberate attempts to cheapen credit by politicians catering to popular inflationist ideology or on attempts at inflationary finance. For a valuable survey article explaining both the incentive and information problems of central banking, see Pamela Brown, "Constitution or Competition? Alternative Approaches to Monetary Reform," *Literature of Liberty* 5 (Autumn 1982): 7–52.

27. On this point see the remarkably perceptive statements of Samuel Bailey, *A Defence of Joint-Stock Banks and Country Issues* (London: James Ridgway, 1840). Several pertinent passages from this work are quoted in White, *Free Banking in Britain*, 130–33.

28. I have given a similar list, and further discussed the question addressed by this section, in "Gold, Dollars, and Private Currencies," *Policy Report* 3 (June 1981): 6–11. Some combination of the fourth and fifth sorts of

nonfiat currency has recently been suggested by Robert E. Hall, "Explorations in the Gold Standard and Related Policies for Stabilizing the Dollar," in *Inflation: Causes and Effects*, ed. Robert E. Hall (Chicago: University of Chicago Press, 1982), 111–22. Hall proposes a basket standard composed of ammonium nitrate, copper, aluminum, and plywood.

29. A base freeze is proposed by R.H. Timberlake, Jr., "Monetization Practices and the Political Structure of the Federal Reserve System," Cato Institute *Policy Analysis* (12 August 1981): 12. The idea of a cashless competitive payments system is explored by Robert L. Greenfield and Leland B. Yeager, "A Laissez-Faire Approach to Monetary Stability," *Journal of Money, Credit, and Banking* 15 (August 1983): 302–15, and proposed as a reform by Leland B. Yeager, "Stable Money and Free-Market Currencies," *Cato Journal* 3 (Spring 1983): 323–25. I criticize on evolutionary grounds the idea that competition would give rise to a cashless payments system, or to a basket standard, in "Competitive Payments System and the Unit of Account."

30. The *locus classicus* for this theory of the origin of money is Carl Menger, "On the Origin of Money," *Economic Journal* 2 (1892): 239–55.

31. Sweden, for example, had a copper standard in early times. The relative cumbersomeness of this should be obvious.

III

The Theory of Competitive Monetary Arrangements

9

Competitive Payments Systems
and the Unit of Account

Recent competitive innovations in payment mechanisms, particularly the checkable money-market mutual fund, seem to have blurred the edges of the category of assets properly called "money." These innovations have coincided with new attempts by economists to reconstruct monetary theory and policy using competitive models. Several authors have conceived of competitive payments systems seemingly devoid of any outside currency, base money, or standard medium of exchange.[1] The unit of account in these systems is evidently not a common currency unit established outside the banking industry. Yet it can be argued that the use of a common unit of account in decentralized economic calculation presupposes a general medium of exchange.

Lance Girton and Don Roper have recently written: "One observes that most contractual obligations are specified in terms of the units in which the medium of exchange is measured. Further research should provide more insight into why contracts are specified in units in which the medium of exchange is measured" (1981, 20). This essay attempts to provide some insight into this question. By examining whether the above-mentioned cashless competitive payments systems are coherent and operational, it explores the fundamental relationship of the unit of account to the medium of exchange. It specifically examines the plausibility of competition divorcing the unit in which prices are specified (the unit of account) from the medium in which payment is typically made. The argument con-

Reprinted, with permission, from *American Economic Review*, vol. 74, no. 4 (September 1984).

cludes that a payments system not based on convertibility into an outside currency should not be expected to arise in the absence of government intervention.

CASHLESS COMPETITIVE PAYMENTS SYSTEMS: A BRIEF SURVEY

Black

The belief that unrestricted competition would produce a payments mechanism devoid of outside money is expressed already in the title of Fischer Black's 1970 article, "Banking and Interest Rates in a World Without Money: The Effects of Uncontrolled Banking." Black claims that in the world he imagines "money in the usual sense would not exist" (p. 9). Initially he assumes that no currency is used; later he allows for currency, but supposes that its nominal quantity will be determined purely by demand, so that it does not serve as an outside money forming a base for bank liabilities.[2] Payments are made by transfer of this currency and bank liabilities. No mention is made of the redeemability of bank liabilities for this currency or any basic physical monetary asset produced outside the banking industry. I will for brevity's sake refer to such an asset as "outside currency" or "cash."

What serves as the unit of account? Black cannot say "the currency unit," for that is supposed to be subsidiary to the unit in which bank liabilities are denominated. Instead he says: "Goods may be priced in terms of a unit of account that does not fluctuate in value very much, and means of payment may be priced in terms of the same unit of account" (1970, 14). The unit of account in Black's world is clearly not an outside currency unit as it is in our world. It is instead apparently a unit of a distinct numeraire commodity (or bundle of commodities) that does not itself serve as the means of payment. This is indicated by the remark that the means of payment is to be *priced* in terms of the unit of account, as opposed to the unit of account being *defined* in terms of the means of payment. Thus Black's system divorces the unit of account from the characteristic units of the system's exchange media.

It is not at all clear in terms of what numeraire commodity the unit of account would be defined in Black's world, or how that numeraire would be selected. He conducts a thought experiment in which the means of payment successively assumes five forms: (1) barter; (2) shares of common stock; (3) corporate bonds; (4) corporate bonds certified by "banks"; (5) pure bank liabilities. The passage quoted above appears in his discussion of the second form. In that discussion, Black makes it clear that the hypothesized unit of account is not the characteristic unit of the means of payment (a share of a stock portfolio). At no later stage in his experiment is this divorce mended.

The logic of Black's construction receives fuller criticism below. But one curious feature of his exposition deserves mention here. He speaks of "the dollar price" of a medium-of-exchange unit and the "dollar price" of a commodity, thus clearly designating "the dollar" as the unit of account. He suggests that transactors in his system may use these "dollar" prices to compute a commodity's price in terms of the medium of exchange. Yet there is nothing called "dollars" actually being traded against the commodities in the system, hence no mechanism for registering the prices of these commodities in terms of dollars. There are no dollar prices established on markets logically or temporally prior to the establishment of medium-of-exchange prices.[3] The problem here is not that the unit of account is divorced from the medium of exchange, but that it is totally abstract, divorced from any traded good. Such an abstract unit of account, as Don Patinkin indicates (1965, 16), can have no operational significance for market participants. It can be meaningful only to a Walrasian auctioneer or other outside observer.

Fama

Black's article went uncited in the literature for a decade, until the appearance of Eugene Fama's "Banking in the Theory of Finance" (1980).[4] Fama, like Black, considers outside money inessential to the competitive payments mechanism he hypothesizes. He posits a "pure accounting system of exchange" (p. 42) in which the function of banks is to operate "a system of accounts in which transfers of wealth are carried out with bookkeeping entries" (p. 39). This method of wealth transfer is asserted to be "entirely different" in relevant respects from the use of cash. Fama claims that the transactions industry in the world he examines can dispense entirely with cash: "An accounting system works through bookkeeping entries, debits and credits, which do not require any physical medium or the concept of money" (p. 39). Hence, in Fama's world, as in Black's, bank liabilities need not constitute claims to cash: "In a pure accounting system of exchange, the notion of a physical medium or temporary abode of purchasing power disappears" (p. 42).

Unlike Black, Fama is explicit in stipulating that the unit of account in his world should be thought of as the unit of a commodity that plays no medium-of-exchange role: "it could well be tons of fresh cut beef or barrels of crude oil" (p. 43). He explicitly recognizes that bank "deposits"—which would be heterogeneous, being essentially shares in various mutual funds and not claims to a common currency—are not a suitable candidate for numeraire.

Prices of commodities are stated in terms of the numeraire. Fama recognizes that an economy of this sort "is basically non-monetary." There is no question of price-level determination: since there is no money commodity trading against other goods, there is no money price level. There are only numeraire or relative prices to be determined. The determination of relative prices is apparently thought of as a function of the Walrasian auctioneer. Fama speaks of the system posing "a standard problem concerning the existence of a stable general equilibrium in a nonmonetary system" (1980, 44).

Like Black, Fama leaves both the particular numeraire commodity ("some real good") and its method of selection unspecified. This is of no concern so long as we take the auctioneer construct seriously. The auctioneer's choice of a numeraire is of no consequence. But Fama implicitly slips out of this construct. He suggests that agents in his world face genuine calculational problems, and that they deal with one another in decentralized markets rather than with the auctioneer alone. He says of the accounting system of exchange, for instance, that "its efficiency is improved when all prices are stated in units of a common numeraire" (1980, 43).

After analyzing banking in a nonmonetary setting, Fama introduces currency in the form of "a non-interest-bearing fiat currency produced monopolistically by the government" (1980, 50). The unit in which currency is measured may then serve as the economy's numeraire. The real value of a currency unit in terms of goods and services is determined in familiar fashion, as a determinate demand for real currency balances confronts a fixed nominal stock of currency.

Fama suggests that banks in the world with currency provide a "currency convertibility service" for their customers. But it is unclear whether he means "convertibility" in the usual sense of an obligation to *redeem* deposits on demand for outside currency. Banks taking on such an obligation have an inventory demand to hold currency as reserves against stochastic redemption outflows.[5] Limitation of the quantity of reserve currency available to the banks then limits the quantity of deposits that banks can prudently create. Fama states that banks would indeed "inventory currency on behalf of depositors" (1980, 50), but at the same time implicitly denies that the banks of an unregulated system would hold any non-interest-bearing reserves. Yet a bank's vault cash should be considered the primary component of its reserves where its deposits are convertible in the usual sense of constituting sight claims to predetermined quantities of currency.[6] By "convertibility," Fama must mean only that the banks act in the manner of money-market mutual funds. Bank liabilities in his analysis are not claims to outside currency, as they are today, but are on the order of shares in a mutual fund's portfolio of interest-bearing assets. These funds (or Fama's "banks") stand ready to liquidate their shares (his "deposits") on demand by selling the assets to which the deposits constitute a claim and then turning over the proceeds to the shareholder ("depositor"). Fama is explicit in a more recent paper that this is what he envisions. He states that in his world: "Deposits are just claims against other claims (securities, loans, etc.)" (1982, 6). That is, they are not redeemable claims to outside currency. Fama's propositions that "deposits issued competitively should not be called money" and that "the concept of money plays no role in the transactions services accessed through deposits" (1982, 7) both rest on deposits not being claims to outside currency. The significance of the difference between such assets and deposits in the usual sense is explored below.

It is clear from the "parable" with which Fama concludes his earlier article (1980, 55–56) that he regards the existence of outside money as unnecessary for the operation of an accounting system of exchange. Outside money is to him simply one commodity that, if it exists, may serve as numeraire; however, there is no need for it to exist. Steel ingots or spaceship permits may as well serve as numeraire. This result is arguably not true of any plausible world. There are compelling reasons, discussed below, for outside money to exist and to serve as the unit of account.

Hall

In two recent papers Robert Hall, searching for monetary policies consistent with stable prices and full deregulation of banking and financial markets, has questioned the necessity and desirability of associating the unit of account with a medium-of-exchange currency unit. Citing Fama (1980), Hall states: "It is possible to define the monetary unit [the unit of account] as one unit of a resource called currency, but this is only one of many different definitions" (1981, p. 4). In general the unit is simply "a certain amount of some resource" specified by government; the resource need not be currency. As an example of a noncurrency monetary unit, Hall proposes "defining" the dollar in terms of a composite-commodity unit called the ANCAP, consisting of specified physical quantities of ammonium nitrate, copper, aluminum, and plywood. Beyond defining the dollar in such a way, government is to play no role in the payments industry.

Hall chose the ANCAP unit for its stable purchasing power over the last thirty years. Presumably this stability was measured in terms of some price index. An obvious question therefore arises: Why does Hall not suggest defining the dollar directly in terms of the commodity bundle making up the price index he desires to stabilize? The answer lies in the mechanism he implicitly relies on for tying the value of the unit-of-account dollar to the specified commodity bundle. Only the commodity bundle is to be legal tender for dollar obligations. This means that all holders of contractual claims to receive dollars (or of obligations to pay dollars) are entitled to demand (or make) payment in the physical commodities defining the dollar. Any sufficiently wide divergence between the market price of the standard commodity bundle and one dollar will trigger demands by creditors to receive commodities rather than paper dollars (or deliveries by debtors of commodities in place of paper dollars). Transactors choosing to contract in ANCAP dollars would be exposing themselves to the risk of being forced to deliver, or to accept delivery of, physical bundles of the standard commodities. Every transactor would be taking on bank-like obligations. It is natural to doubt that many transactors would voluntarily do so. An ANCAP obligation seems to be clearly dominated for both creditor and debtor by an obligation indexed to the ANCAP bundle but contractually payable in a common medium of exchange. That is, explicitly transactors would rule out the commodity-delivery possibility, given that a common medium of exchange is by definition more readily accepted than other commodities. The creditor would rather receive, and the debtor rather pay, readily spendable money than a bundle of commodities of equal market value. It is less implausible to suppose that specialized bank-like institutions might issue ANCAP-redeemable obligations. The question that then arises, to be answered below, is whether such obligations would gain currency in an unregulated environment.

Greenfield and Yeager

In a recent paper, Robert Greenfield and Leland Yeager attempt to describe more explicitly how a competitive mutual-funds-type payments system devoid of outside money might operate. They attribute the inspiration behind the cashless competitive payments system to the three authors whose works I have just surveyed. In Greenfield and Yeager's view of that world, banklike mutual funds would develop and operate a sophisticated barter system (1983, 305–8). The unit of account would be an arbitrarily chosen numeraire consisting of a bundle of commodities; the means of payment would be primarily shares of ownership in mutual fund portfolios. They explicitly affirm both the nonexistence of any outside money in which funds' liabilities are redeemable and the divorce of the unit of account from these media of exchange.

Greenfield and Yeager do not examine the question of whether such a system could emerge or survive under competitive conditions. They do consider whether the system's unit of account "has operational meaning" and whether "the level of prices expressed in that unit is determinate" (p. 313). In both cases, they find in the affirmative. But this merely means that they find the concept of keeping track of relative prices by use of a numeraire unit not incoherent or self-contradictory. It remains to be considered whether economic agents in an unregulated world without a central auctioneer would be likely to converge on the use of a unit of account that is not a unit of outside currency.

COMPETITIVE PAYMENTS SYSTEMS IN EVOLUTIONARY PERSPECTIVE

In the monetary systems our world has known, the generally accepted media of exchange have been and are units of outside money and inside-money claims to outside money. Inside money is naturally denominated in units of the cash to which it is a claim, as each bank note or bank deposit is a claim to a particular number of units of outside money. The distinguishing feature of outside money is that it does not constitute a redeemable claim to any physical asset. Whatever may be the bookkeeping conventions with regard to its issue, fiat money, as a form of outside money, is not in fact a contractual debt liability of any agent or institution. The world has known both commodity outside money—gold and silver coins provide the most familiar example—and fiat outside money. The latter typically originated as monopoly issued inside money whose redeemability was suspended after it had gained currency. In all cases the outside monetary unit naturally functions as the unit of account. This is because prices are naturally quoted in the units of the solitary item (or set of items, identically denominated because secondary members of the set are claims to a primary member) that will routinely be accepted as payment.

To mount a critique of cashless payments systems, one must give reasons for the emergence and prevalence of outside money as a generally accepted medium of exchange and unit of account. The reasons given here delve back to the origins of money.

The Origin of Commodity Money

The classic invisible-hand explanation of the emergence of money from an initial state of barter was given by Carl Menger (1892).

Under barter, each agent, attempting to transform his initial endowment into his desired final consumption bundle through direct exchange, confronts the problem of finding a second agent who both offers for sale what the first wishes to buy and is willing to accept in payment what the first has to sell. The typical agent can achieve his goal more economically if, instead of searching for this rare or even nonexistent match, he exchanges his endowment for more widely acceptable commodities that he may in turn readily exchange for the goods he ultimately wishes to consume. Accordingly, he accumulates a trading inventory of highly salable items. These allow him to economize on search costs by raising the probability that he may, in any given number of samplings among sellers, make desired purchases. In this situation, the superior salability of certain items becomes self-reinforcing: the knowledge that other traders will accept an item with high probability raises its acceptability to each particular trader. A network of traders will therefore converge on one or a small number of items as general media of exchange. The supreme salability of these items then distinguishes them from all other commodities. They have spontaneously become money.[7] Historically gold and silver emerged as money in economically advanced nations through this process.

It should be readily apparent by extension of this perspective on the origin of money that a unit of account emerges together with and wedded to a medium of exchange. A seller pursues his self-interest by posting prices in units of the commodities he is routinely willing to accept as media of exchange. This practice economizes on time spent in negotiation over what commodities are acceptable in payment and at what rate of exchange. More importantly, it economizes on the information necessary for the buyer's and the seller's economic calculation. Posting prices in terms of a numeraire commodity not routinely accepted in payment, by contrast, would force buyer and seller to know and agree upon the numeraire price of the payment media due. This numeraire price of the payment medium would naturally be subject to fluctuation, so that updated information would be necessary. Furthermore, a numeraire commodity not accepted as an exchange medium would be subject to greater bid-ask spreads in barter against other commodities, as by hypothesis it is less salable than a generally accepted medium of exchange. It would therefore serve less well as a tool of economic calculation.[8]

It is worth emphasizing, as Menger emphasized with respect to the genesis of a general medium of exchange, that a collective decision is in no way necessary for the emergence of a clearly defined common unit of account. This point seems to have escaped those authors who consider monetary units to be the creatures of government proclamations.

Coinage

The evolution of monetary institutions does not, of course, stop with the emergence of commodity money. One may trace further steps that take place in an uregulated competitive environment. Supposing that gold has emerged as primary money, the next logical step (economization of the costs of using the metal in transactions) is accomplished by the institution of coinage. Coined metal enjoys greater acceptability than uncoined metal (for example, gold dust) due to the lower cost of determining its true bullion content. The ease of authentication is further enhanced by the institution of brand names in minting: once a mint's products are trusted to be of the weight and fineness stated on their face, its coins may pass by tale. Transactors may then forego weighing and assaying each piece of metal tendered in payment. The demand for readily authenticated pieces of gold will therefore give rise to a market in minting services. Each mint strives to maintain a reputation for uniformly high quality, lest it lose customers to its rivals by imposing higher authentication costs.[9] In competitive equilibrium, the mintage fee will be just sufficient to earn each minter the normal rate of return on investment. Self-interest will lead all mints in an economy to denominate coins in terms of a unit of standard weight and fineness. A mint doing otherwise would inconvenience its customers. The precise definition of the unit is itself unimportant; it may be based on preexisting custom in measuring the bullion content of uncoined gold, or it may be adopted from the coinage of an early reputable mint. This unit then serves as the unit of account.

Competitive private minting industries have been comparatively rare historically. Governments have typically monopolized the supply of minting services. In a noncompetitive situation, where debased government-issued coins circulate, the bullion content of an earlier full-weight coin may continue to serve as unit of account though no existing coin measures up to that content. This is the phenomenon of "ghost money," which is sometimes misleadingly cited as an example of divorce between the unit of account and the medium of exchange.[10] In fact, both the unit of account and the medium of exchange continue to be quantities of gold. The unit-of-account value of any particular coin in circulation is a question of its weight and fineness, not of variable market exchange rates. The unit of account and medium of exchange have not become distinct commodities, only distinct quantities of the same commodity. The informational difficulties posed by a numeraire which is not a payment medium, and whose exchange value may vary in terms of payment media, do not arise. The minor inconvenience that does arise may be attributed to the absence of competitive conditions. Under competitive conditions, a debasing mint would find that money users reject its products in favor of full-weight coins.

Bank Liabilities

The emergence of precious metals as money, and subsequently of coins as their common form comes about in a free economy as the undesigned outcome of decentralized pursuit of self-interest. The genesis of inside monies may be similarly explained. Bank liabilities originate as claims to specie deposited with bankers (hence the term "deposits"; Fama's use of this term to denote shares in a money-market fund is misleading). In medieval Italy the first bankers were money changers; in London they were goldsmiths.

Claims to specie assume a monetary character when bankers discover profit in the business of effecting the payments one depositor wishes to make to another by direct transfer of bank balances from the one to the other. Checks are today the familiar means of signaling the bank to perform a transfer of balances, but increasingly common paperless electronic means do nothing to change the essential nature of the transaction. Bank notes—claims to bank specie transferable without bank intervention and payable to the bearer on demand—similarly emerge as a means of payment.[11] Bank notes naturally find the greatest acceptance when denominated as round multiples of the specie unit that has previously become the standard unit of account. Money users find each form of redeemable claim to bank specie more economical to use for many purposes than actual specie. Bankers are recompensed for providing these instruments by the interest they earn on assets corresponding to the fraction of their liabilities not matched by specie on their balance sheets, or (in the case of deposits) by direct fees for the transfer service. In an unregulated system, the banks pay competitive rates of interest on their deposits. Due to the costliness of doing so, they are unlikely to pay interest on their notes.[12]

An invisible-hand process can be shown to account for the emergence of an interbank clearinghouse in a competitive banking system (White 1984, 19–22). Briefly, each member of a pair of banks profitably enhances the moneyness of its notes and deposits relative to specie by agreeing to accept one another's notes and deposits at face value as tendered by customers for deposit or loan repayment. Mutual acceptance of liabilities is naturally accompanied by an arrangement for periodic settlement of the claims each bank collects against the other. The potential gains from these bilateral arrangements are not exhausted until all banking companies in a region belong to a single clearinghouse system.

In the absence of regulation, members of the clearinghouse will be able to economize on specie transshipments by settling balances partly through the transfer of highly marketable interest-bearing assets. Specie redeemability remains essential to the economical functioning of the mutual acceptance arrangement, however, as the means by which all bank liabilities have their value fixed in terms of the unit of account. The acceptance of their notes at fixed par values spares the banks and their customers exchange risk and calculational inconvenience, and is therefore integral to the function of acceptance arrangements in enhancing the moneyness of the participating banks' liabilities.

In the absence of regulation then a competitive banking system of the following sort emerges. The stock of exchange media consists of specie in the hands of the public plus numerous brands of redeemable bank notes plus transferable bank deposits. The self-interest of issuers insures that notes circulate at par, that is, at unit-of-account values fully equal to the number of specie units to which they are claims.[13] Transferable deposits bear a competitive rate of interest, subject to competitive charges for transfer services. The nominal quantities of specie, notes, and transferable deposits held by the public are determined not by government regulation of the monetary base, but by the real demand to hold those assets divided by the purchasing power of specie. Each bank determines its holdings of specie reserves by equating at the margin the cost of foregone interest to the benefit of reduced risk of illiquidity. Total specie reserves are simply a summation of these holdings across banks.[14]

The transition from a specie-based competitive banking system to a fiat-currency-based system is most readily made in two steps: government creation of a central bank, whose specie-redeemable liabilities displace specie as a commercial bank reserve asset; and suspension of redeemability for central bank liabilities. The supply of banking services may continue to be competitive, but the nominal quantity of money is now scaled to the central bank's determination of the monetary base.

Note what happens to the unit of account in the transition of fiat money. At no point does it cease to be defined in units of the basic outside-money medium of exchange. The status of basic medium of exchange, however, passes from specie alone to a straddle between specie and a redeemable central-bank currency denominated in specie units (dollars, pounds sterling, etc.), then exclusively to the no-longer-redeemable central-bank currency (still bearing the same name). In this way the economy acquires a noncommodity outside money with positive exchange value. Paper money is able to function as the basic medium of exchange because it previously functioned as a secondary medium of exchange.[15]

CASHLESS COMPETITIVE PAYMENTS SYSTEMS: CRITIQUE

In light of the evolution of money and banking, models of noncurrency-based payments systems are of doubtful value for modeling current institutions or predicting future arrangements. We lack a coherent account of how a cashless payments system is consistent with or might emerge from the currency-based payments systems the world has known. The various models of cashless payments systems can nonetheless serve a heuristic function: they serve to illuminate monetary institutions in the real world by contrast to the abstractions of a world without outside money. Greenfield and Yeager deliberately put their model to such use. Fama may also have had this purpose in mind, for he later introduces outside currency into his model after first abstracting from it. These models play a similar role in the present discussion: I hope to illuminate the importance of the causal-genetic processes behind monetary institutions, particularly the unit of account, by contrast to models seemingly inconsistent with these processes.[16]

The Disappearance of Demand Deposits

Could a monetary system based on outside currency (specie or fiat currency) spontaneously evolve into a cashless competitive payments system of the sort envisioned by Black, Fama, Greenfield, and Yeager? Three steps are necessary to make the transition: (1) disappearance of ordinary inside money; (2) disappearance of outside money; and (3) redefinition of the unit of account in terms of a numeraire other than outside money. This section considers the first of these steps. For expositional convenience it focuses on demand deposits, though in the past bank notes have also been important as inside money. The term inside money here denotes ready claims to outside currency. These are distinct from shares in a managed portfolio of assets.

Fama envisions a world in which "competitive unregulated banks provide a wide variety of portfolios against which depositors can hold claims" (1982, 15). In other words, bank deposits no longer constitute claims to cash, but are instead akin to transferable shares in mutual funds and, hence, "can be tailored to have the characteristics of any form of marketable wealth" (Fama, 1980, 43). Fama unfortunately fails to show that the outcome of unregulated competition would be the total domination of interest-bearing demand deposits by mutual fund shares. In fact, this outcome is unlikely, even apart from the question of which can provide payments services more efficiently. Demand deposits, being ready debt claims, are potentially superior to mutual fund shares, which are equity claims, in at least one respect. The value of a deposit may be contractually guaranteed to increase over time at a preannounced rate of interest.

Its unit-of-account value at a future date is certain so long as the bank continues to honor its obligation to redeem its deposits on demand. No such contractual guarantee may be made with respect to an equity claim. A mutual fund is obligated to pay out after the fact its actual earnings, so that the yield on fund shares cannot be predetermined. In the absence of deposit-rate-ceiling regulation, the range of anticipated possible returns from holding fund shares need not lie entirely above the deposit interest rate. Risk-diversifying portfolio owners might therefore not divest themselves entirely of demand deposits, even given a higher mean yield on mutual funds. It is true that the characteristic pledge of money-market mutual funds to maintain a fixed share price (or rather the policy of investing exclusively in short-term highly reputable securities so that the pledge can be kept) makes fund shares akin to demand deposits in having near-zero risk of negative nominal yield over any period. The difference between predetermined and postdetermined yields—between debt and equity—nonetheless remains. The historical fact is that deposit banking did not naturally grow up on an equity basis.[17]

The more important reason why demand deposits may survive even under unregulated competition is that the payments system they provide is, given the conditions that lead to the emergence of money, less costly. This cost differential is suggested by the fact that a checkable money-market fund today typically imposes a $500 minimum on checks written against shares in the fund. The comparative costliness of check-writing against money-market funds in their present form arises from the fact that checks written against a fund require it either (1) to incur the transactions costs of selling securities plus the cost of transmitting the receipts to the payee, or (2), what is presumably less costly and the method actually used, to draw against a demand deposit with a commercial bank held as one of the fund's assets.[18] It is evident that effecting a payment by writing a check against a fund, which in turn draws down its demand deposit, must be more costly than directly effecting the payment by writing a check against the payer's own demand deposit. In the present world the checkable money market fund rides piggyback upon the banking system.

The check-writing feature of money market mutual funds relies on a money-transfer system for the obvious reason that sellers of commodities generally wish to be paid in money and not in other assets. Checks written on a money-market fund are generally acceptable in payment only because to the recipient they represent a transfer of inside money, that is, of cash-redeemable bank deposits. Money's unique acceptability as a routine means of payment is, as we have seen, an essential property conferred on it by the Mengerian convergence process that engenders money. Every form of marketable wealth could serve generally as a medium of exchange only in a world where all forms of wealth begin and remain equally marketable. Outside a Walrasian general equilibrium setting, this is difficult to imagine.

There are no obstacles in principle to the spontaneous emergence of an interfund clearing system that does not rely on transfers of inside money. If mutual funds really could provide payments services efficiently, it would be natural to expect money-market funds in the present system, unless prevented by law, to begin announcing bilateral or multilateral arrangements to permit check-writing in any amount for purposes of transferring wealth to accounts in participating funds. By this device, each participating fund would enhance the spendability and, hence, desirability of its shares relative to nonparticipating shares and demand deposits. As yet this has not happened. At present, money market funds rarely allow check-writing for unlimitedly small amounts, even for transfer of shares to another customer of the same fund. This is difficult to reconcile with the idea that fund shares are so routinely acceptable that they could dominate inside money as a means of payment.

This argument does not rule out the development of an interfund money-transfer system that allows cash withdrawals, or what would be identical, banks offering checkable mutual fund accounts with direct access to an interbank clearing mechanism. The analytical question—why money-transfer and cash-inventory services should be jointly produced with deposits at lower cost than with mutual fund shares—awaits further research. But it seems clear that the major impetus to the use of mutual funds for check-writing purposes, a use negligible before 1974, has been Regulation Q's prohibition of competitive interest rates on checkable bank deposits. With this ceiling largely lifted, the rationale for joining money-transfer services to mutual funds has largely disappeared.[19]

In a model competitive payments system devoid of cash or genuine demand deposits, payments effected via check-writing against fund shares obviously do not work by transfers of money. Instead, a check written against Fund A in favor of a customer of Fund B is supposed to occasion a transfer of nonmonetary assets from Fund A to Fund B via a clearing arrangement (Greenfield and Yeager, p. 307). These two funds must have previously entered a mutual acceptance arrangement of the sort (described earlier) arising in a free-banking system. The clearing mechanism has to be slightly different, however, in the following respect. Fund B, in accepting checks written on Fund A, does not possess a claim to Fund A's vault cash of a specific quantity. Instead, Fund B possesses a claim to Fund A's assets of a specific value. Checks are written, and interbank clearing balances computed in units of account, as at present. But a check no longer transfers a claim to so many physical units of outside currency; it instead transfers ownership of earning assets with a market value of so much. The interfund clearing arrangement has to specify what types of assets are acceptable in settlement of adverse balances. So does an interbank clearing arrangement, if it is to economize on physical transfers of non-interest bearing currency. But in doing so, the interbank clearing arrangement does not reduce its reliance on cash redeemability as the means by which the unit-of-account value of bank liabilities is fixed and the general acceptability of bank liabilities is maintained.

An apparent disadvantage of bank deposits in the form of ready claims to predetermined quantities of currency, in contrast to fund shares, is the possibility that a bank might become insolvent and thereby unable to honor all the claims presented to it for redemption. (Illiquidity is no greater problem for a bank than for a mutual fund that allows check-writing and cash withdrawals.) A mutual fund cannot become insolvent: as it issues no liabilities in the strict sense, but only equities, it cannot have liabilities in excess of its assets. A money-market fund can legally break its pledge to maintain a fixed share price if a sharp fall in the value of its assets makes a reduction necessary. A bank lacks the flexibility to reduce its deposit liabilities in a similar way without going into bankruptcy. In a laissez-faire monetary system, bank deposits would not be government insured. Depositor's fears of insolvency might be adequately addressed, however, by high capital-asset ratios, by private deposit insurance, by forms of organization giving the bank's stockholders extended personal liability for its debts, or by some other means.[20] Hence it is not obvious that checkable mutual funds would dominate demand deposits on grounds of lesser risk. The debt form of deposits does insulate depositors from sharing in portfolio losses that leave equity positive.

The difference between demand deposits and fund shares, and the plausible nondisappearance of demand deposits under freely competitive conditions, requires the revision of several propositions put forth by Fama (1982, pp. 2–8). First, while outside currency and fund shares are indeed not perfect substitutes whose supplies may with any obvious sense be aggregated, and while outside currency and demand deposits are also not perfect substitutes, demand deposits (and bank notes) may sensibly be aggregated with outside currency held by the nonbank public in a measure of the quantity of money. The econometric use of this aggregate is a separate question. Second, the supply of demand deposits will likely be important in the determination of the price level for a closed economy with a competitive, unregulated banking system. Even if the determination of the price level in that economy is most appropriately modeled in terms of the supply and demand for outside money alone, demand deposits are presumably a close substitute on the demand side. Third, the concept of money clearly does play a role in the transactions services made available through demand deposits. Fourth, a bank using the clearing mechanism of an unregulated banking system holds claims against the cash reserves of other banks, not against their portfolios.[21]

The Disappearance of Outside Money

Might outside money disappear with the evolution of competitive payments mechanisms? This question boils down to the disappearance of outside currency. In the present American banking system, the deposits of member banks with the Federal Reserve may be regarded as a form of outside money (though they are claims to Federal Reserve notes, their quantity is not regulated by the existing quantity of those notes). This form of outside money is an artifact of regulation, however; in an unregulated banking system with a private clearing mechanism and no central bank, outside currency (say, specie or fiat currency) would be the only form of outside money.

The authors whose models have been considered here all recognize that currency will continue in use so long as manual transfer of currency remains the least costly method for accomplishing certain transactions. Not only is currency (1) more convenient to use in small payments, but (2) its acceptance, unlike acceptance of personal checks, entails no risk that the payer's funds may be insufficient, and (3) its use leaves behind no possibly incriminating records of payment. These authors all think it coherent, however, to suppose that all currency is inside currency. Pieces of such currency would be akin to bank notes, except that they would constitute claims against the portfolios of the issuing funds rather than claims to cash.[22]

Cashlessness has an interesting implication. Bonds in the cashless world cannot be what they are in our world, claims to future streams of money payments. Instead, they must be claims to future payments of fund shares. This may seem to raise a problem of circularity where fund shares are in turn claims to ownership of bonds. It may seem that we would then have bonds which are merely indirect claims to numbers of similar bonds, leaving the value of all such bonds undetermined. As Greenfield and Yeager (p. 313) indicate, however, bond coupons and all other contractual payments would not be specified in portfolio fractions (so many other bonds), but instead in numeraire units (so many "bundles-worth"). With coupon payments denominated in units of account, the prices of bonds would be determined just as they are today. With bonds having determinate unit-of-account prices, claims against funds (including pieces of inside currency) could sensibly be claims to so many units-of-account-worth of bonds, rather than to so many bonds. Circularity is thereby avoided.[23]

The natural question to ask from an evolutionary perspective is whether there is any plausible reason for outside currency to disappear in a payments system freed from anticompetitive regulation. I have explained above that the emergence of particular commodities as money is not wholly accidental, but a consequence of their superior saleability. Black (1970, 14) hypothesizes the use of shares of a portfolio of common stock as money, that is, as a generally accepted medium of exchange. There are good reasons, however, to doubt that such an item would ever become the most salable in an economy. The primary reason is that the institution of common stock is unlikely to arise in a premonetary economy because the division of labor it presupposes would not exist there. Even were stock shares to emerge in a barter economy, it is difficult to conceive of their being more salable than the most widely salable of commodities. Arising in an already monetized economy (this is Black's scenario), shares of stock are from the outset routinely sold against money and not against any other good. They lack the saleability of money. And this inferior salability is self-reinforcing: no trader routinely accepts shares of stock or shares of a portfolio of stocks when he cannot expect to be able to spend them easily. Each trader finds the use of shares an inefficient medium of exchange due to high information and search costs. The "inefficiencies" of commodity money cited by Black would exceed the inefficiencies of common-stock money only in a world in which common stock approached the salability of commodity money.

For analogous reasons it should be apparent that a currency system in which the basic money is redeemable for a basket of nonmonetary commodities would not arise spontaneously in an unregulated setting. A claim to a basket of commodities would not originally emerge as money, since in a barter setting it would be less salable then the most salable of its components. Nor would it supplant the original monetary commodity. This is not to deny, however, that one money (say, silver or domestic fiat currency) may be spontaneously supplanted by another (say, gold or foreign fiat currency) in a region where both have been circulating internally, or where external trade with neighboring regions is conducted in their different money. A switch may come about because the transactions conducted in the second money grow in relative importance, or because the first money experiences an exogenously caused ongoing relative decline in purchasing power.

The Divorce of the Unit of Account from the Medium of Exchange

For reasons already suggested, a unit of account emerges wedded to a general medium of exchange. Prices are universally posted in the characteristic units of a medium or set of media that sellers are routinely prepared to accept in exchange. This process is self-reinforcing: a buyer or seller who communicated bid or ask offers in nonstandard units would impose calculation costs on potential trading partners. For this reason the unit of account remains wedded to the medium of exchange.

In an inflationary environment it is certainly possible for a unit of stable purchasing power to dispace the depreciating currency unit as the unit of account voluntarily adopted in contracts calling for payments at future dates. An example of a stable unit would be the "constant dollar" defined by a base-year price index. There is no tendency for spot prices to be indexed in this way, however. Indeed the perpetuation of nonindexed spot prices is presupposed by indexing, which uses current nominal prices to compute the current-dollar equivalent of a constant-dollar sum.

The unit of account sticks with the medium of exchange even through the transition from commodity-based to fiat currency. A historical example is instructive here. In the suspension period of the Napoleonic Wars, 1797–1819 in Britain, Bank of England notes and deposits became the basic outside money.[24] Gold coins ceased to circulate. The unit of account, the pound sterling, stuck with the actual medium of exchange rather than with a now-abstract gold definition. The pounds-sterling price of gold fluctuated rather than the pounds-sterling price of Bank of England notes. Commodity prices rose with the expansion of Bank of England notes and deposits, while the unit-of-account value of a bank note or deposit remained fixed.

CONCLUSION

In a decentralized and unregulated economy in which all property is not equally saleable, outside money emerges as most the salable commodity and persists as a general medium of exchange. Inside monies arise and persist on the basis of their convertibility into outside money. The characteristic unit of outside money naturally defines the unit of account, as prices are naturally posted by traders in terms of the item sellers will routinely accept in payment.

In a Walrasian world where the auctioneer renders all commodities equally salable, and therefore equally suitable for use in indirect exchange, payment in any commodity can be accepted indifferently. Tatonnement may proceed without outside money. Any commodity or bundle of commodities can serve as unit of account, the auctioneer's choice of a unit of account being unconstrained by any economic considerations. The payments system appropriate for a Walrasian world, however, is inappropriate in our world of decentralized trade involving goods of unequal marketability. The convenience of traders in our world dictates outside money whose units define the unit of account. Deregulation of the payments system in our world does not imply disappearance of outside money, nor divorce of the unit of account from the basic outside-money medium of exchange.

Notes

1. Fischer Black (1970), Eugene Fama (1980; 1982), Robert Hall (1981; 1982a, 1982b), Robert Greenfield and Leland Yeager (1983). At the other extreme, F. A. Hayek (1978) and Benjamin Klein (1974) have conceived of a great multiplicity of parallel base monies and standards. Criticism of the latter models is left implicit in what follows.
2. Currency in this real world is supposed to be issued by the government, but only on request of the banks, in exchange for reduction of government debt with the banks. For criticism, see note 22 below.
3. I am indebted to Robert Greenfield for this point.
4. This result of a search through the literature (by Fama) was reported to me by Bob Hall. It evidently excludes self-citations by Black.
5. See Ernst Baltensperger (1980, 4–6). In the competitive banking system of Scotland prior to 1844, to give a historical example, banks held positive quantities of specie as reserves against redemptions of liabilities despite the absence of reserve requirements and despite the fact, consistent with Fama's hypothesis of how a competitive system would operate, that the banks settled claims among themselves by transfer of readily marketable interest-bearing assets, namely Exchequer bills. On this episode, see my 1984 book, chap. 2.
6. By "predetermined" I do not mean that deposit interest rates never vary, but that rates are contractually set before the period to which they apply. They are not calculated afterward on the basis of portfolio performance, as in the case of mutual fund shares. For further discussion, see "The Disappearance of Demand Deposits."
7. For a modern version of this theory, see Robert Jones (1976). See also Ludwig von Mises (1971, 30–34). Menger defines "salability" more or

less as the narrowness of the effective bid-ask spread, but construes this broadly to include spatial and temporal dimensions.

8. This paragraph supposes a world in which fiduciary payment media have not yet appeared. To avoid a possible misinterpretation (Mott 1989; Yeager 1989) let me note that the problems of transactional and calculational inconvenience it cites are not necessarily present in an advanced system in which physical specimens of the numeraire are not routinely accepted. So long as the common payment media are meaningfully denominated in units of the numeraire, that is, do not have a bid-ask spread or fluctuating price in terms of the numeraire, the unit of account remains in the relevant sense "wedded to" the media of exchange.

9. For examples of this process at work in the United States, where some three dozen private mints operated in the gold rush regions of the nineteenth century, see Donald Kagin (1981). Black (1972, 811) inaccurately identifies privately minted coins as a form of inside money. Armen Alchian's (1977) account of the selection of a commodity money relies solely on economization of authentication costs. In my view, this explains the emergence of standardized forms of money. But as far as the origin of money itself goes, economization of authentication costs is subsidiary to economization of search costs through holding of highly salable commodities. Easy authentification is simply one among several properties contributing to ready salability.

10. On "ghost monies," see Carlo Cipolla (1956, chap. 4). The misleading claim that these represent abstract units of account is made by Patinkin (1965, 15). While it is true that a unit of ghost money had no exact counterpart among existing coins, each of these coins bore a fixed value relationship to the unit based on relative silver bullion content. For purposes of pricing and calculation, the situation is similar to that prevailing today in the Italian monetary system, where one-lira coins and notes no longer circulate.

11. On the early history of European banking, see Raymond de Roover (1956, chap. 5).

12. See my book (1984, 8–9). Fama (1982, 14–15) comes to the same conclusion for currency that is not a claim to outside money. Note that today's traveler's checks do not bear interest.

13. That bank notes fell below par when they crossed state borders— reflecting risk and transportation costs of accomplishing redemption— in the American "free-banking" era was due to the legal prohibition on interstate branch banking. In the freer Scottish system, no such inconvenience was experienced.

14. This system is spelled out in my book (1984, chap. 1). The statement of marginal conditions in the text assumes equal marginal operating costs of holding various assets. The basic paradigm of bank optimization is set forth by Baltensperger.

15. This historical account may explain more plausibly than the overlap-ping-generations model of fiat money why intrinsically useless fiat money has positive value. For the overlapping-generations model, see Neil Wallace (1980).
16. Greenfield and Yeager also use the cashless competitive payments sys-tem as a model for political reform of payments practices. Criticism of that use is left to the following chapter.
17. In medieval times bank deposits were treated as equity claims, but this treatment was devised to evade church and state prohibitions against the payment of interest on debt. Again see de Roover (1956, 201–2).
18. All funds whose prospectuses I have examined hold a small percentage of their assets (less than one percent) in the form of a demand deposit with a commercial bank for the purpose of honoring redemption checks (and purchasing securities).
19. Two caveats are in order: (1) The 1982 Garn-St. Germain Act authoriz-ing Super NOW accounts (checking accounts with no legal interest ceiling) denies these accounts to business firms, leaving firms a reason for using money-market-fund or sweep accounts for check-writing. (2) So long as demand deposits are in effect taxed by the imposition of reserve requirements, there remains a rationale for hybrid accounts. The reason why money-market mutual funds (like banks) do not price their money-transfer services explicitly may be found in the taxation of ex-plicit interest but nontaxation of gratuitous services.
20. Unlimited liability was a feature of the Scottish free-banking system. Depositors' losses due to bank insolvencies were completely negligible, as failures were rare and the losses fell upon shareholders.
21. Only the last of these sentences rectifies an incorrect statement Fama makes about a banking system. The others contrast a banking system to his characterization of a payments system operated by mutual funds.
22. Fama (1982, 9–11) and Greenfield and Yeager (1983, 307–8) clearly envision currency issued exclusively by mutual funds. Black (1970, 13–14) introduces government-issued currency, but erroneously believes that the nominal quantity of this currency will be endogenously deter-mined. He apparently fails to see or denies that an excess of supply of government-issued currency at a given level of prices will be worked off through a rise in prices, not through retirement of the excess currency. In another paper (1972), Black advances a doctrine of the passivity of outside money.
23. This paragraph replaces a misconceived paragraph in the earlier pub-lished version of this essay.
24. Technically they were not fiat money, for resumption at a later date was both anticipated and realized. In von Mises' terminology they were credit money (1971, 483).

References

Alchian, Armen. 1977. "Why Money?" *Journal of Money, Credit, and Banking*, 9: 133–40.

Baltensperger, Ernst. 1980. "Alternative Approaches to the Theory of the Banking Firm." *Journal of Monetary Economics*, 6:1–37.

Black, Fischer. 1970. "Banking and Interest Rates in a World Without Money: The Effects of Uncontrolled Banking." *Journal of Bank Research*, 1: 9–20.

———. 1972. "Active and Passive Monetary Policy in a Neoclassical Model." *Journal of Finance*, 27: 801–14.

Cipolla, Carlo M. 1956. *Money, Prices, and Civilization in the Mediterranean World: Fifth to Seventeenth Century*. Princeton: Princeton University Press.

de Roover, Raymond. 1956. *Business, Banking, and Economic Thought in Late Medieval and Early Modern Europe*. Chicago: Chicago University Press.

Fama, Eugene F. 1980. "Banking in the Theory of Finance." *Journal of Monetary Economics*, 6: 39–57.

———. 1982. "Fiduciary Currency and Commodity Standards." Mimeograph.

Girton, Lance, and Roper, Don. 1981. "Theory and Implications of Currency Substitution." *Journal of Money, Credit, and Banking*, 13: 12–30.

Greenfield, Robert L., and Yeager, Leland B. 1983. "A Laissez-Faire Approach to Monetary Stability." *Journal of Money, Credit, and Banking*, 15: 301–15.

Hall, Robert E. 1981. "The Government and the Monetary Unit." Mimeograph.

———. 1982a. "Explorations in the Gold Standard and Related Policies for Stabilizing the Dollar." In *Inflation: Causes and Effects*, edited by Robert E. Hall. Chicago: Chicago University Press for the National Bureau of Economic Research.

———. 1982b. *"Monetary Trends in the United States and the United Kingdom:* A Review from the Perspective of New Developments in Monetary Economics." *Journal of Economic Literature*, 20: 1552–56.

Hayek, F. A. 1978. *The Denationalisation of Money*, 2d ed. London: Institute of Economic Affairs.

Jones, Robert A. 1976. "The Origin and Development of Media of Exchange." *Journal of Political Economy*, 84: 757–75.

Kagin, Donald H. 1981. *Private Gold Coins and Patterns of the United States*. New York: Arco Publishing.

Klein, Benjamin. 1974. "The Competitive Supply of Money." *Journal of Money, Credit, and Banking*, 6: 423–53.

Menger, Carl. 1892. "On the Origin of Money." *Economic Journal*, 2: 239–55.

Mott, Tracy. 1989. "A Post Keynesian Perpective on a 'Cashless Competitive Payments System.' " *Journal of Post Keynesian Economics,* in press.

Patinkin, Don. 1965. *Money, Interest, and Prices,* 2d ed. New York: Harper & Row.

Von Mises, Ludwig. 1971. *The Theory of Money and Credit,* trans. H. E. Batson, rev. ed. Irvington-on-Hudson, N. Y.: Foundation for Economic Education.

Wallace, Neil. 1980. "The Overlapping Generations Model of Fiat Money." In *Models of Monetary Economics,* edited by John H. Karekan and Neil Wallace. Minneapolis: Federal Reserve Bank of Minneapolis.

White, Lawrence H. 1984. *Free Banking in Britain: Theory, Experience, and Debate, 1800–1845.* Cambridge: Cambridge University Press.

Yeager, Leland B. 1989. "A Competitive Payments System: Some Objections Considered." *Journal of Post Keynesian Economics,* in press.

10

Competitive Payments Systems: Reply

My 1984 article, "Competitive Payments Systems and the Unit of Account," critically reviewed the work of several authors who have conceived of competitive payments systems devoid of outside money and free of any link between payment media and the unit of account. I concluded that cashlessness, and the divorce of the unit of account from own-units of payment media, are not natural products of unrestricted competition. Further, some imagined systems incorporating these features suffer from internal incoherence. Robert Greenfield and Leland Yeager (1986) register three principal complaints about my treatment of their 1983 contribution to this literature. First, I did not appreciate just how operational they think the unit of account in their system (what they call the "BFH system") really is. Second, I made an argument, concerning the circularity of bonds payable only in bonds, which they find difficult to understand. Third, and evidently most importantly, they believe that I argued "as if" to question the desirability of their system as a serious proposal for monetary reform. I will respond to each of these complaints in turn.

OPERATIONALITY

The issue of whether the unit of account in a Greenfield-Yeager system is operational, that is, fit for proper functioning, can be framed in various ways. The narrowest of these is whether a Walrasian auctioneer could coherently use the unit. Greenfield and Yeager apparently agree with me that an affirmative answer to that question does not establish very much, for they insist (justifiably) that they

Reprinted, with permission, from *American Economic Review*, vol. 76, no. 4 (September 1986).

have framed the issue more broadly than that. They argue that "honest-to-goodness" decentralized trading would not pry the unit denominating payment accounts (demand deposits or checkable equity holdings) away from a commodity-bundle definition of the unit of account initially adopted. No divorce could come about, they say, because the only plausible alternative unit for denominating payment accounts would be some quantity of a common medium of exchange, and their system has no common medium of exchange.

Let us suppose, for the sake of argument, that a Greenfield-Yeager system has been established. Would market forces subsequently promote the emergence of a common medium of exchange, or would they prevent such a development? As far as I can tell, Greenfield and Yeager have not addressed this question. (Nor have I previously.) They do state that "under [our] system, which would eschew government money, no such single homogeneous medium of exchange would exist" (p. 848). But surely absence of government money does not insure absence of *any* homogeneous outside money: a specie standard with private mints and no government bank furnishes a conceptual counterexample.[1]

In Carl Menger's theory of the origin of money, which my article recounted, the needs of hand-to-hand traders promote the emergence of a common medium of exchange which eventually takes the form of an outside currency. For present purposes, however, I grant the assumption that in a sophisticated payments system the public can happily do without an outside currency. Market pressure for a common medium of exchange would instead be felt most strongly at the clearinghouse. (For simplicity, assume that a single clearinghouse covers the entire economy.) Greenfield and Yeager speak of clearing balances being settled by transfer of nonhomogeneous "redemption property" (1986, 848; 1983, 307). They do not further elaborate except to speculate that the settlement assets agreed upon by member funds might consist of "specified securities." Already this recognizes the crucial point that not all assets are equally acceptable to all traders as payment.

How then are settlement assets and their values agreed upon? Certainly it would not be feasible to negotiate each settlement individually. Suppose instead that there is a pre-approved list of specified securities. Who chooses the securities to be remitted in a particular day's settlement? It does not seem workable to let the paying member fund make the choice. Assuming end-of-day settlement using securities evaluated at closing prices, the fund would have an incentive to remit securities which up-to-the-minute news indicated would be likely to lose the most value between that day's (or the most recent market day's) closing and the next market day's opening. And it could profit the fund to bid up a closing security price in order to lock in an artificially high price at which to unload a great quantity of the security (including the quantity it had just purchased). There would be even graver problems with evaluation and choice of securities for purposes of intraday settlement, when the spread between bid and ask prices is obvious. For these reasons, there would be market pressure for a homogeneous settlement asset. The clearinghouse can provide such an asset by holding member fund redemption property on account, and pooling it, giving each fund homogeneous shares in the clearinghouse portfolio (hereafter *CP*). The clearinghouse can then make settlement instantaneously by transfer of *CP* shares between accounts. That ability is important in light of the fact that wire transfers account for approximately three-fourths of all transactions in the United States today in unit-of-account volume (Maxwell Fry and Raburn Williams 1984, 6).

This arrangement makes the participating funds themselves owners of shares in a funds' fund, just as clearing banks today own deposits at a bankers' bank. More importantly, it gives *CP* shares many of the characteristics of outside money. The *CP* shares are effectively a redemption medium for transfers among ordinary commercial payment accounts, just as deposits at the Federal Reserve are in the present American banking system. Over-the-counter redeemability might also emerge. *CP* shares are routinely accepted as a medium of exchange, because no one will refuse to accept the ultimate clearing asset. A question requiring further thought is whether *CP* shares can be spent into existence, and, if so, with what consequences.

Does the *CP* share constitute a unit which could rival the government-chose commodity bundle as a unit of account? It does if the clearinghouse defines the *CP* share in "physical" terms, for example, one *CP* share equals 1.0 shares Alcoa common stock, 2.5 shares Burlington Northern stock, 1.7 shares Conoco stock, and so on down a list. The price of a *CP* share in terms of the government-stipulated numeraire would then vary day to day. Correspondingly, the *CP* share price of the commodity bundle to which all government accounting and obligations were indexed would vary from day to day. If, on the other hand, the clearinghouse were to denominate *CP* shares in unit-of-account terms, just as the typical money market mutual fund today fixes its share price at one dollar, then no rivalry would exist. The clearinghouse might well choose not to do so, however, in order to avoid the awkwardness of posting a price for acquisition and surrender of *CP* shares by funds, which could only be paid in bundles of primary securities, in units other than the units it would routinely accept and pay.

CIRCULARITY

I argued (in a misconceived paragraph, which I have now replaced) that there is a circularity problem in a Greenfield-Yeager system if two conditions simultaneously hold: (1) bonds are exclusively claims to streams of payment in fund shares; and (2) fund shares are claims to portfolios consisting exclusively of bonds. The problem as I saw it may perhaps be grasped more clearly by considering the absurdity of consols which are exclusively claims to future streams of similar consols.[2] Who would want to buy such a claim? A transactor attempting to value it faces an infinite regress. I now recognize (and have revised the previous essay to reflect the recognition) that no such circularity problem exists so long as a bond's coupons and principal are not specified in portfolio fractions (so many other bonds), but instead in numeraire units (so many "bundles-worth"). No infinite regress occurs when coupon payments are denominated in units of account. Bond prices can be determined just as they are today. All that is necessary is that transactors be able to form expectations regarding the purchasing power of the unit of account at each prospective date the bond promises to make a payment. Greenfield and Yeager are correct in suggesting that the pricing of bonds in their system poses no greater problem than the pricing of present-day bonds payable in fiat money. In fact the positive value of fiat money presents a seeming "bootstrap" paradox (the fiat dollar is valued by each person as a medium of exchange only because it is similarly valued by others) not encountered with a commodity-defined unit of account. This paradox can be resolved, as I argued in the previous essay (note 15) by understanding the historical transition from redeemable to irredeemable central bank liabilities. But to resolve it in this way is not to find any great solace in fiat money's iredeemability.

REFORM

Contrary to the first sentence of Greenfield and Yeager's comment, I did not treat their 1983 piece as a proposal for monetary reform. I therefore did *not* intend my conjectures about spontaneous evolution to "form the centerpiece of judgments about what is desirable now," as they suppose (p. 849). Instead, I deliberately and explicitly limited my critique of their system, and of the cashless competitive payments systems of Fisher Black and Eugene Fama, to questioning "their applicability for modeling current arrangements or predicting future arrangements" (p. 706). I thought that a purely analytical approach was consistent with the approach of Greenfield and Yeager who in their opening paragraph remark: "Regardless of who if anyone may actually advocate the system, contemplating it is instructive. It illuminates, by contrast, some characteristics of our existing and recent systems" (1983, 302). I agree fully with that. And I would add that most readers will probably find the idea of a cashless competitive payments system easier to contemplate seriously when it is presented as an analytical construct than when it is presented as a reform proposal. But I am willing to deviate from my original purely analytical orientation in order to address briefly here the issues raised by cashlessness as a reform proposal.

I do not at all wish to question Greenfield and Yeager's preference for "dismantling government domination of the existing system" (p. 849), that is, for moving to a private and unregulated payments system. (For what it is worth, I share that preference.) We agree that doing this entails deregulating banks and other financial institutions. There remains, however, the question of how to undo government's current control over the quantity of basic money. As they correctly insist, any approach requires deliberate policy actions that will condition the successor system. One avenue of reform (the one I happen to favor) is to take steps to enable private competitively issued money to supplant government fiat money. Commodity money, having historical precedent, is the most obvious form private outside money might take, but noncommodity monies as imagined by F. A. Hayek (1978) are also worth consideration. Greenfield and Yeager's alternative avenue is simply to abolish money.

In its starkest outlines, Greenfield and Yeager's argument for reform runs as follows: (1) Monetary payments systems inherently have important features which are socially undesirable. (2) Therefore it is desirable to abolish money. In advancing these two propositions their argument reminds me of S. Herbert Frankel's characterization of Keynes' outlook: "[I]t rests on the fear of money itself. . . . Keynes . . . sees money as distorting everything and wants the authority of the state to force money to reflect a less disturbing image" (1977, 3). Greenfield and Yeager, while fearing money, instead want the state to facilitate the abandonment of money. They propose that an effective and desirable way to abolish money is to have government announce and use a unit of account defined in terms of a bundle of goods so wide as to be totally unusable as a basic medium of exchange or outside money.[3]

The logical gap between steps 1 and 2 should be obvious. Granting that the use of money carries with it certain social costs (foregone benefits of barter) does not compel one to conclude that its costs outweigh its benefits. One of my purposes in tracing the spontaneous evolution of money, and in emphasizing the supreme salability of money, was to indicate that there are important benefits to using a common medium of exchange, namely in facilitating transaction. These benefits are never mentioned by Greenfield and Yeager, and seem to have been overlooked.[4] Such an oversight is surprising, given that Yeager is the author of a classic account of "the essential properties of a medium of exchange" which emphasizes money's supreme salability in comparison with other assets. In that paper, Yeager recognizes that money has uniquely low transactions costs, and explains that for an asset to have "the lowest transactions costs" means that "loosely speaking, it is the most convenient medium of exchange" (1968, 67). Surely the extra convenience of using money —of having a generally accepted asset for ultimate settlement—is a genuine benefit that ought not to be neglected in the evaluation of monetary versus nonmonetary payments systems.

Most of the advantages that Greenfield and Yeager (1983, 308–

11) claim for their system may be attained, I believe, without abolishing money. Reasonable stability in the purchasing power of the numeraire, an end to inflationary finance, competitive innovation in payments institutions, resistance to financial panics, and mitigation of macroeconomic difficulties through a demand-elastic supply of particular forms of payment media, would all be promoted by deregulation of banking (including the private issue of currency) combined with freezing or denationalizing outright the supply of base money.[5] In addition, either freezing or denationalizing the monetary base (the latter by redeeming fiat dollars for some commodity presently stockpiled by government) avoids an important disadvantage of cashlessness: the transition to cashlessness implies significant wealth losses to relatively heavy base-money holders.

Notes

1. Greenfield and Yeager (1986) add that payment account holdings would be nonhomogeneous, differing according to issuer. But this is logically unrelated, as the same counterexample shows, to the existence of a homogeneous outside money.
2. I borrow this example from Kevin D. Hoover (1985, 55).
3. Greenfield and Yeager (1983, 303) explicitly eschew state force against money users. Yet citizens will presumably be forced to pay taxes in media denominated in commodity bundles. It is nonetheless far from obvious, to anyone skeptical of the state of theory of money, that these measures would be sufficient to make private traders abandon dollars in order to adopt the new system.
4. Greenfield and Yeager do assert that their system would retain "convenient methods of payment" (1986, 848), for example, check-writing, but they evidently see no convenience in a common *medium* of payment.
5. George Selgin (1988) provides detailed arguments for these results, particularly the first, fourth, and fifth.

References

Frankel, S. Herbert. 1977. *Money: Two Philosophies.* Oxford: Basil Blackwell.

Fry, Maxwell J., and Williams, Raburn M. 1984. *American Money and Banking.* New York: John Wiley & Sons.

Greenfield, Robert L., and Yeager, Leland B. 1983. "A Laissez-Faire Approach to Monetary Stability." *Journal of Money, Credit, and Banking* 15: 302–15.

———. 1986. "Competitive Payments Systems: Comment." *American Economic Review* 76: 848–49.

Hayek, F. A. 1978. *The Denationalisation of Money*, 2d ed. London: Institute of Economic Affairs.

Hoover, Kevin D. 1985. "Causality and Invariance in the Money Supply Process." Ph.D. diss., Oxford University.

Selgin, George A. 1988. *"The Theory of Free Banking."* Totowa, N.J.: Rowmar and Littlefield.

White, Lawrence H. 1984. "Competitive Payments Systems and the Unit of Account." *American Economic Review* 74: 699–712.

Yeager, Leland B. 1968. "Essential Properties of a Medium of Exchange." *Kyklos* 21: 45–69.

11

A Subjectivist Perspective on the Definition and Identification of Money

In a clear statement of the subjectivist research program in economics, Professor Ludwig M. Lachmann instructed us that there are dual aspects to economic inquiry:

> Economics has two tasks. The first is to make the world around us intelligible in terms of human action and the pursuit of plans. The second is to trace the unintended consequences of such action.[1]

The present paper attempts to take these tasks seriously in discussing two very basic questions in the economics of money. The first question asks: What is the proper definition of money? The second question asks: What actual items in the modern economies of the nineteenth and twentieth centuries meet this definition?[2]

DEFINING MONEY

The question of the proper definition of money is really a question of the attributes essential to an item's being properly considered to be money. This question has been widely debated among economists. Dale K. Osborne has recently identified no fewer than ten approaches to the definition of money, each emphasizing a particular attribute.[3] From a subjectivist perspective, it is clear that the defining set of attributes of money is to be sought in the role that money plays (and alone plays) in the plans of individual economic agents. This immediately rules out approaches that focus on the statistical behavior of an aggregate as the essential criterion for deciding whether

Reprinted, with permission, from *Subjectivism, Intelligibility, and Economic Understanding*, ed. Israel M. Kirzner (New York: New York University Press, 1986).

components of that aggregate ought to be considered money. Moneyness is a property conferred on an item by individuals' plans, not by the econometric performance of an aggregate containing that item relative to an aggregate omitting it.

It should not be surprising or objectionable to many students of money that the definition of money must invoke subjective purposes. After all, it is a commonplace observation that money has taken widely varying physical forms, from shells to metal disks to imprinted slips of paper, in various historical economies. At least since the early medieval period in Europe there have been non-tangible assets (transferable deposits at commercial or central banks) which most economists would identify as a form of money. Thus it should not be controversial to recognize that money cannot be defined by its physical attributes. It must instead be defined by its role in purposive human activity. In this respect money is like capital. The definition of each necessarily refers to the plans of its respective owners.[4] Because these plans are not directly observable, there may be some practical difficulty in identifying or counting up the units of money (or capital) in an economy. But this does not bear on the proper choice of a definition of money (or capital).

Several potential definitions of money can pass through this subjectivist filter. Obviously a supplemental criterion for choosing among definitions is needed. It seems natural to suggest choosing the definition of money that best captures what monetary economists have generally meant in using the term "money," though the consensus may be less than complete.[5] Rather than take the space necessary for an exhaustive comparative study ranking the major candidate definitions on this score, I will simply propose that the following definition is both compatible with subjectivism and represents the most standard usage among experts: The money of an economy consists of its *generally accepted media of exchange.*[6] In what follows I will refer to this as the GAMOE definition of money. The terms making up this acronym clearly require further definition themselves.

A *medium of exchange*, following what I take to be standard economics usage, is an item acquired through exchange with the intention of later disposal in exchange for some further good, i.e., acquired in order to be spent.[7] In still other words, a medium of exchange is an item acquired as an intermediate link in a planned chain of exchanges. Normally this chain is intended to transform an agent's initial endowment into the goods he ultimately desires to consume. In a premonetary economy there may be many media of exchange. One trader may exchange his wares for salt with the intention of exchanging the salt for the food and clothing he wants; another may trade his produce for nails which he plans to trade for whatever he may want subsequently. Though his plans may be more or less successful, a single agent's plan to use a good as a medium of exchange is sufficient to make that good a medium of exchange for that agent.

Money, by contrast, is a social institution. It is not the case that whatever any individual in an economy plans to use as money is properly considered part of the economy's stock of money. A Rip van Winkle awakening today with a pocketful of gold coins (from a slumber that began in 1920) would not, despite his natural beliefs and plans for disposal, have a pocketful of money. Moneyness depends not merely on one person's plans, but no an interwoven net of many individuals' plans. This is the import of the modifiers "generally accepted" in the definition of money. A generally accepted medium of exchange is a good which not only plays an intermediate role in one agent's plans, but which other agents are routinely ready to accept in trade. This definition of money reflects its intersubjective and not merely subjective character.[8]

Once it is granted that the essential or defining function of money is its function as a generally accepted medium of exchange, it is easy to show that the other functions of money commonly mentioned in old and new textbooks are implied by, or subsidiary to, the essential function.[9] Any item that serves as money must also serve as a "store of value," i.e., must be an asset held for positive lengths of time. A unit of money is naturally used as the "unit of account" because buyers and sellers naturally find it convenient to denominate their prices in terms of the media of exchange they are routinely ready to accept. Profit-and-loss accounts are in turn most conveniently kept in the same units as buying and selling prices and cash balances.[10] The use of money as a "standard of deferred payments," or denominator for long-term contracts, is in turn subsidiary to its general use as the unit of account. Finally, the function of money as a "means of payment" or "means of *final* payment" is nothing other than its function as a generally accepted medium of exchange in the context of transactions where one party's (the "buyer's") receipt of the (nonmoney) good for which he has traded is separated form the other party's (the "seller's") receipt of the (money) good for which he has bargained.

A proper definition of money is important principally because the definition necessarily guides the identification of items as part of the stock of money or not. (A secondary function of the definition is that it allows critical scrutiny of how closely what is called "money" in an abstract economic model really resembles money as we think of it.) The proper identification of the components of the money stock is in turn vitally important for the application of monetary theory to historical experience. Statistical and other historical work in monetary economics needs to know to what items the propositions of theory are supposed to apply. This is true both for research into the evolution of payments systems and for the more common sorts of work on the relationship of changes in money stock to change in price indices, interest rates, measures of nominal and real income, and other aggregates.

IDENTIFYING MONEY

In identifying the assets that serve as money in today's economy it is natural to consider the easiest case first. Clearly hand-to-hand fiat currency (in the United States, Federal Reserve notes and token coins) is generally accepted and serves as a medium of exchange. Currency is not *universally* accepted, as some sellers (e.g., mail-order outlets) require other payment media, but it is nearly so. There is no controversy over including fiat currency as part of the stock of money.

In considering the commodity-based monetary systems of the past, the case for including coins in the money stock is equally compelling. Gold coins clearly were acquired as a media of exchange and were near-universally accepted in exchange. The case for banknote currency is somewhat less straightforward in that the notes of a particular issuer were not always generally accepted outside the vicinity of the bank's offices.[11] If we define the sphere of acceptance for a type of assets as the set of markets within which transactors are routinely ready to accept those assets in exchange for what they are selling, it seems proper to say that bank notes were money within their sphere of acceptance. Recall that our definition of money began: "The money *of an economy* is. . . ." The notion of a sphere of acceptance is simply a subjectivist way of delimiting "an economy" within which a set of items is to be identified as money.

The boundaries of a sphere of acceptance need not be purely geographical. There would be no semantic impropriety in saying (though it may or may not be a fact) that Bank of Ireland notes in 1800 were money among the merchants, manufacturers, and landed gentry of County Cork, but they were not money among the wage laborers and small farmers of the same area who insisted on payment in gold. The notion of a sphere of acceptance can be applied to demand deposits as readily as to banknotes. Today, for instance, the sphere of acceptance for ordinary bank checks does not encompass capital markets, where securities dealers insist on payment in Immediately Available Funds.[12] We consider other questions regarding the moneyness of demand deposits below.

The inclusion of raw gold and gold bullion in the stock of money under a gold standard raises a problem (almost a logically necessary feature of any commodity money system) for the would-be quantifier of the money stock. Some of the metal commodity was acquired and held not for the purpose of using it as a medium of exchange, but for the purpose of using it as an input in a noncoinage production process (e.g., filling molars) or as a consumption good (e.g., jewelry). It may not always be easy to distinguish cleanly in practice between gold bullion holdings intended as a medium of exchange and gold inventories that were not to be exchanged. (Indeed, some plans may have been intentionally flexible enough to allow for either possible use, depending on the realization of certain contingencies.) But to the extent that such a distinction can be made, an uncoined monetary gold stock can be identified, a subset of the total gold stock and a component of the stock of money within its sphere of circulation. In historical practice its sphere was largely limited to international trade.

The inclusion of traveler's checks in today's money stock has been a subject of controversy. Examining this question at some length—a length disproportionate to its relative magnitude as a potential component of the money stock, to be sure—may therefore prove instructive. Certainly traveler's checks serve as a medium of exchange. People purchase the checks with the intention of later spending them. Within their sphere of acceptance (retail transactions, at least), it seems clear that they ought to be considered money. In a classic article Leland B. Yeager has argued the contrary on two grounds. The first ground is that traveler's checks do not *circulate,* i.e., they are not routinely "accepted with the intention of passing them along to others and without anyone's asking the issuer to redeem them."[13] This raises intricate issues. It is certainly neither antisubjectivist (note Yeager's reference to intentions) nor logically unsound to take repeated circulation rather than merely general acceptance to be a defining characteristic of money. This definition is, however, narrower than the GAMOE definition. It requires of money not only that it be used as a medium of exchange, but that it be generally intended to be used as a medium of exchange by those who accept it. For instance, it would rule out any gold bullion being considered money, even if gold bullion is generally accepted in trade and some fraction is intended to be reeexchanged, if a sizable enough fraction of those accepting it intended to use it for industrial purposes. Or, it would rule out considering any subway (or pay-telephone) tokens to be money, even if some individuals do acquire them purely for reexchange and find them generally accepted in exchange at their par value, if the preponderance of their acceptors intend to redeem them for rides (or calls). The GAMOE definition would allow that some fraction of the stock of gold bullion, or of subway tokens, should be considered money if generally accepted in trade, namely, that fraction acquired with the intention of use as a medium of exchange. The task of measuring the stock of money will be naturally more difficult in the case that something like gold or subway tokens has both a monetary and a nonmonetary use, but that may be the way the economy is. The purpose of a definition of money is not to make the statistician's measurements as easy as possible, but to help them be as meaningful as possible.

Another way of highlighting the comparative narrowness of Yeager's definition is by pointing out his unusual (nonstandard) construal of the term "medium of exchange." He writes that only if traveler's checks were passed from party to party without encashment would they constitute "an actual medium of exchange."[14] This builds routine circulation into the definition of a medium of exchange. But in standard usage a medium of exchange is anything acquired with the intention of later disposal in exchange for something new, regardless of how the eventual acceptor of the thing disposes of it. In a nonmonetary economy, corn serves as a medium of exchange for Smith if he trades his wool for corn in order to trade corn for fish with Jones (who has no interest in wool), even if Jones intends to eat the corn rather than pass it along. It is surely a defect of Yeager's usage that we must come up with some new term to describe the role of corn in this situation. It is convenient, for example, to summarize Carl Menger's theory of the origin of money as an explanation of why traders in a barter setting would individually (like Smith) begin to use commodities as media of exchange and would then eventually converge socially on a few commodities or a single commodity as the generally accepted media or medium of exchange. When routine circulation is taken to be a defining characteristic of any medium of exchange, however, no distinction can be made between *a* medium of exchange and a generally accepted medium of exchange.

A strict insistence on routine circulation without redemption as a defining characteristic of a medium of exchange, or of money, limits the identification of money to those items acquired repeatedly with the intention of direct disposal in trade. No one-use-only means of payment may be considered money. Under a preferably broader interpretation, by contrast, an item counts as a medium of exchange provided that any one party acquires it with the intention of spending it for some further good.

Strictly applied, Yeager's criterion would have the surprising implication that checkable demand deposits in a multibank system are not money, contrary to Yeager's own readiness to include them.[15] Demand deposit claims on Bank *A* are not accepted by customers of other banks with the intention of passing them along without redemption. When a customer of Bank *B* accepts a check written against an account balance in Bank *A*, he accepts it only because he can readily convert it via deposit into an account balance at Bank *B*. When he deposits the check into his Bank *B* account, he thereby initiates a collection process which does result in the issuer Bank *A* being asked to redeem the check. Bank *A* must transfer reserves through the clearinghouse to Bank *B* in the amount of the check.

On average, of course, most deposit outflows of the sort just described are paired off at the clearinghouse against deposit inflows, and net adverse or positive clearings on any day are a small fraction of total funds cleared. But at the economically relevant margin, the adverse clearing takes place just as indicated.

Elsewhere in his discussion Yeager recognizes general acceptability as the defining characteristic of money. He quite rightly notes that "an asset cannot be a generally acceptable means of payment if some inducement is required not merely to persuade people to hold it for some time but even to persuade them to accept payment in that particular form in the first place." He now argues that a traveler's check is not money on the second ground that merchants who may accept it "have to be persuaded to take it . . . by the prospect of losing a sale if the seller did not thus accommodate the customer." It is difficult to distinguish this from the sense in which merchants "have to be persuaded" to take a regular bank check. More to the point, given that these statements occur in the context of a discussion of transactions costs, it is not at all apparent why taking (and subsequently depositing to one's bank account) a traveler's check is generally any more troublesome or costly than taking a regular bank check. Physical handling procedures would appear to be identical. So would the process of depositing the check to one's own bank account and receiving a positive clearing. Casual empiricism suggests that the transactions costs associated with accepting traveler's checks may in fact be lower: many establishments accept traveler's checks while refusing regular bank checks.[16] The reason is presumably that there is less risk of having a traveler's checks "bounce" due to insufficient funds.

If the foregoing argument is correct, it is clearly invalid to exclude traveler's checks from the category of money while including checkable demand deposits (transactions balances). On the GAMOE definition of money advanced here, the case for acknowledging checkable bank balances (as well as traveler's checks) to be money is straightforward. Checkable balances (including NOW accounts, Super NOW accounts, and money market deposit accounts) are acquired with the intention of later exchange; hence they are media of exchange.[17] If checks written against balances at a particular bank are generally accepted in most exchanges conducted within an economic sphere (the vicinity of the bank, say), then they are money within that sphere.

The inclusion of checkable demand deposits is not uncontroversial, however. It has been challenged by Dale K. Osborne on the "simultaneity" criterion, which he attributes to G. L. S. Shackle, that the actual stock of means of payment existing at any moment is equal to the total of payments that could be made simultaneously under any conceivable pattern of payments. Osborne argues that checkable transactions balances (in excess of bank reserves) in a multibank system fail to meet this criterion applied strictly because a bank could not execute outflowing payments beyond the quantity of its reserves in the event that it received no inflowing deposits.[18] It would be a fallacy of composition, however, to suppose that since any *single* bank could thus be depleted, all banks together could thus be depleted by check-writing, and therefore that the volume of simultaneous payments always possible is no greater than the volume of bank reserves. In fact the volume of payments always possible through simultaneous check-writing is equal to the volume of reserves in other banks plus the volume of demand deposits in the smallest bank. This is because the worst-case scenario (generating the maximum of adverse clearings against banks) is one in which customers of every other bank attempt to transfer their entire balances to customers of the smallest bank. Only transfers equal to the volume of those banks reserves can actually be excuted for their customers in this case. But customers of the smallest bank can at the same time spend their entire balances without hindrance. (In a single-bank system, the monopoly bank would be the smallest bank, because it was the only bank, and hence the entire volume of demand deposits would always be simultaneously spendable.)[19] Surely the identification of the stock of money as the sum of the monetary base plus the smallest bank's demand deposits (minus its reserves) is unappealing.

Osborne notes that if cash redemption of demand deposits for the sake of their holders is considered a form of payment, the worst-case scenario is one in which redemption of all checking balances is simultaneously demanded. In that case only a volume of payments equal to the monetary base is possible. If redemption is considered a payment, then under the simultaneity criterion the money stock equals the monetary base.[20] We could also reach this conclusion under the GAMOE definition by stipulating that an item is not to be considered "generally accepted" in exchange unless it is accepted in "exchanges" where banks deposits are being redeemed. But this is an unduly restrictive way of defining acceptance and therefore of defining money in general.

With redemptions included, what the simultaneity criterion really helps to identify is not the stock of money as such, but the stock of *outside money*. Outside money is a subset of money, namely, money that is nonredeemable. Under a gold-coin standard the stock of outside money equals the stock of monetary gold. Under the present American fiat money system it equals the stock of currency plus bank reserves held at the Federal Reserve.[21] The concept of outside money is crucial for monetary theory in at least two ways. (1) The number of units of outside money must be considered the basic nominal scalar for an economy using a fiat monetary unit as its unit of account. (2) As Osborne indicates, monetary disequilibria are most consistently analyzed in terms of positive or negative excess demand for outside money.[22] Outside money plays these theoretical roles better than the total of outside plus inside money simply because its composition is more uniform in terms of the plans of economic agents. Changes in the desired composition of total money balances, as between outside and inside (redeemable) money, can cause changes in the size of the stock of money (by changing the "money multiplier"), but changes in the desired composition of outside-money balances cannot change the size of the stock of outside money. Despite these differences, however, both outside and inside money share the property of being generally accepted media of exchange, and therefore both are properly called money. It would be not only inappropriate but awkward to introduce another phrase to cover the sum of (outside) money plus redeemable claims that serve as generally accepted media of exchange.[23]

Having now identified outside currency, inside currency, and checkable demand deposits as money, the next candidate to consider is the checkable money-market mutual fund (MMMF). Its inclusion may be plausible because it functions for its owner very much like a checking account.[24] MMMF shares are acquired with the intention of later being spent, so that they do function as media of exchange. The sticky question, however, is whether MMMF shares are generally accepted in exchange *as such*. When a check is written on an MMMF, the recipient does not acquire a claim on the fund's portfolio; rather, he acquires an inside-money claim against the bank which the fund uses to hold its transactions balances and to clear its checks. The check travels through the clearing mechanisms in the usual fashion, with the fund's bank redeeming it by transferring reserves to the recipient's bank, and debiting the fund's deposit balance. The fund in turn replenishes its deposit account (at the margin) by selling securities out of its portfolio (or rather, when a day's net daily clearings are less than the value of its maturing assets, by reinvesting less than all of its maturing funds.)[25] In this way the item that the check-writing MMMF customer relinquishes (ownership of shares in a portfolio of assets) is not what the payee accepts (ownership of an inside-money claim to bank reserves). Because the actual MMMF shares are not what the second party accepts (or intends to accept), MMMF shares cannot be considered a generally accepted medium of exchange; hence, they are not money.

By a similar argument it can be seen that time deposits such as certificates of deposit, passbook savings accounts, and other non-checkable claims on banks, should not be identified as money. Because these claims are not directly transferable, they do not serve as media of exchange, let alone as generally accepted media.[26] If they were transferable, the situation might conceivably be different,[27] though there are fairly obvious reasons why a ready claim should be more generally accepted than a future-dated claim.[28]

Finally, credit cards present an interesting case. The credit card itself never changes hands, of course. But it might be argued that the merchant does acquire the signed charge slip as a medium of exchange since he uses it as a link in a planned chain of transactions leading him to exchange for other goods. Within the retail sphere where an individual's debt instruments in the form of signed charge slips are generally acceptable, then, they should qualify as a form of money. The flaw in this argument cannot be quite as simple as conflating debt items with money since demand deposits are both money and a liability (debt) of the issuing bank. The flaw is rather that the debt instrument in this case is not *acquired through trade in order to be spent* by anyone. The card holder exchanges or "spends" the debt instrument, if you like, but he does not acquire it through trade. The merchant acquires the instrument (the charge slip) in trade, but does not intend to spend it. The merchant must redeem the instrument, receiving guaranteed reimbursement from the issuer of the credit card who in turn seeks reimbursement from the card holder. Redemption does not count as spending. It is a transaction, perhaps, but not a link in a chain of exchanges. In general, a debt instrument can satisfy the medium-of-exchange aspect of the GAMOE definition of money only if it is spent, and therefore acquired in order to be spent, by someone other than the debtor.

CONCLUSION

This essay proposes defining money in a way (though certainly not the only way) consistent with the methodological subjectivism espoused by Ludwig M. Lachmann. In particular, it defines money as the generally accepted media of exchange in an economy. Together with supplemental subjectivist-oriented definitions of "medium of exchange" and "generally accepted in an economy," this definition of money allows identification of the components of the stock of money in present and past economies. In the present United States economy, considered as the union of various economic spheres, the stock of money consists of currency, traveler's checks, and checkable claims on banks. Noncheckable bank liabilities and money-market mutual fund shares are not money because they are not directly spendable, and hence not generally accepted in exchange. The stock of money thus identified, it turns out, corresponds to the official monetary aggregate M_1, (as defined in 1985), plus money-market deposit accounts. (The inclusion of MMDAS is perhaps debatable, but only because their checkability is artificially limited by legislated restrictions on the number of transfers per month from any account.) If this identification of the stock of money, and the definition of money underlying it, are intelligible in terms of human action and the pursuit of plans, this essay will have accomplished its task.

Notes

1. Ludwig M. Lachmann, "Sir John Hicks as a Neo-Austrian," in *Capital, Expectations, and the Market Process*, ed. Walter E. Grinder (Kansas City: Sheed Andrews & McMeel, 1977), 261–62.

2. The distinction between *defining* money (the first question) and *identifying* money (the second question) is cogently made by Dale K. Osborne, "Ten Approaches to the Definition of Money," Federal Reserve Bank of Dallas *Economic Review* (March 1984), p. 2. The title of the article by Murray N. Rothbard, "Austrian Definitions of the Supply of Money," in *New Directions in Austrian Economics*, ed. Louis M. Spadaro (Kansas City: Sheed Andrews & McMeel, 1978), 143–56, actually refers to identifications of money.

3. Osborne, "Ten Approaches to the Definition of Money," 1–23. The ten candidates are (1) tangible media of exchange, (2) liquid assets, (3) *any* routine means of payment, (4) means of *potentially simultaneous* payment, (5) means of *final* payment, (6) the set of liquid assets most highly correlated with national income, (7) a set of liquid assets exhibiting a stable demand function, (8) routinely circulating exchange media, (9) temporary abodes of purchasing power, and (10) nondebt assets with legally fixed interest yield.

4. On the definition of capital see Ludwig M. Lachmann, *Capital and Its Structure* (Kansas City: Sheed Andrews & McMeel, 1978), 11–12.

5. We do not want a definition that tries to capture whatever the man in the street may mean in using the term, for he is likely to use "money" when he means income, wealth, profits, or cash. In deferring to monetary economists on the meaning of "money" one respects the linguistic division of labor in society. On this division, and on the value of making sense of past endeavors in a discipline, see Hilary Putnam, *Meaning and the Moral Sciences* (London: Routledge, 1978), 114 and 22–25.

6. This definition seems to be implicit in the discussion of Ludwig von Mises, *The Theory of Money and Credit* [1912] (Irvington-on-Hudson, N.Y.: Foundation for Economic Education, 1971), 29–37. It also seems consistent with the entry "Money, functions of" in G. Bannock, R. E. Baxter, and R. Rees, *A Dictionary of Economics* (Harmondsworth: Penguin, 1972), 287.

7. A lot is packed into these words. "Some *further* good" is meant to exclude an asset which is bought with money (or good X) and later sold for money (or X) from being considered a medium of exchange since it is not used as a vehicle for carrying forward the exchange process. (This raises difficulties in interpreting formal economic models containing only two goods, one of them labeled "money." A charitable interpretation, since typically there there no rationale for holding the money

unless it can be carried between periods more cheaply than the other consumption good, is that the consumption good in period *t* and the consumption good in period *t* + 1 are two different goods, economically speaking.) "Disposal *in* exchange for" something else does not include disposal via redemption. But an item "acquired *through* exchange" may have been acquired by redeeming a claim itself acquired *in* exchange.

8. In its intersubjectivity, money is unlike capital. It is perfectly sensible to speak of an autarkic Robinson Crusoe's using certain items as capital goods but not of his using money.

9. This point is made by Carl Menger, *Principles of Economics* (New York: New York University Press, 1981), 272–80, and by Mises, *Theory of Money and Credit*, 34–37.

10. Menger, *Principles of Economics*, 276–77; see also Lawrence H. White, "Competitive Payments Systems and the Unit of Account," *American Economic Review* 74 (September 1984): 704. Jurg Niehans, *The Theory of Money* (Baltimore: Johns Hopkins University Press, 1978), 118, makes the point that money per se is not a unit of account because money is not a unit; money is rather "the good whose unit is used as the unit of account." Niehans calls money itself the "medium of account."

11. The Scottish banking system as it developed in the nineteenth century eventually eliminated this problem, principally by branch banking and a systemwide arrangement among banks for reciprocal par acceptance of notes. In the United States and England, the problem persisted because branch banking and nationwide clearing arrangements were artificially stunted by legislated restrictions.

12. Dale K. Osborne, "What is Money Today?" Federal Reserve Bank of Dallas *Economic Review* (January 1985), p. 3.

13. Leland B. Yeager, "Essential Properties of the Medium of Exchange," *Kyklos* 21 (1968): 57. Osborne, "Ten Approaches to the Definition of Money," 19, cites this passage and elaborates upon Yeager's argument.

14. Yeager, "Essential Properties of the Medium of Exchange," 66.

15. Osborne, "Ten Approaches to the Definition of Money," accepts without argument the idea that demand deposits circulate. But the simple fact of the matter is that the deposits of any particular bank do not circulate in Yeager's sense.

16. Yeager, "Essential Properties of the Medium of Exchange," 67, n. 28, notes: "Currency has the lowest transactions costs—loosely speaking, it is the most convenient medium of exchange—in some types of transactions, and demand deposits have the lowest costs in others. But no other asset has lower transactions costs than currency and demand deposits, respectively, in the types of transactions in which each predominates." Yes, and traveler's checks have the lowest costs in still other types of transactions, namely, the ones in which *they* predominate.

17. Money market deposit accounts (MMDAS) are restricted (by the Garn-St.

Germain Act) from being drawn upon by check more than three times a month. Some holders of MMDAS may, especially if automated teller machines make it easy to transfer balances between MMDAS and regular checking accounts, never write checks against them or even have checks printed. In principle one would like to exclude at least the MMDAS for which checks are never ordered, because they are not immediately checkable, from a measure of the stock of money.

18. Osborne, "What is Money Today?" 3.
19. Osborne ibid., 5, considers the case of the monopoly bank.
20. As Osborne, ibid., concludes.
21. These reserve balances may be converted into fiat currency, and vice versa, but they are not *redeemable* for any asset not also a figment of the Federal Reserve's balance sheet. (I assume that coins are issued by the Treasury acting passively as an agent of the Federal Reserve.)
22. Osborne, "What is Money Today?" 8–9.
23. Mises, *Theory of Money and Credit*, 133 and 482–83, for example, refers to "money in the narrower sense" *(Geld in engeren Sinne)* plus "money-substitutes" *(Geld-surrogaten)* equalling the sum of "money in the broader sense" *(Geld in weiteren Sinne).* This is confusing because the term "money-substitutes" suggests nonmoneyness, yet these items are counted as part of "money in the broader sense." It is much easier to speak simply of outside money and inside money together constituting money.
24. Its weekly yield is known only after the week is over, rather than before the week begins (as with MMDAS), but that feature is not relevant to the present question.
25. See Gerald P. O'Driscoll, Jr., "Money in a Deregulated Financial System," Federal Reserve Bank of Dallas *Economic Review* (May 1985): 1–12.
26. Rothbard, "Austrian Definitions of the Supply of Money," in Spadaro ed., 146–48, argues that passbook accounts should be considered money because they can be redeemed on demand for cash. But this feature is irrelevant when they fail to satisfy the medium of exchange criterion for money, which Rothbard himself (p. 144) enunciates.
27. It is thus conceivable (it may or may not be a fact) that bills of exchange, short-maturity IOUS issued by merchants and manufacturers, transferable by consecutive endorsement, served as money within a limited sphere of nineteenth-century Britain. Mises, in *Theory of Money and Credit*, 284–86, argues that in fact they naturally did *not* serve as money because they could not be routinely accepted even in that sphere.
28. First, the acceptor of a certificate of deposit must remain a creditor of the bank that issued it until he can trade it away; he cannot cash or deposit it in order to realize funds in another form. Second, there are inconveniences associated with recalculating the present value of the claim with each passing day and with every change in interest rates.

12

The Evolution of a Free Banking System

with George A. Selgin

INTRODUCTION

In recent years monetary theorists have produced a substantial literature on the properties of a completely unregulated monetary system.[1] Their assumptions concerning the institutional features of such a system have ranged from the proliferation of numerous competing private fiat currencies at one extreme to the complete disappearance of money at the other. While these assumptions have generated clear-cut and provocative conclusions, their plausibility or realism in light of historical experience is open to serious doubt. These doubts may unfortunately suggest that any discussion of an unregulated monetary system (or free banking system) must be tenuous and highly speculative. This study shows, to the contrary, that important institutional features of a free banking system, in particular the nature of payment media, can be realistically grounded by constructing a logical explanation of its evolution.

The method of logical evolutionary explanation has previously been applied to monetary institutions by John Hicks (1967) and Carl Menger (1892), among others. The present study integrates and extends work along their lines. The method is imployed here in the belief that it has been unduly neglected in recent work, not that it is the only valid method for theoretically explaining institutional arrangements. The more standard method of building explicit transactions costs or informational imperfections or asymmetries into an optimization model has unquestionably been useful in the task of

Reprinted, with permission, from *Economic Inquiry*, vol. 25 (July 1987).

explaining why banks exist as intermediaries (Anthony Santomero [1984, 577–80] surveys this literature).

Our investigation derives arrangements that would have arisen had state intervention never occurred. The results should therefore help to identify the degree to which features of current monetary and banking institutions are rooted in market forces and the degree to which they have grown out of regulatory intervention. Such information gives important clues about how future deregulation would modify institutions. We show that sophisticated monetary arrangements emerge in the absence of regulation. No strong claims are advanced here about the welfare properties of these arrangements.[2] We aim to establish the most credible path for unrestricted monetary evolution, but certainly not the only possible path. Economists who find other institutional outcomes more plausible for an unregulated system will, we hope, similarly try to explain why and how those outcomes would emerge.

The evolution of a free banking system, following the emergence of standardized commodity money, proceeds through three stages. These are, first, the development of basic money-transfer services which substitute for the physical transportation of specie; second, the emergence of easily assignable and negotiable bank demand liabilities (inside money); and third, the development of arrangements for the routine exchange ("clearing") of inside monies among rival banks. The historical time separating these stages is not crucial. The path of development, rather than being one of steady progress as pictured here, may in practice involve false starts or creative leaps. What is essential is that, by an invisible-hand process, each stage is the logical outgrowth of the circumstances that preceded it. In other words, each successive step in the process of evolution originates in individuals' discovery of new ways to promote their self-interest, with the outcome an arrangement at which no individual consciously aims.

COMMODITY MONEY

Because the use of money logically and historically precedes the emergence of banking firms, we begin with an account of the origin of money. Our account follows that of Menger (1892), who furnished an invisible-hand explanation, consistent with historical and anthropological evidence, of how money originated as a product of undesigned or spontaneous evolution.[3] Menger's theory shows that no state intervention is necessary in order to establish a basic medium of exchange or unit of account. It also provides a useful prototype for our explanations of how subsequent banking institutions evolve in spontaneous fashion.

In premonetary society, traders relying upon barter initially offer goods in exchange only for other goods directly entering their consumption or household production plans. The number of bargains struck this way is small, owing to the well-known problem of finding what William Stanley Jevons termed a "double coincidence of wants." Before long some frustrated barterer realizes that he can increase his chances for success by adopting a two-stage procedure. He can trade his wares for some good, regardless of its direct usefulness to him, which will more easily find a taker among those selling what he ultimately wants. It follows that the earliest media of exchange are simply goods perceived to be in relatively widespread demand. The widening of demand for these things owing to their use as media of exchange reinforces their superior salability. Other traders eventually recognize the gains achieved by those using indirect exchange, and emulate them, even though they may be unaware of the reason for the advantages of using a medium of exchange. This emulation further enhances the acceptance of the most widely accepted media, elevating one or two goods above all others in salability. The snowballing of salability results in the spontaneous appearance of generally accepted media of exchange. Eventually traders throughout an economy converge on using a single commodity as a generally accepted medium of exchange, i.e., as money.

Historical evidence on primitive monies indicates that cattle were often the most frequently exchanged commodity, and that a standardized "cow" was the earliest unit of account. Cattle were a poor general medium of exchange, however, because of their relative nontransportability and nonuniformity. Not until the discovery of metals and of methods for working them did the use of money replace barter widely.[4] According to Jacques Melitz (1974, 95), common attributions of moneyness to primitive media, especially nonmetallic "moneys" (with the exception of cowries in China), warrant skepticism because many of these media (e.g., the Yap stones of Melanesia) do not meet any reasonably strict definition of money.

The emergence of coinage can also be explained as a spontaneous development, an unplanned result of merchants' attempts to minimize the necessity for assessing and weighing amounts of commodity money received in exchange. Merchants may at first mark irregular metallic nuggets or pieces after having assessed their quality. A merchant recognizing his own or another's mark can then avoid the trouble and cost of reassessment. Marking gives way to stamping or punching, which eventually leads to specialists making coins in their modern form. Techniques for milling coin edges and covering the entire surface with type provide safeguards against clipping and sweating and so allow coinage to serve as a guarantee of weight as well as of quality. Arthur R. Burns (1927a, 297–304; 1927b, 59) has illustrated this process with evidence from ancient Lydia, where coins of electrum (a naturally occurring silver-gold alloy) came into early use.

Absent state interference, coinage is a private industry encompassing various competing brands. Under competition coins are valued according to bullion content plus a premium equal to the marginal cost of mintage. The demand for readily exchangeable coins promotes the emergence of standard weights and fineness. Nonstandard coins must circulate at a discount because of the extra computational burden they impose, so that their production is unprofitable. States seem to have monopolized coinage early in history, but not by outcompeting private mints. Rather, the evidence suggests that state coinage monopolies were regularly established by legal compulsion and for reasons of propaganda and monopoly profit. State-minted coins functioned both as a symbol of rule and as a source of profits from shaving, clipping, and seigniorage. For these reasons coinage became a state function throughout the world by the end of the seventh century (Burns 1927a, 308; 1927b, 78).

BANKING FIRMS

The counting and transporting of coin entail considerable inconvenience. Traders, particularly those frequently making large or distant exchanges, will naturally seek lower-cost means of transferring ownership of money. One likely locus for development of such means is the market where local coins are exchanged for foreign coins. Standard coins may differ interlocally even in the absence of local state interventions because of geographic diseconomies in reputation building for mints. A coin-exchange market then naturally arises with interlocal trade. A trader who uses a money changer must initially count and carry in local coin each time he wants to acquire foreign coin, or vice versa. He can reduce his costs by establishing a standing account balance, to build up at his convenience and draw upon as desired. The money changer's inventories equip him to provide such accounts, which constitute demand deposits, and even to allow overdrafts. These deposits may originally be nontransferable. But it will soon be apparent, where one customer withdraws coins in order to pay a recipient who redeposits them with the same exchange banker, that the transfer is more easily made at the banker's place of business, or more easily yet by persuading the banker to make the transfer on his books without any handling of coins. Thus trading individuals come to keep money balances with agencies which can make payments by ledger-account transfers.

Money-transfer services of this sort, provided by money changers and bill brokers in twelfth-century Genoa and at medieval trade fairs in Champagne, mark the earliest recorded forms of banking.[5] In time all the major European trading centers had what Raymond de Roover (1974, 184) calls "transfer banks." De Roover comments that "deposit banking grew out of [money-changing] activity, because the money changers developed a system of local payments by book transfer." In our view, however, the taking of deposits on at least a small scale logically *precedes* the development of book-transfer methods of payment.

Money-transfer services may also develop in connection with deposits made for safekeeping rather than for money changing. The well-known story of the origins of goldsmith banking in seventeenth-century England illustrates this development. Wealthy persons may temporarily lodge commodity money with scriveners, goldsmiths, mintmasters, and other reputable vault-owners for safekeeping. Coin and bullion thus lodged must be physically withdrawn and transferred for its owner to use it as a means of payment. Exchanges in which the recipient redeposits the coins or bullion in the same vault (like redeposits with a money changer or bill broker) can obviously be accomplished more easily by making the transfer at the vault, or better yet by simply notifying the vault's custodian to make the transfer on his books. In England, scriveners were the earliest pioneers in the banking trade; in Stuart times they were almost entirely displaced by goldsmith bankers. English goldsmiths evidently became transfer bankers when they "began to keep a 'running cash' for the convenience of merchants and country gentlemen" (de Roover 1974, 83–84). The confiscation by Charles I of gold deposited for safekeeping at the royal mint ended that institution's participation in the process of banking development. Private mints, had they been permitted, would have been logical sites for early banking activities.

Transfer banking is not connected with intermediation between borrowers and lenders when the banker acts strictly as a warehouseman, giving deposit receipts which are regular warehouse dockets. The strict warehouse banker is a bailee rather than a debtor to his depositors and can make loans only out of his personal wealth. Two conditions make it possible, however, to take advantage of the interest income available from lending out depositors' balances, even while satisfying depositors' desire to have their funds withdrawable on demand: (1) money is fungible, which allows a depositor to be repaid in coin and bullion not identical to that he brought in, and (2) the law of large numbers with random withdrawals and deposits makes a fractional reserve sufficient to meet actual withdrawal demands with high probability even though any single account may be removed without notice. (Interestingly, these conditions may also be met in the warehousing of standard-quality grain, so that fractional-reserve "banking" can likewise develop there, as Jeffrey C. Williams [1984] has shown.) The lending of depositors' balances is an innovation that taps a vast new source of loanable funds and alters fundamentally the relationship of the banker to his depositor customers.

Historically in England, according to R. D. Richards (1965, 223), "the bailee . . . developed into the debtor of the depositor; and the depositor became an investor who loaned his money . . . for a consideration." Money "warehouse receipts" became merely ready promissory notes. W. R. Bisschop (1910, 50n) reports that English warehouse bankers had become intermediaries by the time of Charles II (1660–85): "Any deposit made in any other shape than ornament was looked upon by them as a free loan." Competition for deposits prompted the payment of interest on deposits, and the attractiveness of interest on safe and accessible deposits in turn apparently made the practice of depositing widespread among all ranks of people (Powell 1966, 56–57).

TRANSFERABLE INSTRUMENTS

Under these circumstances the effective money supply obviously becomes greater than the existing stock of specie alone. The most important banking procedures and devices, however, have yet to develop. Many purchases are still made with actual coin. Bank depositors, in order to satisfy changing needs for money at hand, make frequent withdrawals from and deposits into their bank balances. These actions may in the aggregate largely cancel out through the law of large numbers. But they require the banks to hold greater precautionary commodity money reserves, and consequently to maintain a larger spread between deposit and loan rates of interest, than is necessary when payments practices become more sophisticated. Greater sophistication comes with the emergence of negotiable bank instruments, able to pass easily in exchange from one person to another, which replace coin and nonnegotiable deposit receipts in transactions balances. The use of coin is also superseded by the development of more efficient means for the bank-mediated transfer of deposits.

Assignability and negotiability may develop through several steps. Initially the assignment of deposited money (whether "warehoused" or entrusted to the banker for lending at interest) by the depositor to another party may require the presence of all three parties to the exchange or their attorneys. Money "warehouse receipts" (or promissory notes) and running deposit balances cannot be assigned by the owner's endorsement without the banker acting as witness. An important innovation is the development of bank-issued promissory notes transferable by endorsement. Assignable notes in turn give way to fully negotiable bank notes assigned to no one in particular but instead payable to the bearer on demand. A parallel development is the nonnegotiable check enabling the depositor to transfer balances to a specific party, in turn giving way to the negotiable check which can be repeatedly endorsed or made out "to cash."[6] Thus the modern forms of inside money—redeemable bearer bank notes and checkable deposits—are established. Once this stage is reached it is not difficult for bankers to conceive what Hartley Withers (1920, 24) has called "the epoch-making notion"—in our view it is only an incremental step—of giving inside money not only to depositors of metal but also to borrowers of money. The use of inside money enhances both customer and bank profits, so that only the possible reluctance of courts to enforce obligations represented by assigned or bearer paper stands in the way of its rapid development.

In England bearer notes were first recognized during the reign of Charles II, about the time when warehouse banking was giving way to fractional-reserve transfer banking. At first the courts gave their grudging approval to the growing practice of repeated endorsement of promissory notes. Then after some controversy, fully negotiable notes were recognized by Act of Parliament. In France, Holland, and Italy during the sixteenth century merchants' checks "drawn in blank" circulated within limited circles and may have cleared the way for the appearance of bank notes (Usher 1943, 189; Richards 1965, 46, 225).

REGULAR NOTE-EXCHANGE

Further economies in the use of commodity money require more complete circulation of inside money in place of commodity money, and more complete development of bank note and check clearing facilities to reduce the need for commodity money reserves. It is relatively straightforward to show that bankers and other agents pursuing their self-interest are indeed led to improve the acceptability of inside money and the efficiency of banking operations.

At this stage, although bank notes are less cumbersome than coin, and checkable deposits are both convenient for certain transactions and interest paying, some coin still remains in circulation. Consumers trust a local bank's notes more than a distant bank's notes because they are more aware of the local notes' likelihood of being honored and more familiar with their appearance (hence less prone to accepting forgeries). It follows that the cost to a bank of building a reputation for its issues—particularly regarding note convertibility —is higher in places further from the place of issue and redemption. The establishment of a network of bank branches for redemption is limited by transportation and communication costs. In the early stages of banking development the par circulation of every bank's notes and checks is therefore geographically relatively limited.[7] People who generally hold the inside money of a local bank but who do business in distant towns must either take the trouble to redeem some of their holdings for gold and incur the inconvenience of transporting coin, or suffer a loss in value on their notes by carrying them to a locale where they are accepted only at a discount, if at all. (The alternative practice of keeping on hand notes from each locality they deal with is likely to be prohibitively costly in terms of foregone interest.) In general, a brand of inside money will initially be used only for transactions in the vicinity of the issuer, and coin will continue to be held alongside notes of like denomination. The use of commodity money in circulation requires banks to hold commodity reserves greater than those required by the transfer of inside money, because the withdrawal of commodity money for spending generates more volatile reserve outflows than the spending of notes or deposits.

In this situation, profit opportunities arise which prompt actions leading to more general acceptance of particular inside monies. The discounting of notes outside the neighborhood of the issuing bank's office creates an arbitrage opportunity when the par value of notes (i.e., their face redemption value in commodity money) exceeds the price at which they can be purchased for commodity money or local issues in a distant town plus (secularly falling) transaction and transportation costs. As interlocal trade grows, "note brokers" with specialized knowledge of distant banks can make a business, just as retail foreign-currency brokers do today, of buying discounted nonlocal notes and transporting them to their par circulation areas or reselling them to travelers bound for those areas. Competition eventually reduces note discounts to the level of transaction and transportation costs plus a factor for redemption risk. By accepting the notes of unfamiliar banks at minimal commission rates, brokers unintentionally increase the general acceptability of notes, and promote their use in place of commodity money.

To this point we have implicitly assumed that banks refuse to accept one another's notes. This is not unreasonable; banks have as many reasons as other individuals do to refuse notes unfamiliar to them or difficult to redeem. They have in addition a further incentive for refusing to accept notes from rival banks, which is that by doing so they help to limit the acceptability of these notes, thereby enhancing the demand for their own issues. To cite just one historical illustration of this, the Bank of Scotland and the Royal Bank of Scotland—the first two banks of issue located in Edinburgh—refused to accept the notes of "provincial" banks of issue for a number of years (see Checkland [1975, 126]).

Nevertheless note brokerage presents opportunities for profit to bankers. Banks can out-compete other brokers because, unlike other brokers, they can issue their own notes (or deposit balances) to purchase "foreign" notes and need not hold costly till money. Each bank has an additional incentive to accept rival notes: larger interest earnings. If the notes acquired are redeemed sooner than the notes issued, interest-earning assets can be purchased and held in the interim. This profit from "float" can be continually renewed. In other words, a bank can maintain a permanently larger circulation of its own notes by continually replacing other notes with its own, and correspondingly can hold more earning assets than it otherwise could. If other banks are simultaneously replacing Bank A's notes with their own, there may be no absolute increase in A's circulation compared to the situation in which no bank accepts rival notes. But there will be an increase compared to Bank A not accepting, given whatever policies rivals are following, so that the incentive remains. (We argue below that in fact an indirect consequence of *other* banks' par acceptance of Bank A notes will be an absolute increase in A-note-holding in place of specie-holding.) Where transaction and transportation costs and risks are low enough, competition for circulation will narrow the brokerage fee to zero, that is, will lead the banks to general acceptance of one another's notes at par. The development of par acceptance by this route does not require that the banks explicitly and mutually agree to such a policy.

An alternative scenario, which assumes strategic behavior by the banks, leads to the same result. A bank may aggressively purchase foreign notes in the markets, and then suddenly return large quantities to their issuers for redemption in commodity money, hoping to force an unprepared issuer to suspend payments. The aggressor hopes to gain market share by damaging a rival's reputation or even forcing it into liquidation. These tactics, historically known as "note-picking" and "note-duelling," initially provoke the other issuers to respond in kind. Collecting and redeeming the first bank's notes not only returns the damage, but helps replenish the other banks' reserves. Purchasing its rivals' notes at par allows a bank to collect them in greater quantities, and may therefore be adopted. (Arbitrage-redemption of notes paid out precludes paying a price above par.) In the long run, nonaggression among banks should emerge, being less costly for all sides. Note-picking and note-duelling are costly and ineffectual ways to promote circulation when others do likewise. Banks thus find it profitable to take rivals' notes only as these are brought to them for deposit or exchange, and to return the collected notes to their issuers promptly in exchange for commodity money reserves. This result is contrary to Eugene Fama's (1983, 19) suggestion that note-duelling will persist indefinitely. It is an example of the "tit for tat" strategy, as discussed by Robert Axelrod (1984), proving dominant in a repeated-game setting.[8] Again, no explicitly negotiated pact is necessary. It only takes a single bank acting without cooperation from other banks to nudge the rest toward par acceptance (zero brokerage fees) as a defensive measure to maintain their reserves and circulation.

In New England at the beginning of the nineteenth century the Boston banks gave the nudge that put the whole region—with its multitude of "country" banks of issue far removed from the city— on a par-acceptance basis (Trivoli 1979). In Scotland the Royal Bank, when it opened for business in 1727, immediately began accepting at par the notes of the Bank of Scotland, at that time its only rival, and instigated a short-lived note duel. One response by the Bank of Scotland, later widely adopted, is notable: the bank inserted a clause into its notes giving it the option (which it did not normally exercise) of delaying redemption for six months, in which event it would pay a bonus amounting to 5 percent per annum

(Checkland 1975, 60, 67–68). In both places, established banks, even after they had begun accepting each other's notes at par, sometimes refused to take the notes of new entrants. They soon changed their policies because the new banks that accepted and redeemed their notes were draining their reserves, while the established banks could not offset this without engaging in the same practice.

Banks that accept other banks' notes at par improve the market for their own notes and, unintentionally, for the notes that they accept. This makes a third scenario possible: If two banks both understand these circulation gains, they may explicitly enter a mutual par-acceptance arrangement. Others will emulate them, leading to general par acceptance. This explanation, previously offered by White (1984a, 19–21), assumes slightly more knowledge on the part of banks than the first two scenarios. Historical evidence of such explicit arrangements in Scotland is provided by Munn (1975).

Statistics from Boston dramatically illustrate the mutual circulation gains from acceptance arrangements. From 1824 to 1833 the note circulation of the Boston banks increased 57 percent, but the Boston circulation of country banks increased 148 percent, despite the Boston banks' intent to drive the country banks out of business (Lake 1947, 186; Trivoli 1979, 10–12). There is room for all banks to gain because the spread of par acceptance makes inside money more attractive to hold relative to commodity money. Since notes from one town are now accepted in a distant town at par, there is no longer good reason to lug around commodity money. As par note acceptance developed in Scotland, Canada, and New England— places where note issue was least restricted—during the nineteenth century, gold virtually disappeared from circulation. (Small amounts of gold coin were still used in these places at least in part because of restrictions upon the issue of "token" coin and of small-denomination notes. In an entirely free system, such restrictions would not exist.) In England and the rest of the United States, where banking (and note issue in particular) were less free, gold remained in circulation.

Even the complete displacement of commodity money in circulation by inside money does not, however, exhaust the possibilities for economizing on commodity money. Much of the specie formerly used in circulation to settle exchanges outside the banks may still be

needed to settle clearings among them. Banks can substantially reduce their prudentially required holdings of commodity money by
making regular note exchanges which allow them to offset their
mutual obligations. Only net clearings rather than gross clearings are
then settled in commodity money. The probability of any given-sized
reserve loss in a given period is accordingly reduced (by the law of
large numbers) and each bank can prudently reduce its ratio of
reserves to demand liabilities.

The gains to be had from rationalization of note exchange are
illustrated by the provincial Scottish banks before 1771, which practiced par acceptance without regular exchange. Note duelling among
these banks was not uncommon (Leslie 1950, 8–9; Munn 1981, 23–
24), and to guard against redemption raids they had to keep substantial reserves. Munn's figures (1981, 141) show that their reserves
during this period were typically above 10 percent of total liabilities.
This contrasts with reserve ratios of around 2 percent that were
typical after note clearings became routine. The advantages of regular
note exchange are great enough to have secured its eventual adoption in every historical instance of relatively free plural note issue.

CLEARINGHOUSES

The most readily made arrangements for note exchange are bilateral.
In a system of more than two issuers, however, multilateral note
exchange provides even greater economies. Reserve-holding economies result from the offsetting of claims that would otherwise be
settled in specie. Multilateral clearing also allows savings in time and
transportation costs by allowing all debts to be settled in one place
and during one meeting rather than in numerous scattered meetings.

The institutional embodiment of multilateral note and deposit exchange, the clearinghouse, may evolve gradually from simpler note-
exchange arrangements. For example, the note-exchange agents of
banks A and B may accidentally meet each other at the counter of
bank C. The greater the number of banks exchanging bilaterally, the
less likely it is that such an encounter could be avoided. It would be
natural for these two agents to recognize the savings in simple time
and shoe-leather costs from settling their own exchange then and
there, and from agreeing to do it again next time out, and then

regularly. From a set of there bilateral settlements around one table it is not a large step toward the computation and settlement of combined net clearing balances. Once the advantages of this arrangement become clear to management, particularly the reserve-holding economies which may not have concerned the note porters, the institution will spread. Fourth, fifth, and subsequent banks may join later meetings. Or similar regular few-sided exchanges may be formed among other groups of banks, either independently or by one of the first three banks, whose meetings are later combined with the meetings of the original group. Eventually all the banks within an economy will be connected through one or a small number of clearinghouses.

The histories of the best-known early clearinghouses, in London, Edinburgh, and New York, all conform to this general pattern. J. S. Gibbons (1858, 292) reports that in New York the impetus for change from numerous bilateral exchanges to combined multilateral exchange came from note porters who "crossed and re-crossed each other's footsteps constantly." Among the London check porters, as related by Bisschop (1910, 160), "occasional encounters developed into daily meetings at a certain fixed place. At length the bankers themselves resolved to organize these meetings on a regular basis in a room specially reserved for this purpose."

The settlement of interbank obligations is initially made by physical transfer of commodity money at the conclusion of clearing sessions. Banks will soon find it economical to settle instead by means of transferable reserve accounts kept on the books of the clearinghouse, echoing the original development of transfer banking. These accounts may be deposits or equity shares denominated in currency units. As a transfer bank, the clearinghouse need not hold 100 percent reserves, and can safely pay its members a return (net of operating costs) by holding safe earning assets. This development reduces a member bank's cost of holding reserves, but does not eliminate it because alternative assets yield a higher return. Unless regulated directly by the clearinghouse, a bank's reserve ratio is determined by precautionary liquidity considerations depending mainly on the volume and volatility of net clearings and the clearinghouse penalty for reserve deficiency (see Ernst Baltensperger [1980, 4–9] and Santomero [1984, 584–86]).

Once established, a clearinghouse may serve several purposes beyond the economical exchange and settlement of interbank obligations. It can become, in the words of James G. Cannon (1908, 97), "a medium for united action among the banks in ways that did not exist even in the imagination of those who were instrumental in its inception." One task the clearinghouse may take on is to serve as a credit information bureau for its members. By pooling their records, banks can learn whether loan applicants have had bad debts in the past or are overextended to other banks at present, and can then take appropriate precautions (Cannon 1910, 135). Through the clearinghouse banks can also share information concerning bounced checks, forgeries, and the like.

The clearinghouse may also police the soundness of each member bank in order to assure the other member banks that notes and deposits are safe to accept for clearing. As part of this function, banks may be required to furnish financial statements and may have their books audited by clearinghouse examiners. The Chicago clearinghouse insisted on statements as early as 1867, and in 1876 gained the right to carry out comprehensive examinations whenever desired, to determine any member's financial condition (James 1938, 372–73, 499). Regular examinations began in 1906 (Cannon 1910, 138–39). Other clearinghouses, such as the Suffolk Bank and the Edinburgh clearinghouse, took their bearings mainly from the trends of members' clearing balances and traditional canons of sound banking practice. Those two clearinghouses enjoyed such high repute as certifying agencies that to be taken off their lists of members in good standing meant a serious loss in reputation and hence business for an offending bank (Trivoli 1979, 20; Graham 1911, 59).

It is possible that a clearinghouse may attempt to organize collusive agreements on interest rates, exchange rates, and fee schedules for its members. However, rates inconsistent with the results of competition would tend to break down under unregulated conditions, for the standard reason that secretly underbidding a cartel has concentrated benefits and largely external costs. A clear example of this comes from Scottish experience (Checkland 1975, 391–427). The Edinburgh banks set up a committee in 1828 to set borrowing and lending rates. The Glasgow banks joined a new version of the committee in 1836, at which time it represented the preponderance of Scottish banks in number and in total assets. Though not a clearinghouse association itself, the committee had much the same membership as the Edinburgh clearinghouse. In spite of repeated formal agreements, the committee could not hold members to its recommended interest rates. Not until after entry to the industry was closed in 1844 did the agreements become at all effective.

Perhaps the most interesting of all the roles a clearinghouse may perform is to assist its members in times of crisis (see Cannon [1910, 24]). If a bank or group of banks is temporarily unable to pay its clearing balances, or if it experiences a run on its commodity money reserves, the clearinghouse can serve as a medium through which more liquid banks lend to less liquid ones. It provides the framework for an intermittent, short-term credit market similar to the continuous federal funds market from which reserve-deficient American banks presently borrow. Another possible emergency function of clearinghouses is note issue. This function is called for when member banks are artificially restricted from issuing, as for example U.S. banks were by the bond-collateral requirements of the National Banking Acts, so that the banks are not able independently to fulfill all of their depositors' requests for hand-to-hand means of payment. Currency shortages occurred frequently in the United States during the second half of the nineteenth century, and clearinghouses helped to fill the void caused by deficient note issues of the National Banks.[9]

THE MATURE FREE-BANKING SYSTEM

We are now in a position to describe a mature free banking system, using historical evidence to illuminate its likely structural and operational characteristics. Evidence on industry structure from Scotland, Canada, Sweden, and elsewhere indicates that unregulated development does not produce natural monopoly, but rather an industry consisting of numerous competing banking firms, most having widespread branches, all of which are joined through one or more clearinghouses. In Scotland there were nineteen banks of issue in 1844, the final year of free entry. The largest four banks supplied 46.7 percent of the note circulation. In addition to their head offices the banks had 363 branch offices, 43.5 percent of which were owned by the largest (measured again by note issue) four banks.[10]

The banks in the mature system issue inside money in the shape of paper notes and demand deposit accounts (checkable either by paper or electronic means) that circulate routinely at par. Banks may also issue redeemable token coins, more durable but lighter and cheaper, to take the place of full-bodied coins as small change. Each bank's notes and tokens bear distinct brand-name identification marks and are issued in the denominations the public is most willing to hold. Because of the computational costs that would be involved in each transfer, interest is not likely to accrue on commonly used denominations of bank notes or tokens, contrary to the hypothesis of Neil Wallace (1983) that all currency would bear interest under laissez-faire.[11] Checkable accounts, however, provide a competitive yield reflecting rates available on interest-earning assets issued outside the banking system.

Checkable bank accounts are most familiarly structured as demand deposits, i.e., liabilities having a predetermined payoff payable on demand. An important reason for this structure is that historically a debt contract has been easier for the depositor to monitor and enforce than an equity contract which ties the account's payoff to the performance of a costly-to-observe asset portfolio. The predetermined payoff feature, however, raises the possibility of insolvency and consequently of a run on the bank if depositors fear that the last in line will receive less than a full payoff. One method of forestalling runs that may prevail in an unregulated banking system is the advertised holding of a large equity cushion, either on the bank's books or off them in the form of extended liability for bank shareholders. If this method were inadequate to assure depositors, banks might provide an alternative solution by linking checkability to equity or mutual-fund-type accounts with postdetermined rather than predetermined payoffs. The obstacles to such accounts (asset-monitoring and enforcement costs) have been eroded over the centuries by the emergence of easy-to-observe assets, namely publicly traded securities. Insolvency is ruled out for a balance sheet without debt liabilities, and the incentive to redeem ahead of other account holders is eliminated. An institution that linked checkability to equity accounts would operate like a contemporary money-market mutual fund, except that it would be directly tied into the clearing system (rather than having to clear via a deposit bank). Its optimal reserve holdings would be determined in the same way as those of a standard bank.

The assets of unregulated banks would presumably include short-term commercial paper, bonds of corporations and government agencies, and loans on various types of collateral. Without particular information on the assets available in the economy, the structure of asset portfolios cannot be characterized in detail, except to say that the banks presumably strive to maximize the present value of their interest earnings, net of operating and liquidity costs, discounted at risk-adjusted rates. The declining probability of larger liquidity needs, and the trade-off at the margin between liquidity and interest yield, suggest a spectrum of assets ranging from perfectly liquid reserves, to highly liquid interest-earning investments (these constitute a "secondary reserve"), to less liquid higher-earning assets. Thus far, because the focus has been on monetary arrangements, the only bank liabilities discussed have been notes and checking accounts. Unregulated banks would almost certainly diversify on the liability side by offering a variety of time deposits and also traveler's checks. Some banks would probably become involved in such related lines of business as the production of bullion and token fractional coins, issue of credit cards, and management of mutual funds. Such banks would fulfill the contemporary ideal of the "financial supermarket," with the additional feature of issuing bank notes.

Commodity money seldom if ever appears in circulation in the mature system, virtually all of it (outside numismatic collections) having been offered to the banks in exchange for inside money. Some commodity money will continue to be held by clearinghouses so long as it is the ultimate settlement asset among them. At the limit, if inter-clearinghouse settlements were made entirely with other assets (perhaps claims on a super-clearinghouse which itself holds negligible commodity money), and if the public were completely weaned from holding commodity money, the active demand for the old-fashioned money commodity would be wholly nonmonetary. The flow supply formerly sent to the mints would be devoted to industrial and other uses. Markets for those uses would determine the relative price of the commodity. The purchasing power of monetary instruments would continue to be fixed by the holder's contractual right (even if never exercised) to redeem them for physically specified quantities of the money commodity. The problem of meeting any significant redemption request (e.g., a "run" on a bank) could be contractually handled, as it was historically during note-duelling episodes, by invoking an "option clause" that allows the bank a specified period of time to gather the necessary commodity money while compensating the redeeming party for the delay. The clause need not (and historically did not) impair the par circulation of bank liabilities.

This picture of an unregulated banking system differs significantly in its institutional features from the visions presented in some of the recent literature on competitive payments systems. The system described here has assets fitting standard definitions of money. Banks and clearinghouses hold (except in the limit), and are contractually obligated to provide at request, high-powered reserve money (commodity money or deposits at the clearinghouse), and they issue debt liabilities (inside money) with which payments are generally made. These features contrast with the situation envisioned by Black (1970) and Fama (1980), in which "banks" hold no reserve assets and the payments mechanism operates by transferring equities or mutual fund shares unlinked to any money.

Bank reserves do not disappear in the evolution of a free banking system, as analyzed here, because the existence of bank liabilities that are promises to pay presupposes some more fundamental means of payment that is the thing promised. Individuals may forgo actual redemption of promises, preferring to hold them instead of commodity money, so long as they believe that they will receive high-powered money if they ask for it. Banks, on the other hand, have a competitive incentive to redeem one another's liabilities regularly. So long as net clearing balances have a positive probability of being nonzero, reserves will continue to be held. In a system without reserve money it is not clear what would be used to settle clearing balances. In a commodity-money system, the scarcity of the money commodity and the costliness of holding reserves serve to pin down the price level and to limit the quantity of inside money. In moneyless systems it is not always clear what forces limit the expansion of payment media nor what pins down the price level. Nor are these things clear, at the other extreme, in a model of multiple competing fiat monies.[12]

Our analysis indicates that commodity-based money would persist in the absence of intervention, for the reason that the supreme salability of the particular money good is self-reinforcing. This result contradicts recent views (see Black [1970], Fama [1980], Greenfield and Yeager [1983], Yeager [1985]) that associate complete deregulation with the replacement of monetary exchange by a sophisticated form of barter. (To be sure, Greenfield and Yeager recognize that their system would be unlikely to emerge without deliberate action by government, particularly given a government-dominated monetary system as the starting point.) In an economy with commodity-based money, prices are stated in terms of a unit of the money commodity, so the question of using an abstract unit of account does not arise as it does in a sophisticated barter setting.[13] Even if actual commodity money were to disappear from reserves and circulation, the media of exchange would not be "divorced" from the commodity unit of account; they would be linked by redeemability contracts. We can see no force severing this link. Contrary to Woolsey (1985), the renunciation of commodity redemption obligations is not compelled by economization of reserves. Thus we find no basis for the spontaneous emergence of a multicommodity monetary standard or of any pure fiat monetary standards, such as contemplated in works by Hall (1982), Woolsey (1984), Klein (1974), and Hayek (1978). In short, unregulated banking would be much less radically unconventional, and much more akin to existing financial institutions than recent literature on the topic suggests.

One important contemporary financial institution is nonetheless missing from our account, namely the central bank. We find no market forces leading to the spontaneous emergence of a central bank, in contrast to the view of Charles Goodhart. (For this discussion a central bank is closely enough defined, following Goodhart [1985, 3–8], as an agency with two related powers: monetary policy, and external regulation of the banking system.) Goodhart (1985, 76) argues that the development of a central bank is "natural" because "the natural process of centralization of interbank deposits with leading commercial banks tends toward the development of a banks' club" which then needs an independent arbiter. But even on his own account the forces that historically promoted centralized interbank deposits were *not* "natural" in any laissez-faire sense. They stemmed crucially from legal restrictions, particularly the awarding of a monopoly of note issue or the suppression of branch banking. Where no legislation inhibits the growth of branched banking firms with direct access to investment markets in the economy's financial center, and able to issue their own notes, it is not at all apparent that profit seeking compels any significant interbank depositing of reserves. Walter Bagehot (1873, 66–68) argued persuasively that "the natural system—that which would have sprung up if Government had let banking alone—is that of many banks of equal or not altogether unequal size" and that in such a system no bank "gets so much before the others that the others voluntarily place their reserves in its keeping." None of the relevant historical cases (Scotland, Canada, Sweden) shows any significant tendency toward interbank deposits.

We have seen that reserves do tend to centralize, on the other hand, in the clearinghouses. And clearinghouses, as Gorton (1985a, 277, 283; 1985b, 274) has recently emphasized, may take on functions that are today associated with national central banks: holding reserves for clearing purposes, establishing and policing safety and soundness standards for member banks, and managing panics should they arise. But these functional similarities should not be taken to indicate that clearinghouses have (or would have) freely evolved into central banks. The similarities instead reflect the preemption of clearinghouse functions by legally privileged banks or, particularly in the founding of the Federal Reserve System (Gorton 1985a, 277; Timberlake 1984), the deliberate nationalization of clearinghouse functions. Central banks have emerged from legislation contravening, not complementing, spontaneous market developments.[14]

Notes

The authors are indebted to the Institute for Human Studies for the opportunity to work together on this article, and to Chris Fauvelas, David Glasner, Israel Kirzner, Hu McCulloch, Mario Rizzo, Kurt Schuler, Richard J. Sweeney, and anonymous referees for useful comments. The Scaife Foundation provided support for White's research.

1. See for example Black (1970), Klein (1974), Hayek (1978), Fama (1980), Greenfield and Yeager (1983), Wallace (1983), White (1984b), O'Driscoll (1985), and Yeager (1985).
2. We have each made normative evaluations of free banking elsewhere: Selgin (1988, chaps. 8–10); White (1984a, chap. 5; 1984b).
3. See also Menger (1981, 260–62). The same view appears in Carlisle (1901, 5) and Ridgeway (1892, 47). A more recent version of Menger's theory is Jones (1976). For a secondary account of Menger's theory, see O'Driscoll (1986).
4. See Menger (1981, 263–66); Ridgeway (1892, 6–11); and Burns (1927a, 286–88). On some alleged nonmetallic monies of primitive peoples, see Quiggen (1963).
5. See Usher (1943), de Roover (1974, chaps, 4, 5), and Lopez (1979).
6. On the historical development of bank notes and checks in Europe, see Usher (1943, 7–8, 23).
7. See White (1984a, 84–85) for nineteenth-century views on geographic diseconomies in note circulation.
8. An example of the explicit adoption of "tit for tat" by an exhausted note-duelling bank is given by Munn (1981, 24).
9. See Cannon (1908), Andrew (1908), Smith (1936), Timberlake (1984), and Gorton (1985a).
10. These figures are based on data in White (1984a, 37). A recent econometric study of economics of scale in banking is Benston, Hanweck, and Humphrey (1982).
11. See White (1984a, 8–9; 1987).
12. Taub (1985) has shown that a dynamic inconsistency facing issuers in Klein's (1974) model will lead them to hyperinflate.
13. This point is emphasized by White (1984c). For additional criticism of the Black-Fama-Yeager literature, see O'Driscoll (1985), Hoover (1985), and McCallum (1984).
14. On the appearance of central banks in several nations, see Smith (1936); on Canada in particular see Bordo and Redish (1985).

References

Andrew, A. Piatt. 1908. "Substitutes for Cash in the Panic of 1907." *Quarterly Journal of Economics* (August): 497–596.

Axelrod, Robert. 1984. *The Evolution of Cooperation*. New York: Basic Books.

Bagehot, Walter. 1873. *Lombard Street: A Description of the Money Market.* London: Henry S. King.

Baltensperger, Ernst. 1980. "Alternative Approaches to the Theory of the Banking Firm." *Journal of Monetary Economics* 6 (January): 1–37.

Benston, George, J., Gerald A. Hanweck, and David B. Humphrey. 1982. "Scale Economies in Banking: A Restructuring and Reassessment." *Journal of Money, Credit, and Banking* (November): 435–54.

Black, Fischer. 1970. "Banking and Interest Rates in a World Without Money: The Effects of Uncontrolled Banking." *Journal of Bank Research* 1 (Autumn): 9–20.

Bisschop, W. R. 1910. *The Rise of the London Money Market, 1640–1826.* London: P. S. King & Son.

Bordo, Michael, and Angela Redish. 1985. "Why Did the Bank of Canada Emerge in 1935?" Manuscript.

Burns, A. R. 1927a. "Early Stages in the Development of Money and Coins." In *London Essays in Economics in Honour of Edwin Cannan,* edited by T. E. Gregory and Hugh Dalton. London: George Routledge & Sons.

———. 1927b. *Money and Monetary Policy in Early Times.* New York: Alfred E. Knopf.

Cannon, James G. 1908. "Clearing Houses and the Currency." In *The Currency Problem and the Present Financial Situation,* edited by E.R.A Seligman. New York: Columbia University Press.

———. 1910. *Clearing Houses.* Washington, D. C.: Government Printing Office.

Carlisle, William. 1901. *The Evolution of Modern Money.* London: Macmillan.

Checkland, S. G. 1975. *Scottish Banking: A History, 1695–1973.* Glasgow: Collins.

de Roover, Raymond. 1974. *Business, Banking, and Economic Thought in Late Medieval and Early Modern Europe,* edited by Julius Kirshner. Chicago: University of Chicago Press.

Fama, Eugene F. 1980. "Banking in the Theory of Finance." *Journal of Monetary Economics* 6 (January) 39–57.

———. 1983. "Financial Intermediation and Price Level Control." *Journal of Monetary Economics* (July): 7–28.

Gibbons, J. S. 1858. *The Banks of New York: Their Dealers, the Clearing House, and the Panic of 1857.* New York: D. Appleton Co.

Goodhart, Charles. 1985. *The Evolution of Central Banks: A Natural Development?* London: Suntory-Toyota International Centre for Economics and Related Disciplines/London School of Economics and Political Science.

Gorton, Gary. 1985a. "Clearinghouses and the Origin of Central Banking in the United States." *Journal of Economic History* 42 (June): 277–83.

———. 1985b. "Banking Theory and Free Banking History: A Review Essay." *Journal of Monetary Economics* 16 (September): 267–76.

Graham, William. 1911. *The One Pound Note in the History of Banking in Great Britain*, 2d ed. Edinburgh: James Thin.

Greenfield, Robert L., and Leland B. Yeager. 1983. "A Laissez-Faire Approach to Monetary Stability." *Journal of Money, Credit, and Banking* 15 (August): 302–15.

Hall, Robert E. 1982. "Explorations in the Gold Standard and Related Policies for Stabilizing the Dollar." In *Inflation: Causes and Effects*. edited by Robert E. Hall. Chicago: Chicago University Press for the National Bureau of Economic Research.

Hayek, F. A. 1978. *The Denationalisation of Money*, 2d ed. London: Institute of Economic Affairs.

Hicks, John. 1967. "The Two Triads, Lecture I." In *Critical Essays in Monetary Theory*. Oxford: Clarendon Press.

Hoover, Kevin D. 1985. "Causality and Invariance in the Money Supply Process." Doctoral dissertation, Oxford University.

James, F. Cyril. 1938. *The Growth of Chicago Banks*. New York: Harper & Brothers.

Jones, Robert. 1976. "The Origin and Development of Media of Exchange." *Journal of Political Economy* 84 (November): 757–75.

Klein, Benjamin. 1974. "The Competitive Supply of Money." *Journal of Money, Credit, and Banking* 6 (November): 423–53.

Lake, Wilfrid S. 1947. "The End of the Suffolk System." *Journal of Economic History* (November): 183–207.

Leslie, J. O. 1950. *The Note Exchange and Clearing House Systems*. Edinburgh: William Blackwood.

Lopez, Robert S. 1979. "The Dawn of Medieval Banking." In *The Dawn of Modern Banking*. New Haven: Yale University Press.

McCallum, Bennett T. 1984. "Bank Deregulation, Accounting Systems of Exchange, and the Unit of Account: A Critical Review." Carnegie-Rochester Conference Series on Public Policy (Autumn): 3–45.

Melitz, Jacques. 1974. *Primitive and Modern Money*. Reading, Mass.: Addison-Wesley.

Menger, Carl. 1892. "On the Origin of Money," translated by Caroline A. Foley. *Economic Journal* 92 (June): 239–55.

———. 1981. *Principles of Economics* [1871]. New York: New York University Press.

Munn, Charles. 1975. "The Origins of the Scottish Note Exchange." *Three Banks Review* 107: 45–60.

———. 1981. *The Scottish Provincial Banking Companies, 1747–1864*. Edinburgh: John Donald.

O'Driscoll, Gerald P., Jr. 1985. "Money in a Deregulated Financial System." Federal Reserve Bank of Dallas *Economic Review* (May): 1–12.

———. 1986. "Money: Menger's Evolutionary Theory." *History of Political Economy* 18 (Winter): 601–16.

242 *The Theory of Competitive Monetary Arrangements*

Powell, Ellis T. 1966. *The Evolution of the Money Market, 1385–1915.* New York: Augustus M. Kelley.

Quiggen, A. Hingston. 1963. *A Survey of Primitive Money: The Beginning of Currency.* London: Methuen.

Richards, R. D. 1965. *The Early History of Banking in England.* New York: Augustus M. Kelley.

Ridgeway, William. 1892. *The Origin of Metallic Currency and Weight Standards.* Cambridge: Cambridge University Press.

Santomero, Anthony M. 1984. "Modeling the Banking Firm: A Survey." *Journal of Money, Credit, and Banking* (November): 576–602.

Selgin, George A. 1988. *The Theory of Free Banking.* Totowa, N. J.: Rowman and Littlefield.

Smith, Vera C. 1936. *The Rationale of Central Banking.* London: P. S. King & Son.

Taub, Bart. 1985. "Private Fiat Money with Many Suppliers." *Journal of Monetary Economics* 16 (September): 195–208.

Timberlake, Richard H. 1984. "The Central Banking Role of Clearing-House Associations." *Journal of Money, Credit, and Banking* 16 (February): 1–15.

Trivoli, George. 1979. *The Suffolk Bank: A Study of a Free-Enterprise Clearing System.* Leesburg, Va.: Adam Smith Institute.

Usher, Abbott Payson. 1943. *The Early History of Deposit Banking in Mediterranean Europe.* Cambridge: Cambridge University Press.

Wallace, Neil. 1983. "A Legal Restrictions Theory of the Demand for "Money" and the Role of Monetary Policy." *Federal Reserve Bank of Minneapolis Quarterly Review* (Winter): 1–7.

White, Lawrence H. 1984a. *Free Banking in Britain: Theory, Experience, and Debate, 1800–1845.* Cambridge: Cambridge University Press.

———. 1984b. "Free Banking as an Alternative Monetary System." In *Money in Crisis: The Federal Reserve, the Economy, and Monetary Reform,* edited by Barry N. Siegel. Cambridge, Mass.: Ballinger Publishing.

———. 1984c. "Competitive Payments Systems and the Unit of Account." *American Economic Review* (September): 699–712.

———. 1987. "Accounting for Non-interest-bearing Currency: A Critique of the Legal Restrictions Theory of Money." *Journal of Money, Credit, and Banking* 19 (November): 448–56.

Williams, Jeffrey C. 1984. "Fractional Reserve Banking in Grain." *Journal of Money, Credit, and Banking* (November): 488–96.

Withers, Hartley. 1920. *The Meaning of Money.* London: John Murray.

Woolsey, W. William. 1984. "The Multiple Standard and the Means of Exchange." Manuscript, Talledega College, Al.

———. 1985. "Competitive Payments Systems: Comment." Manuscript, Talledega College.

Yeager, Leland B. 1985. "Deregulation and Monetary Reform." *American Economic Review* (May): 103–7.

13

Accounting for Non-interest-bearing Currency: A Critique of the Legal Restrictions Theory of Money

In a series of articles, Neil Wallace and his collaborators have developed a "legal restrictions theory" of the demand for money which leads to several provocative conclusions.[1] The primary conclusion is that the difference between the rates of return on money and bonds is due entirely to certain legal restrictions on private intermediation, so that in the absence of legal restrictions the difference would go to zero. To put it another way, distinctive money would cease to exist under laissez-faire. Two further conclusions follow: (1) because the effectiveness of open-market operations depends on the existence of distinctive money, open-market operations would have no effect on the price level in the absence of legal restrictions; (2) the interest rate on Treasury bills measures the bindingness of the legal restrictions.

I shall first attempt to reconstruct briefly the theory's primary conclusion, then cite historical evidence which indicates that the conclusion is empirically falsified. In the third section I try to explain where the theory goes wrong, and to account for the "paradox" of non-interest-bearing currency coexisting with interest-bearing bonds even in the absence of the legal restrictions cited by Wallace. There I identify conceivable future conditions under which this account might no longer be valid, so that coexistence might indeed constitute a paradox. A final section restates the major points.

Reprinted, with permission, from *Journal of Money, Credit, and Banking*, vol. 19, no. 4 (November 1987).

THE LEGAL RESTRICTIONS THEORY

In the legal restrictions framework, money and other assets "are valued only in terms of their payoff distributions" (Bryant and Wallace 1980), that is, only in terms of explicit pecuniary yields. It follows immediately from this assumption that a non-interest-yielding financial instrument of constant nominal value, e.g., a $100 Federal Reserve note, is strictly dominated by an interest-yielding asset of the same denomination and with the same default risk and legal negotiability characteristics. e.g., a $100 Treasury bearer bond.[2] For Wallace (1983) "it is hard to see why anyone would hold non-interest-bearing currency instead of the interest-bearing securities" unless the securities were somehow legally prevented from playing the same role in transactions. He argues that securities in the United States today *are* legally prevented from playing a transactions role by virtue of (1) the Treasury's refusal to issue any small-denomination bearer bonds, and (2) the prohibition on private issue of small-denomination bearer bonds.

The second restriction prevents a form of intermediational arbitrage whereby a private firm could offer small-denomination bearer bonds presenting a default risk no greater (fraud aside) than that of the safest large-denomination bonds (e.g., Treasury bills) available in the economy. To do so a firm would hold as assets only such large-denomination bonds timed to mature simultaneously with its own small-denomination bonds. Wallace (1983) analogizes this sort of arbitrage to converting hundred-pound packages of butter into one-pound packages. Competition would force the interest rate paid on the small-denomination bonds to equal the rate on large-denomination bonds minus only the cost of intermediation, which he estimates to be less than one percent.

Were competition in this sort of intermediation allowed, Wallace argues, safe, small-denomination interest-yielding bearer bonds would dominate non-interest-yielding currency and thereby drive it out of circulation. Non-interest-yielding currency could survive only if the yield on the small-denomination bonds were also zero, which would require that the yield on large-denomination securities be very close to zero (no greater than the cost of intermediation). Thus he concludes: "Either nominal interest rates go to zero or existing government currency [non-interest-bearing, and no freer from default risk than private notes backed exclusively by Treasury securities] becomes worthless."[3] The latter case implies adoption of a monetary unit other than the fiat dollar, such as the gold ounce (Wallace 1983).

HISTORICAL EVIDENCE

The legal restrictions theory makes a clear and falsifiable prediction: non-interest-yielding paper currency should not be able to coexist with positive-interest-yielding securities carrying equal default risk in the absence of legal restrictions against the sort of intermediation that could produce interest-yielding bearer bonds backed by those same securities.[4] The prediction, as stated here (though not by Wallace), specifies *paper* currency (or more precisely, non-commodity currency) because commodity money's complete freedom from default risk cannot be equaled, even assuming away fraud. The legal restrictions theory therefore does not imply the disappearance of commodity outside money.[5]

An obvious place to look for possible falsification of the non-coexistence prediction is in historical cases of laissez-faire in money and banking. The clearest such case is the Scottish free banking system from 1716 to 1844 (see Checkland 1975 or White 1984). The Scottish experience does appear to falsify the non-coexistence prediction of the legal restrictions theory. Non-interest-yielding paper currency coexisted with interest-yielding assets, despite the absence of any legal impediments to entry into banking, to the issue of circulating liabilities (of £1 or larger), or, in particular, to the production of interest-yielding bearer bonds backed by interest-yielding assets. The typical private bank note promised only to be redeemable on demand for specie of a constant specified amount. Such a note neither paid coupon interest nor enjoyed any nominal appreciation. No law directly discouraged the payment of interest on bank notes. Note-issuing Scottish banks did offer interest on demand deposit accounts and, as Adam Smith ([1776] 1981) reports, private bankers did pay interest on promissory notes which were redeemable on demand. At the same time, the banks' assets included essentially risk-free government bonds yielding 3 to 4 percent annually, and high-quality short-term commercial bills of exchange yielding around 5 percent.[6] This conjunction of events represents a serious paradox for the legal restrictions theory.

Scotland was not an absolutely pure case of laissez-faire banking, as two restrictions were placed on note issue by a Parliamentary Act of 1765. Neither restriction, however, eliminates the empirical challenge to the legal restrictions theory. First, the act outlawed the use of an "optional clause" in bank notes. The clause had typically reserved to the issuer the option of delaying redemption for six months, in which case a 2.5 percent premium over par would be paid (Checkland 1975). By requiring that bank notes be redeemable on demand, the act may have ruled out one method of paying interest, namely the circulation of postdated bearer instruments at a discount. (It is not clear whether a bank-issued bearer bond not redeemable on demand would have been considered an illegal bank note under the act.) It left open the payment of interest by other means, such as promising redemption on demand for the note's initial value plus a premium that would grow over time. The latter method, to be sure, may not allow the intermediation perfectly matched in maturity that Wallace supposes possible. On the other hand, Scottish currency was non-interest-bearing before 1765 as well. Second, the act prohibited bank notes smaller than £1, a sizable sum relative to per capita income. Large-denomination notes, however, should most clearly be interest-bearing under the legal restrictions theory.[7]

The paradox appears in all other historical systems (e.g., nineteenth-century United States, Canada, Sweden, England) which, despite their other infringements of laissez-faire, have allowed competitive note issue, have not banned interest-bearing notes, and yet have produced non-interest-bearing notes.

ACCOUNTING FOR THE "PARADOX" OF NON-INTEREST-BEARING CURRENCY

By assuming that money is valued only according to its risk-return characteristics and legal negotiability, the legal restrictions theory excludes consideration of the liquidity services or nonpecuniary yield provided by money.[8] If currency yields services that interest-bearing bonds do not, then non-interest-bearing currency (like non-interest-bearing oil paintings) can find willing holders and clearly *can* coexist with interest-bearing assets even in the absence of legal restrictions. One needs to explain, of course, the nature of these services and the inability of bearer securities to provide them. Well-known accounts of the nature and definition of money (e.g., Yeager 1968) have stressed money's supreme salability in comparison with all other assets. Money balances provide a liquidity service yield because, given that sums of money alone are generally or routinely accepted in exchange, their possession puts one in the position of being able to make any potential purchase with minimum inconvenience.[9]

This conception of the unique salability of money is fundamentally at odds with the legal restrictions approach. So, too, is the complementary theory of the origin of money, whereby an invisible-hand market process elevates one commodity from superior salability under barter to the status of supreme salability or moneyness (Menger 1892; Jones 1976). Wallace implicitly assumes that all goods are equally salable, as, for example, they would be in a Walrasian general equilibrium setting where the auctioneer absorbs all the costs of finding a buyer at the most advantageous price available. In his view (1983), "the only significant frictions are those created by legal restrictions." In other words, in the absence of legal restrictions there are no greater transaction costs involved in spending securities than in spending money. Wallace sees no reason why interest-yielding bearer bonds would be any less readily exchangeable for goods than would non-interest-yielding currency (assuming like denomination and identical default risk).[10]

An obvious and credible reason for the superior salability of non-interest-yielding currency is surely the simplicity of transacting with it. Transacting with an interest-yielding bank note (or small-denomination bearer bond) requires both parties to perform a cumbersome calculation or other routine for discovering its present value at the moment of transfer. If the date of original issue, initial value, and stipulated rate of appreciation were stated on the note, accumulated interest would have to be calculated. If a redemption date and terminal value were stated, the present discounted value would have to be calculated using an agreed-upon discount rate.[11]

Alternative devices can also be imagined, but none would be costless to use. Fama (1983) hypothesizes currency denominated in portfolio-share units, with the (rising) numeraire redemption value of the unit reported daily in the newspapers, but he himself notes the inconvenience of having to check the up-to-date numeraire value of the unit. A calendar of nominal values at various dates might be carried in small print on the back of a bank note, but then the current value would have to be tediously looked up. Cash registers might be equipped to read the issue (or redemption) date and initial (or terminal) value from a "zebra" bar code on the face of a bank note, and to compute and display its present value, but reading such information by machine would still take time. The fixed cost of installing such a cash register furthermore suggests that it would not be economical to install one at every point of sale.

Under any of these technologies for paying interest on currency, the indicated calculations or operations would have to be performed not just once in each transaction, but separately for each note tendered by the buyer and for each note offered by the seller in exchange. This process recalls the inconvenience historically involved in transacting with coins, each of which had to be tested for weight and possibly fineness.[12]

For competition to compel bank-note issuers in practice to offer interest-bearing notes, bank-note users must find the interest-bearing feature worthwhile. The expected interest receivable at each note-transfer occasion must at least compensate both the holder and the recipient of the note for the time and trouble of computing and collecting it. Because the time cost of collecting interest is presumably the same for every denomination of bank note, whereas the benefit to the note holder declines proportionately with the size of the note, there must under any concrete set of circumstances be some threshold denomination of currency below which it will *not* pay an average-time-cost individual to bother about collecting interest.[13]

A thumbnail calculation indicates that this threshold value would in practice exceed historically common currency sizes, given historically common interest rates. On a note whose initial value equals two hours' wages, held one week while yielding interest at 5 percent per annum, accumulated interest would amount to less than 7 seconds' wages. If the note holder's wage rate indicates the opportunity cost of his time, then he will not find it worthwhile to compute and collect interest if to do so twice (once at the receiving end and once at the spending end) takes 7 seconds or more, i.e., if it takes 3.5 seconds or more per note-transfer. To give a specific example, a $20 note held one week at 5 percent interest would yield less than 2 cents. Notes held in cash registers by retailers generally turn over much more rapidly than once a week, of course, so that the threshold denomination may well be extremely high.

The legal restrictions theorists simply overlook the significant costs involved in collecting interest on hand-to-hand currency. They do recognize a minor production cost to the intermediation which splits large interest-yielding assets into smaller assets. As a measure of this cost, Bryant and Wallace (1980) and Wallace (1983) look to the spread at which competitive mutual funds presently operate, which is said to be 1 percent or less. This spread would be relevant for predicting the spread between bank asset yields and deposit yields under laissez-faire, for the technology of paying interest on a bank deposit is not significantly different from that of adding earnings to a mutual fund account. Currency *is* different, however. Because the holder of a bank note at any moment is anonymous to the bank, the bank cannot simply make a bookkeeping entry to add interest to an account which it holds for him or her. Neither Bryant and Wallace (1980) nor Wallace (1983) recognizes any technological difference between demand deposits and currency with respect to the ease of paying interest. The only cost Wallace (1983) mentions with direct reference to currency is the cost to the issuer of replacing worn notes.

Two potential objections to the argument advanced here need to be addressed. First, the implication that paper currency under laissez-faire would circulate at par might seem itself to be readily falsified by a historical example: the existence of variable discounts on bank notes, as recorded by "bank note reporter" publications, during the "free banking" period in the United States. Those publications only indicate, however, that discounts from par were charged by specialized brokers who purchased "foreign" notes with local notes or specie (Rockoff 1974). They do not indicate that notes routinely circulated at variable discounts. Indeed, the existence of the brokerage business reflects travelers' needs to get hold of "current" money (accepted at par) for convenient local spending. That well-known brands of notes were not current across wide areas of the country (as they were in Scotland) is to be explained at least in part by the departures from laissez-faire that prevented interstate branch banking in the United States.

Second, it might be objected that unlimited profits are available to firms that hold interest-bearing assets and issue non-interest-bearing bank notes. On average and at the margin, of course, the profit from note issue must be zero in competitive equilibrium. The limiting factors are fixed costs and marginal diseconomies of scale in issuing notes and keeping them in circulation in the face of (non-price) competition from rival issuers. Outlays, which may rise at the margin, must be made on numerous services to attract note-holding customers: longer banking hours, more tellers and machines, and additional branch offices to make redemption easier; advertising to make notes more familiar or trusted; special engraving of notes to make them attractive and counterfeit-proof (White 1984). These services are similar to the familiar features of non-price competition among banks for depositors when interest rate ceilings are legally imposed on bank deposits.

Technological progress may one day render microchips and associated display equipment so cheap that tamper-proof chips may be economically implanted into currency (much as they are currently implanted at considerable cost into France's "smart" credit cards), thereby enabling an interest-bearing bank note to calculate and display its own present value continuously. On that day, which has certainly not yet arrived, the continued existence of non-interest-bearing currency might constitute a paradox. On the other hand, the simple ease of working with round denominations might well preserve a demand to hold non-interest-bearing notes, at least in the smaller denominations. If *all* pieces of currency were interest-bearing, locating exact change would become prohibitively costly or even impossible.

CONCLUSION

The legal restrictions theory of money accounts for the existence of non-interest-bearing paper currency by referring to legal barriers against certain forms of private intermediation. Yet we find that non-interest-bearing paper currency has existed historically even in the absence of such barriers. Non-interest-yielding paper currency can be accounted for without invoking legal restrictions on private intermediation once we drop the assumption that transaction and computation costs are universally zero. Interest on at least some smaller denominations of currency is not worth collecting because its transfer is too cumbersome. Hence non-interest-bearing currency can survive even in the absence of legal restrictions.

Notes

The author thanks Fernando Alvarez, John Bryant, Clive Bull, Ty Cowen, David Glasner, Robert Greenfield, Daniel Klein, Randy Kroszner, John Lott, Jr., Gerald O'Driscoll, Jr., Hugh Rockoff, George Selgin, Neil Wallace, seminar participants at Texas A&M University, and anonymous referees for comments. He also thanks the Scaife Foundation for research support, the Institute for Humane Studies for a congenial writing environment, and the C. V. Starr Center for Applied Economics for clerical support.

1. In particular see Wallace (1983). This article lists (p. 3) as "some applications of the legal restrictions theory" the following articles: Bryant and Wallace (1983), Karaken and Wallace (1978, 1981), Sargent and Wallace (1982, 1983), and Wallace (1979, 1981). An early and detailed presentation of the theory is offered by Bryant and Wallace (1980). Intellectual predecessors of the legal restrictions theory are surveyed by Cowen and Kroszner (1987).
2. A "bearer bond" is a security conveyed without endorsement or supplementary documentation. In this respect it resembles a bank note.
3. This statement suggests that competitive free banking might itself force the risk-free interest rate on large securities down to zero (i.e., down to the cost of intermediation), or, in other words, that the phenomenon of interest (beyond default risk and intermediation costs) may be simply a product of currency scarcity. Such a view is startling, but criticism of it here would require a major digression.
4. Makinen and Woodward (1986) offer anecdotal evidence contradicting the legal restrictions theory in a different way, relating a case in which small-denomination bearer bonds issued by the French government failed to circulate as a medium of exchange.
5. Consequently Wallace (1983, 1 n. 2) is not strictly correct in identifying Fama's (1980) and Hall's (1982) discussions of *purely* moneyless payments systems as "discussions of the legal restrictions theory."

A referee of this paper, agreeing that the coexistence of specie with interest-bearing assets is not inconsistent with the legal restrictions theory, argues that because bank notes are essentially default-free claims to specie, the coexistence of non-interest-bearing bank notes is also consistent with the theory. The theory insists, however, that a note-issuing bank would be forced by competition to pay out to note holders the anticipated net earnings on its asset portfolio. If there were literally no risk differential between specie and bank notes, then the theory moreover implies that specie would be dominated by such interest-bearing notes and could *not* coexist.

6. Government bond yields and open-market discount notes on short-term commercial bills in London are given by Homer (1977). The discount rate in Glasgow was 5 percent on the highest quality bills in 1800 (Anonymous 1960). The same figure is reported by Adam Smith (1981). Smith unfortunately does not provide details concerning the promissory notes of private (non-bank-note-issuing) bankers but they apparently did not circulate as a medium of payment.

7. In fact, the "price discrimination" story told by Bryant and Wallace (1983) has large-denomination notes bearing interest even in the presence of legal restrictions.

8. On the same score McCallum (1983, 1986) criticizes the overlapping-generations model of Sargent and Wallace (1982), and O'Driscoll (1985) criticizes cashless payments models.

9. On this point, see the important piece by Hutt (1956) which contrasts the idea of a service yield from money balances with the idea that money is "barren." Hutt shows that the latter idea has been endorsed by a long line of economists, to which we may add the legal restrictions theorists.

10. Bryant and Wallace (1980) quite explicitly make the assumption of zero transactions costs part of their analytical framework: "Under laissez-faire, no transactions costs inhibit the operation of markets and, in particular, the law of one price." As they recognize, this assumption clearly contradicts the spirit of Hicks's 1935 article, which they in other respects aim to follow, and the title of which they appropriate.

11. Bryant and Wallace (1980) suggest that unregulated bank notes could take the form of "titles to, say, $20 of U. S. currency payable to the bearer in, say, 30 days or thereafter." Wallace (1983) similarly hypothesizes bank notes with definite maturity dates.

12. This cumbersome-transfer argument does not apply, however, to McCulloch's (1986) imaginative suggestion that interest in an expected-value sense could efficiently be paid on bank notes by means of a periodic lottery on their serial numbers. Under that technology winning notes would be withdrawn from circulation, and remaining notes would presumably circulate at their face value. A version of the threshold argument of the next two paragraphs does apply, but the relevant

threshold would be much lower. A (possibly minor) drawback of the scheme for the issuer is the incentive it gives for periodic surges and declines in bank note holding as the lottery date approaches and passes.
13. Fama (1983) has arrived at a similar conclusion.

References

Anonymous. 1960. "The Glasgow Financial Scene: Early Nineteenth Century." *Three Banks Review* 45 (March): 33–40.

Bryant, John, and Neil Wallace. 1980. "A Suggestion for Further Simplifying the Theory of Money." Manuscript, Federal Reserve Bank of Minneapolis and University of Minnesota.

———. 1983. "A Price Discrimination Analysis of Monetary Policy." Federal Reserve Bank of Minneapolis Research Department Staff Report 51.

Checkland, S. G. 1975. *Scottish Banking: A History, 1695–1973.* Glasgow: Collins.

Cowen, Tyler, and Randall Kroszner. 1987. "The Development of the New Monetary Economics." *Journal of Political Economy* 95 (June): 567–90.

Fama, Eugene F. 1980. "Banking in the Theory of Finance." *Journal of Monetary Economics* 6 (January): 39–57.

———. 1983. "Financial Intermediation and Price Level Control." *Journal of Monetary Economics* 12 (July): 7–28.

Hall, Robert E. 1982. "Monetary Trends in the United States and the United Kingdom: A Review from the Perspective of New Developments in Monetary Economics." *Journal of Economic Literature* 20 (December): 1552–56.

Hicks, John. 1935. "A Suggestion for Simplifying the Theory of Money." *Economica* (N. S.) 2 (February): 1–19.

Homer, Sidney. 1977. *A History of Interest Rates,* 2d ed. New Brunswick, N. J.: Rutgers University Press.

Hutt, W. H. 1956. "The Yield from Money Held." In *On Freedom and Free Enterprise,* edited by Mary Sennholz, 196–223. Princeton: D. Van Nostrand.

Jones, Robert. 1976. "The Origin and Development of Media of Exchange." *Journal of Political Economy* 84 (November): 757–75.

Karaken, John, and Neil Wallace. 1978. "International Monetary Reform: The Alternatives." Federal Reserve Bank of Minneapolis *Quarterly Review* 2 (Summer): 2–7.

———. 1981. "On the Indeterminacy of Equilibrium Exchange Rates." *Quarterly Journal of Economics* 96 (May): 207–22.

Makinen, Gail E., and G. Thomas Woodward. 1986. "Some Anecdotal Evidence Relating to the Legal Restrictions Theory of the Demand for Money." *Journal of Political Economy* 94 (April): 260–65.

McCallum, Bennett T. 1983. "Comments [on Sargent and Wallace (1983)]." *Journal of Monetary Economics* 12 (July): 189–96.

————. 1986. "Some Issues Concerning Interest Rate Pegging, Price Level Determinancy, and the Real Bills Doctrine." *Journal of Monetary Economics* 17 (January): 135–60.

McCulloch, J. Huston. 1986. "Beyond the Historical Gold Standard." In *Alternative Monetary Regimes,* edited by Colin Campbell and William R. Dougan, 73–81. Baltimore: Johns Hopkins University Press.

Menger, Carl. 1892. "On the Origin of Money," translated by Caroline A. Foley. *Economic Journal* 92 (June): 239–55.

O'Driscoll, Gerald P., Jr. 1985. "Money in a Deregulated Financial System." Federal Reserve Bank of Dallas *Economic Review* (May): 1–12.

Rockoff, Hugh. 1974. "The Free Banking Era: A Reexamination." *Journal of Money, Credit, and Banking* 5 (May): 141–67.

Samuelson, Paul A. 1947. *Foundations of Economic Analysis.* Cambridge: Harvard University Press.

Sargent, Thomas, and Neil Wallace. 1982. "The Real-Bills Doctrine versus the Quantity Theory: A Reconsideration." *Journal of Political Economy* 90 (December): 1212–36.

————. 1983. "A Model of Commodity Money." *Journal of Monetary Economics* 12 (July): 163–87.

Smith, Adam. 1981. *An Inquiry into the Nature and Causes of the Wealth of Nations* [1776], edited by R. H. Campbell, A. S. Skinner, and W. B. Todd Indianapolis: Liberty Classics.

Wallace, Neil. 1979. "Why Markets in Foreign Exchange are Different from Other Markets." Federal Reserve Bank of Minneapolis *Quarterly Review* 3 (Fall): 1–7.

————. 1981. "A Modigliani-Miller Theorem for Open-Market Operations." *American Economic Review* 71 (June): 267–74.

————. 1983. "A Legal Restrictions Theory of the Demand for 'Money' and the Role of Monetary Policy." Federal Reserve Bank of Minneapolis *Quarterly Review* (Winter): 1–7.

White, Lawrence H. 1984. *Free Banking in Britain: Theory, Experience, and Debate, 1800–1845.* Cambridge: Cambridge University Press.

Yeager, Leland B. 1968. "Essential Properties of the Medium of Exchange." *Kyklos* 21: 45–69.

Index